The Prince of Frogtown

The Prince
of Frogtown

Rick Bragg

Alfred A. Knopf   *New York* 2008

This Is a Borzoi Book Published by Alfred A. Knopf

www.aaknopf.com

Knopf, Borzoi Books, and the colophon are registered trademarks of
Random House, Inc.

Portions of this work originally appeared in Best Life magazine.

Library of Congress Cataloging-in-Publication Data
Bragg, Rick.
The prince of Frogtown / Rick Bragg.—1st ed.
p.   cm.
"A Borzoi Book."
ISBN 978-1-4000-4040-7
1. Bragg, Rick. 2. Fathers and sons. 3. Stepfathers. 4. Journalists—
United States—Biography. 5. Working class whites—Alabama—
Biography. 6. Alabama—Biography. I. Title.
CT275.B594643 2008
976.1'063092—DC22
[B]   2007038884

Manufactured in the United States of America

First Edition

FOR RANDY HENDERSON

Get six jolly cowboys to carry my coffin
Get six pretty girls to carry my pall
Put bunches of roses all over my coffin
Put roses to deaden the clods as they fall

"Streets of Laredo"

Contents

CONTENTS

The Prince of Frogtown

The Stream

I N WATER SO FINE, a few minutes of bad memory all but disappear downstream, washed away by ten thousand belly busters, a million cannonballs. Paradise was never heaven-high when I was a boy but waist-deep, an oasis of cutoff blue jeans and raggedy Converse sneakers, sweating bottles of Nehi Grape and Orange Crush, and this stream. I remember the antidote of icy water against my blistered skin, and the taste of mushy tomato and mayonnaise sandwiches, unwrapped from twice-used aluminum foil. I saw my first water moccasin here, and my first real girl, and being a child of the foot washers I have sometimes wondered if this was my Eden, and my serpent. If it was, I didn't hold out any longer than that first poor fool did. It took something as powerful as that, as girls, to tug me away from this tribe of sunburned little boys, to scatter us from this place of double-dog dares, Blow Pops, Cherry Bombs, Indian burns, chicken fights, and giggling, half-wit choruses of "Bald-Headed Man from China." Maybe we should have nailed up a sign—NO GIRLS ALLOWED—and lived out our lives here, to fight mean bulls from the safe side of a barbed-wire fence with a cape cut from a red tank top, and duel to the death with swords sliced off a weeping willow tree. I don't know what kind of man I turned out to be, but I was good at being a boy. Then, a thrust to the heart only bent against my chest, in a place where I could look straight into the Alabama sun through a water-smoothed nugget of glass, and tell myself it was a shipwrecked emerald instead of just a piece from a broken bottle of Mountain Dew.

The stream began in a jumble of rocks beside the Piedmont Highway, bubbling up cold and clear a half mile from my grandmother's house. The air always smelled of coconut-scented suntan lotion and lighter fluid, and in summer the white gravel parking lot filled with church buses, poodle walkers, and weekend Hells Angels who might have been born to run, but now lugged along well-fed wives in white go-go boots and polyester pantsuits rolled to the knee. It was a lovely park, but a boy, a genuine boy, can have no real fun with so many Presbyterians puttering around, and so many mommas in one tight place.

But if you followed the water a meandering half mile to the west, through a dark, spiderwebbed, monster-infested culvert tall enough for a small boy to run through, all the picnickers and weenie roasters vanished behind a curtain of gnarled, lightning-blasted cedars and thick, dark pines. The stream passed under four strands of barbed wire, flowed through a sprawling pasture studded with wicked blackberry thickets and the rusted hulks of old baling machines, then rushed into a dogleg against a high, red clay bank. Here, the shin-deep water pooled into a clear, cold swimming hole, made deeper by the ragged dam of logs, rocks and sandbags we built just downstream.

This was our place. From a running start, I could leap clear across it, heart like a piston, arms flailing for distance, legs like shock absorbers as I finally, finally touched down. This is where I learned to take a punch and not cry, how to dodge a rock, sharpen a knife, cuss, and spit. Here, with decrepit cowboy hats and oil-stained BAMA caps on our burr heads and the gravel of the streambed sifting through our toes, we daydreamed about Corvettes we would drive, wondered if we would all die in Vietnam and where that was, and solemnly divined why you should never, ever pee on an electric fence.

This is the last place I remember having much peace of mind. It is where I lay still shaking from the water and let the sun simmer me to sleep, my feet and legs slicked by nail polish to suffocate the chiggers that had hitched a ride on me the day before. I would wake, hard, to the bite of a horsefly, or soft, to a faint, far-off rumbling in still-blue skies and the frightened calls of a mother who always, somehow, foretold the storm. A few times I took a book, but it was hard to read with your brothers pelting you with day-old cow patties and green pinecones. And besides, in those days of bloody adventure, the Boxcar Children moved a little slow, and the Hardy Boys didn't have nothin' on me.

My mother had tried to open the outside world to me in the only way she could, by taking home a volume every Friday morning from the discount encyclopedia sale at the A&P, but the sale ended too soon and the world stopped at the letter K—Kyoto, Kyushu and Kyzyl Kum. I didn't miss the rest of the alphabet or the world, not here. The only thing that could force an end to perfect days in the perfect stream was the dipping of that almighty sun, sinking into *Gunsmoke,* hot cornbread and cold buttermilk, and a preemptive "If I should die before I wake" as a shorted-out electric fan droned off and on in a window by my bed. Somewhere out there, my father drifted from ditch to ditch in a hundred-dollar car, but we were free of him then, free of him for good.

Yet sometimes, when I am wading through my memories of this place, I find the pieces of another day, a day told to me as much as it was truly remembered, because I was so small. My father was still with us then, his loafers spit-shined, his creases sharp enough to cut you in two, and he would have smelled of Ivory soap and Old Spice and a faint, splashed-on respectability. It is not the best or worst story I have of my father, but is worth telling if only because, this time, he was innocent.

———·———

I WAS NOT A TODDLER ANYMORE, but not yet school-age. Mostly, I remember the weather. It was late spring, after the blackberries bloom. Summer does not wait on the calendar here, and by the end of May the heat has settled across the foothills of the Appalachians like a damp dishrag. By Memorial weekend, the flies have discovered every hole in the screen doors, and the grass has been cut six times. But some years, just before four solid months of unrelenting sweat, a cool, delicious wind blows through the hills, mixes with the brilliant sunshine, and provides a few, final sips of dry, breezy, perfect weather. The old people call it blackberry winter.

It is fine sleeping weather and even better for visiting, and that is what brought us together in the early 1960s. By midmorning, the chert drive in front of my grandmother Ava's house was crowded with fifties-model Chevrolets and GMC pickups loaded with chain saws, rusted picks and shovels, logging chains and battered toolboxes. There was work in the American South then, good blue-collar work with health insurance and solid pension funds. Smokestacks burned at midnight, and coated the parked cars in a film of black, beautiful, life-giving smut. If a man's family did without, it was his own damn fault.

The hot-grease smell of frying chicken would have leaked from the windows and screen doors, as it did every Sunday, as aunts and cousins twisted the lids off sweet pickles and stirred yellow mustard into big gobs of potato salad. Gospel music from the black-and-white television mixed in the air with the smell from sizzling iron skillets. *". . . and now, folks, from Pensacola, Florida, with sand in their shoes, it's the Florida Boys . . ."* My grandmother Ava, who never really recovered from the death of the one man she ever deemed worthy of a second glance, would nod to the music, and dream.

The yard was chaos and tricycles, the red dirt and spring grass covered in pink-faced children crying, laughing, screaming, fighting, bleeding. Doll heads bounced across the ground, diapers were lost, green plums and some small measure of dirt were eaten. Wagons and Kiddie Kars crashed and overturned in wild onions and ant beds, but no baby's suffering, not even a sweat bee sting, lasted too long. Daddies snatched up the afflicted, baby-talked into their ears, and jiggled them well again.

Older boys walked the nearby field, using Daisy BB guns to harass but miss clean thousands of birds, and shoot each other, giggling, in the behind. My older brother Sam, too grown up even at age seven for all that foolishness, stalked the tall weeds beneath the power lines, knocked big crows off the wire with his air rifle, then nailed them, wings spread, to the side of the barn. A dead dog would break his heart, but he was murder on crows.

My mother would have been beautiful then, her hair the color of fresh-picked corn, and my dark, blue-eyed father would have been the most handsome man in our part of Calhoun County. They belonged together, light and dark, I once believed. As the clock inched toward noon and the sun flushed out every dark corner of my world, he stood gun-barrel straight and stone sober beside my uncles, cousins and the other men. There would have been hangover in his eyes and in the tremble of his hands around his cigarette, but it wasn't anything a little taste of liquor wouldn't heal, once he had shaken free of his wife and kids like a man slipping out of a set of too-tight Sunday clothes.

The men segregated themselves under the chinaberry tree. They wore double-knit slacks and what we called sport shirts, not one necktie or day of college between them, but capable men who fixed their own cars, patched their own water lines and laid their own bricks. They were a mix of the Old and New South, men who drew their paychecks from the cotton mills, pipe shops and steel mills, but still believed that you could make it rain if you hung dead snakes in the branches of trees. They were solid as the steel they rolled or concrete they poured. They did not drink, did not cuss unless they were in the fraternity of like-minded men, and surrendered their paychecks to their wives the minute they walked in the front door. As they talked they clicked chrome Zippo lighters toward thin, tight, hand-rolled cigarettes, and stuffed strings of tobacco into their jaws until they looked deformed. Some were Saved, some backslid and some as yet unaffiliated, but even the ones who walked in the Holy Holy did not preach to the others, out of respect. If you went to work and fed your babies, you were already halfway home. So they spoke of the secular, of the secrets of fuel injection, how to put brake shoes on a '64 Corvair, or the best way to worm a good dog. They believed in General Motors, Briggs & Stratton, Craftsman, Poulan, John Deere, International, Tree Brand, Zebco, Remington and Wolverine, and the bumper stickers on their trucks read WALLACE or nothing at all.

My father was, in the moment, one of them. He was a body and fender man when he was working. He drank, yes, but he had killed a man in Korea by holding his head underwater, and if that didn't earn you a swallow at home, not much did. The truth is none of them knew him well. He was quiet when he was all right—our polite code for the word "sober"—and his close friends, which were few, said he was only at ease in conflict, fighting, taking some risk. He should have joined a circus, they said, and walked a wire.

I guess if we have to place the blame somewhere on how that day just came apart around us, we can blame it on the livestock. My mother had let me play in the dirt with the rest of the yard urchins, until I skinned myself raw on a Kiddie Kar. I had just started to weep when my father reached for me, and began to walk with me toward the pasture and stream beyond. It shamed him, to have his little boy cry in front of the other men.

"I'll take the boy down to the creek and show him the cows, Margaret," he said, and I stopped crying as if I had a switch attached to my simple mind.

"I like to see the cows, Daddy," I said.

"I know, boy," he said.

That was me.

Boy.

I don't think he ever called me son, just "boy," but that was good enough. It's one of those words that bind you to someone strong as nylon cord, if you say it right.

I was too old to carry, surely, but I swung in his arms like a doll. He was a little man, even shorter than my tall mother, but incredibly strong. Through the open neck of his sports shirt you could see the tattoos of bluebirds inked high on his sunburned chest. My mother hated them, but the little boys were fascinated. It was a time when, if you had a tattoo, you had better be a Marine, and if you had an earring, you had better be a pirate.

Ahead of us, across the wire, a rust-and-white Hereford bull the size of a pickup watched over his harem, not far from the stream that would become our swimming hole.

From her chair, her time machine, Ava noticed us. Her screams and curses clawed out at him, and snatched his head around.

She was coming for us. She was short-legged and bowlegged and it took a while, but she caught him at the fence. He took me by one arm and pulled me close just as she grabbed my other arm and almost jerked it out of its socket. "Give me the child," she said as she set her shoes in the grass, ready to pull me in two if it meant saving half of me.

"I'm just takin' him to see the cows, Missus Bundrum," he said.

"Give him to me," she said, pulling.

"I ain't hurtin' him," he said.

Ava read her Bible and sent monthly payments to Oral Roberts for a written guarantee on her immortal soul, but that old woman could cuss like they were handing out money for it, and did, right in his face.

"You can't have him," she said.

It was like she was pulling against Legion himself, and maybe in her mind she was.

He turned loose and she dragged me away. He stood at the barbed wire as if he was caught on it. In the yard, people stared. Had he tried to hurt the boy? Unthinkable. He just hung there in the sunlight and paid for the man he was the night before, when he wobbled into my grandma's yard and threatened to drown us all in that lovely stream.

———

I DO NOT KNOW WHY, in all the train wrecks of gibberish she endured from drunken men, that one splinter of foolishness lodged in her mind. I pity him for being punished so much for just trying to take a walk with his son, but you have to forgive old women, who suffer so many fools. It was a good world for drunks then, and a bad

world for everybody else. A man could rise up in his drunkard's rai-
ment at night, dripping poison, and pull it off in the day like dirty
clothes. I often wondered, if a man could look in the daylight on the
drunk he was, would there be any drunks at all?

Ava made him look. It did not save him, but it was then he stopped
trying to pretend. The immaculate young man began to slough away,
revealing more of the drunk inside. It was the beginning and end of
everything, the end of hope, and the beginning of the days we lived
with him in the absence of it.

I have never dreamed of my father, but there are things that happened in our last year that seemed like dreams. From that time I carried a cloudy memory of choking in his arms, of the whole room
turning red as he clawed at my clenched teeth and poured what
seemed to be sand down my throat. It was the year I realized the TV
preachers' rants on hell were all wrong, that the devil lives in Alabama,
and swims in a Mason jar. He lost his looks, drank his paychecks,
wrecked his old cars, and stiffed the Tennessee Valley Electric until
all they would give us was free dark. My mother lived in fear of him,
and my older brother, more aware of what was going on than me,
lived in pure loathing. I have always felt guilty for the few nights I
enjoyed, the perfume of old beer on floor mats, bald tires hissing on
blacktop as we rode, him and me, to burn time in the company of sorry
men. "You were his favorite," my big brother told me, but I didn't
mean to be.

That is the man I wrote of in my early thirties. I summed him up as
a tragic figure, a one-dimensional villain whose fists and tongue lashed
my mother when he was drunk, who drove us away for months and
years only to reclaim us when we again crossed his mind. Against his
darkness her light was even brighter, as she just absorbed his cruelties
till she could not take them into herself anymore, and wasted her
beauty in a cotton field, picking a hundred pounds a day of a crop that
was light as air. She turned thirty over an ironing board, smoothing
other people's clothes, standing in line for a government check. He
became nothing more than the sledge I used to pound out her story of

unconditional love. I wanted more, of course. I wished he could have been just rewritten. But I got what I needed from him.

It was hypocritical to condemn such a careless man, after my own careless, selfish life, but I did it. I sawed my family tree off at the fork, and made myself a man with half a history. I had just one people, my mother's, and stood apart as my paternal grandmother grew old and died. Velma Bragg lived for over a century, surrounded by the family she watched over long after old age had taken her eyes. I was too stiff-necked to be one of them, one of her great family. I am truly sorry for that.

When Velma died, her youngest daughter, Ruby, gave my mother a small red box that held my father's last possessions, things he owned when he died in the winter of 1975. My mother, not knowing what else to do, gave it to me. Inside it, I found a crumbling, empty wallet, a clip-on tie, and a pair of yellowed, mismatched dice.

I rolled them across my desk.

Seven.

I rolled them again.

Seven.

I do not believe in ghosts, but I do believe in loaded dice. I sat for a long time, clicking them in my hand, touching something he touched. I do not know what I expected to feel, but I did not feel anything good. It was just bones, clean bones. I tossed the dice into a desk drawer to be forgotten with the rest of the junk—.22 rifle bullets, eight-year-old aspirin, foreign coins as worthless as washers from countries I will never see again.

In the last weeks of his life I had reoccurred to him one last time, and he gave me a box of books. For years I lugged the books from city to city, not even sure why. They mattered less, it seemed, with every change of address, and as I got older, meaner, sadder and dumber, most of the books got lost or left behind. I left the last of them on a curb in New Orleans, with a sign that said FREE. By my forty-fourth birthday he had become no more than a question I answered at book signings in nice-sounding clichés.

People who cared about me had, for years, warned me it was stupid to ignore such uneasy dead. One of the most elegant writers I knew, Willie Morris, did believe in ghosts. One night, about a year before his own death, he drank a bottle of whiskey at a restaurant outside Jackson, bounced off the door frame on his way to his car, and told me I would never have any peace until I wrote about my father. Others told me the same, but none as elegantly as him. "My boy," he said, "there is no place you can go he will not be."

But that did not seem true. In my life, I swung a pick, drove a dump truck, ran a chain saw, fist-fought some men, disappointed some women and wrote a billion words. I traveled from Africa to Arabia to Central Asia to make a living, or just to see the elephants before they are gone. I had been happy in New Orleans, broke in L.A., bashed with a rock in Miami, dog-cussed in New York, sick on a bus to Kashmir, lost in London, belligerent at Harvard, and greatly compromised in the Gamecock Motel. I was teargassed in the Bazaar of the Storytellers, enchanted by a magical midget in a Sarasota trailer park, and bit on my privates by a spider in a hotel on St. Charles. In one year, I argued unsuccessfully for my little brother before the Alabama Board of Pardons and Paroles, then gave the after-dinner speech at a banquet to honor a justice of the United States Supreme Court. I flew around the world at least three times and landed upside down in a convertible on Alabama 21, blue lights in my windshield, mud and glass in my mouth, and thinking, Man, this is cool.

He didn't take nothin' from me, really, that little man.

He had been worth three chapters to me, all he would ever be worth. Whole months went by, and I did not think of him at all.

Then, about three years ago, everything bounced, tumbled, rolled. I got a boy of my own.

It is not that I went looking for one. I had never dated, in my disreputable life, a woman with a child, and dreaded women who seemed determined to have one. There was no sadness in it, no hole in my life. I did not want a child, the way I did not want fuzzy pajamas, dishwashers, vacuum cleaners, neckties, sensible cars, department store credit cards, multivitamins, running shorts, umbrellas, goldfish, grown-up shoes, snow skis, and most cats.

I saw her, and I forgot.

I love women, but had seldom been plagued by the debilitating kind of love other men went on about, till it was just nauseating. My attention span, in romance, was that of a tick on a hot rock. Then I met her, and landed with a thud on the altar at the Peabody Hotel. "I have children," she told me, and I am sure I heard that, must have heard it. But by the time I regained what sense I had, I was driving car pool next to a ten-year-old boy who, for reasons I may never truly understand, believes I hung the moon.

I guess it is natural that, in the company of the boy, I almost always think of my father. But if you add all the time I spent with Charles Bragg in the first six years he tore in and out of our lives, it comes to only a few months, not even one whole year. I remember him in fragments, because we left him too soon, and still not soon enough. With the weight of that new boy tugging at my clothes, I went to find him.

———————

I N T H I S B O O K I close the circle of family stories in which my father occupied only a few pages, but lived between every line. In my first book, I tried to honor my mother for raising me in the deprivations he caused. In my second, I built from the mud up the maternal grandfather and folk hero who protected my mother from my father, but died before I was born, leaving us to him. In this last book, I do not rewrite my father, or whitewash him. But over a lifetime I have known a lot of men in prisons, men who will spend their eternity paying for their worst minute on earth. It came when they caught their wife cheating on them and thumbed back the hammer on a gun they bought to shoot rats and snakes, or got cross-eyed drunk in some fish camp bar and pulled a dime-store knife, just because they imagined a funny look or a suspicious smile. You do not have to forgive such men, ever, that minute. You can lock them away for it, put them to death for it, and spend your eternity cursing their name. It is not all they are.

The Boy

———

Y**OU DON'T SLEEP GOOD** in a chair by a hospital bed, but you do dream.

I saw the woman in a bookstore in Memphis. She had the kind of beauty people write songs about, red hair that tumbled to her shoulders in loose curls, jade eyes flecked with gold, lips of the most promising pink. She was tall, and just a little bit slinky.

"Will you marry me?" I asked, smooth as a concrete block tumbling down a hill.

"No," she said.

She taught at a college, and knew a half-wit when she heard one.

I watched her walk away for years, in my mind.

But I persevered, and we had a great, blistering romance. I wrote her love letters that should have made me gag, and she wrote me the same. I even saved one, for when I am old, or alone.

But she had to ask her littlest boy, who was her world, if she could remarry.

"Sure," he said. "Where are we goin' on the honeymoon?"

I turned forty-six in the summer of 2005 and became the closest thing to a father I will ever be, because I loved a woman with a child. I guess it happens all the time.

But a man who chases a woman with a child is like a dog that chases a car and wins. How many times since then have I stared at the boy in dumb wonder, and muttered: "Son, if your momma had just been homely, think how much easier my life would have been."

The idea of having a boy had always nibbled at me. I could imagine us in a boat in the deep blue, casting into lucky water, talking about life. But the idea of a boy is one thing, while the reality is you spend your last spry years at the Sonic, stabbing at a big red button, then watching him baste the interior of your truck in root beer and barbecue sauce as he squeals, whines, pouts and punches every button on the radio till all you can get is static and satanic howls. At least, I thought, there was just the one. Her two oldest boys were all but grown by the time I came along. The oldest referred to me only as "that dude," and the middle one, I still believe, is from another galaxy.

But I would tolerate the little boy, for the woman. I believed I was catching him at a good age. He was house-trained, past diapering but still too young to borrow my car or ask me questions on sex, about which, of course, I would be forced to lie. I did not expect much. All I wanted was a brave, clean boy who would take out the trash, be kind to his mother, and occasionally bathe the big dog, which also came with the marriage and smelled as if it had already died. It would be nice if the boy was coordinated, had good oral hygiene, could catch a football, did his homework, and did not run buck naked in the house.

I should have lowered my expectations a little, to "house-trained."

He refused to hold his fork right, transforming me from what I always believed to be a real man into an etiquette-quoting popinjay. I watched him, amazed, as he chased a single green pea across a plate and dumped a mountain of mashed potatoes on the white tablecloth, all of which he would have scooped up and eaten if I had not threatened him with charm school. He showered as if he were running through a waterfall, barely getting damp before shouting to his beleaguered mother, "Where's my pants?" If she did not respond, he would run naked after all. She had to inspect him after every bath because he would not use soap, or wash his hair, or else wash only the front or back part of his head, hoping that would be the part she chose to inspect. I was a boy once, too, but I did not look greasy *after* a bath, or festoon the backseat in used tissues, or sprinkle the floor mats with takeout biscuit crumbs as if I needed them to find my way home again.

"Enjoy it," said the woman who bore this troglodyte, "because that little boy will disappear before your eyes."

"When?" I asked, hopeful.

I almost ran the first time I saw him eat pancakes. He covered a table—and his upper body—with syrup, then spread it like plague across a new day.

In one restaurant, he managed to get a gob of spaghetti sauce on his underarm. "You got some . . ." I said, pointing.

He licked it off. I did not think it humanly possible.

In another, he blew his nose so loud at the table it trembled the water glasses.

"He's yours," I said to the woman.

If he did not like the taste of something, he just spit it out.

"He is not unusual," the woman told me, but I saw doubt in her eyes.

I hoped a boy so nasty would be tough, gritty, but instead this was a child of piano lessons and gifted schools, a child once rushed to the hospital with a tummy ache, where an X-ray showed that he had merely overdosed on cinnamon Pop-Tarts and Chick-fil-A.

He yelled for his mother to come stomp a spider.

He wept from a boo-boo, or if he was tired.

It seemed too much, that the boy would be gentle, pampered, and nasty. I guess it might have been easier if he had looked, sounded or at least pretended to be a little like me, or the boy I remembered myself to be. But on trips, he traveled with his own pillow and blanket, which he called his "blanky." He needed them, he said, to be "comfy."

"Boys," I said, "do not have a blanky."

"Yes they do," he said.

"No they—" and I gave up and walked away.

He was too pampered, too helpless, I thought, to enjoy or endure the company of men like me. He was a sensitive, loving, gentle boy who said his prayers without being told, loved his momma and, to my horror, attached himself to me with fishhooks I could not pull free.

At night, in front of a television frozen forever on Animal Planet, he used me for a pillow, and no matter how much I chafed or squirmed or shoved, he always came back. I would fret and the woman would smile as he dozed on my shoulder, a toxic wad of neon-green bubblegum hanging half out of his mouth. He followed me like a baby duck, stood glued to me in restaurants and stores, and expected me to hug him, as nasty as he was. I hugged, grimacing, as if I had wrapped my arms around a used Porta Potti. He even expected me to tuck him in at night, and as I did I wondered what had happened to me, and who was this nearly neutered man who stood in line for Day-Glo nachos and sticky juice boxes, and paid good money to see the march of the goddamned penguins.

He did not go on the honeymoon, but we felt so guilty we brought him back the next week to Fort Walton. The Gulf was rough and the boy swallowed a 55-gallon drum of seawater, most of which came up through his nose. He would reach for my hand in the water, but the idea of it still seemed wrong to me. "You just stand close, so I can grab you if you go under," I said. Then a wave knocked him down and beat him up as it rolled him along the bottom, and I had to snatch him up, coughing, spitting. I let him hold my hand for a while as we waded into the shallow water, but as soon as his feet were under him I shook my hand free, because that is not the kind of men we are.

"He's a little boy," the woman said.

"He's a boy," I said.

"He's not a little you," she said. "You can't make him be like you."

I only wanted him to be ready. I just didn't know what for.

I must have dozed awhile. An alarm screamed me awake, my heart jerking in my chest. I expected to see a team of doctors rush in to revive her. But instead a single, solid, middle-aged woman in a sensible smock shuffled in to change out a flattened IV, flicked off the alarm, then shuffled out. I waited for my heart to slow, and caught my mother looking at me. She is seventy now. She likes to quote a poem about an old woman who has come to live uninvited in her house, a wrinkled, ancient woman she can see only in the mirror. I watched her, through the dark and the fog of painkillers, try to figure out who I was. She cannot see a lick without her featherlight, Sophia Loren glasses, but her hearing is fine. She hears with absolute clarity the things she wants to hear, and not one syllable she does not.

It wouldn't be long till the next shift, the next son. I asked how her pain was and she told me not too bad.

"Well," I said, "you ought to be ashamed of your damned self."

My bedside manner was not all it could be in the summer of 2006. I sat by her bed all night for three nights, to watch her breathe. She hated doctors and always had, and that almost killed her. She let a thing as simple as a bad gallbladder degenerate into gangrene, but a sure-handed surgeon in our small-town hospital saved her. I griped in the dark but never told her the truth, how I was never so scared in my life as I was outside her operating room. I mean, didn't that silly old woman know that once she is gone there is nothing left?

But that was not really true, I thought, not anymore.

"Can I get you anything?" I asked.

"You can bring the boy to see me," she said.

My boy.

"I like that boy," she said.

"I know, Momma."

She plies him with biscuits, and watches him read on the floor. Some women melt around little boys. She did not give a damn that he did not look like us, or come to her in the usual way. He looks like my father's people, dark-haired, handsome. How odd, he would look like him.

"He's spoiled," I said. "You helped."

She harrumphed. It is her prerogative to spoil a boy.

"He's not real tough," I said.

"He don't need to be," she said.

The woman says that, that same way. I sat awake another few hours as the window began to glow yellow behind the blinds. My big brother and sister-in-law tapped on the door and came in, half hiding a sack that smelled suspiciously like a sausage biscuit.

"How is she?" he asked.

"Still hurtin'," I said, "but nothin' she can't stand."

He smiled at that.

Once, a long time ago, we were not that tough either, him and me. But she was, or we would have vanished. I walked into the heat of the morning to my truck and drove through the town that had framed our story for a hundred years, past fast-food restaurants and antebellum mansions, rich cousins and poor cousins, waiting for the same parade. I glanced at my phone, knowing that I should check in at home.

This is what it is like, I thought, to be the circus bear. You pace your cage till they let you out to do tricks. You talk about tuition, hardwood floors, braces and sometimes algebra, and see how long you can balance on that wobbling ball before you go berserk and eat the crowd. Sometimes you bust out, but never get further than the Exxon station before you go slouching home, for treats. You are a tame bear now. They will have you riding a red tricycle and wearing a silly hat before too long.

I dialed, a little fearfully. The woman is mad at me a lot. I make her mad, being me.

The boy never is.

I walk in the door, and the boy never looks disappointed in me.

CHAPTER ONE

In a Cloud of Smoke

MAN, I WISH I COULD HAVE SEEN HIM. They say he was slick and pretty in '55, and when he leaned against his black-and-pearl '49 Mercury in his white Palm Beach suit and cherry-red necktie, he looked like he got lost on his way to some-place special and pulled off here to ask the way. He always stole a red flower for his lapel—what magic, to always steal a red one—and cinched up his pants with a genuine leatherette imitation alligator belt. His teeth were too good to be true, his canines long and wicked white, and he wore his wavy, reddish-brown hair swooped up high like the Killer, Jerry Lee. It turned black when he combed it back with Rose hair oil, and when he fought, leading with his right, punishing with his left, all that hair flopped into those blue-flame eyes. He only finished sixth grade but he was drawing good government money then, as a Marine, and drove home every weekend from the base in Macon with one thing on his mind. He liked to pose on the square and see the girls sway by, but wouldn't whistle because he'd already found the one. "He smiled mischievous," my mother said, like he was picking life's pocket, like he was getting away with something by hanging around and breathing air. He was just another linthead kid, but as different from other men she knew, the brush-arbor prophets, pulpwooders and shade-tree mechanics, as the mannequin in Steinberg's department store was from a cornfield scarecrow. When it was time to go he slid behind the wheel and turned the key, and he looked like an angel, one of the fallen kind, as the big engine caught fire and he vanished in a blue-black, oily, noxious cloud.

"His car burnt a lot of oil," she said. "It burnt so much oil that a cloud followed him all around town, burnt so much oil he couldn't keep oil in it, but instead of getting it fixed he'd just go out to that fillin' station out on the highway, you know, where Young's used to be, and he'd pull it up to a barrel of the burnt oil they drained out of people's cars, and he'd dip it out in a bucket and put it in his ol' car, and he'd just ride and ride. People used to laugh at him. They'd say, 'Here comes that Bragg boy, in a cloud of smoke.'

"They ought not laughed at him, though," she said. "People's mean."

The words must have tasted a little stale.

She had not defended him in forty years.

"Now," she said, "it was a pretty car."

She remembers him that way, in smoke.

But sometimes, in a blue moon, she remembers him on his knees.

"It was about four months after we started seein' each other. We was at Germania Springs, and he was gettin' him a drink of water, laying on his belly on the creek bank. You could drink it right out of the creek back then, and it was good 'n' cold. Well, he got a drink, and he turned and looked at me. 'Will you marry me?' he said. And I laughed at him and he got mad. I think he cussed a little, too. But, I mean, who asks somebody to get married while they're on their belly gettin' a drink of water? 'You're kiddin', ain't you?' I told him, and then he cussed again. He said, 'Hell, I was serious. Will you marry me?' But I giggled again. I couldn't quit."

She has tried to forget so much it seems odd to try to remember. But she can still see him pushing himself up to his knees for a little dignity. For a second, just a second, he faced her on one knee, just like in a storybook.

"I mean it, goddammit," he said.

His face was bright, burning red.

"Will you, or not?"

———

H E WAS NOT A MARRYING MAN.

The old men laughed at him, all duded up with that oil bucket in his hand, but the women loved his face. Even men—men so afraid of appearing feminine they would walk a wide loop around the unmentionables in Sears to avoid being in proximity of a panty—would concede that, yeah, that Charles Bragg was a good-looking man. He had a movie star's squared-off chin with a dashing white line across it, like a dueling scar. He got it one night, drunk, when he banged his face on the steering wheel, but it made him look mysterious and a little bit dangerous all the same. He had Indian blood and cheekbones, proud and high, and his face tanned to dark red. His ears and Adam's apple were too big but his hands were as small and delicate as a woman's, yet strong as wire pliers, like his daddy's had been. He talked country but dressed for town, as all the boys from the mill village did back then, a hybrid hillbilly with silver dimes flashing in his black penny loafer shoes. He chain-smoked Pall Malls and toted a thin, yellow-handled knife in his left hip pocket, so he could get at it, quick. He hid a snub-nosed pistol at the small of his back, but only on the weekends, and never when he was with her. He raised fighting dogs, bet on chickens and loved vanilla ice cream, and I guess he was a scoundrel before he knew what a scoundrel was.

"He would cut you, if you hemmed him up," said my father's cousin Carlos Slaght, whose daddy named him after a label he saw on a crate of Mexican apples in Christmas 1932. "But he was a good boy, all in all." If you turned him upside down and shook him, as his older brothers were prone to do, dice and a pint of liquor would have bounced across the floor and fifty-two cards would have fluttered down, or fifty-one, if he had one hid. The darkness he had done an ocean away had left a mark on him, sure, but he hid it then, like his tattoos. Back home, he drew his pocket comb like a gun, and could often be seen slouched at a table in the Ladiga Grill, preening, pretending not to notice the girls who noticed him.

"He walked by me once on the street and didn't speak, and turned around and followed me down the sidewalk," my mother said. She caught him doing that, caught his reflection in a storefront window, but she didn't turn around and embarrass him. She just smiled, and kept walking. He showed up a lot when she was in the café, and he would sit and smoke and drink black coffee and steal looks at her over the top of a paperback western.

He had a reputation of course, but she didn't know, and that is the same as having none at all. "Charles always had the women," said his buddy Jack Andrews. "Nice girls, too, I mean. Church girls. But your momma . . . He fell in love with her. He made up this picture in his head of how he thought his life ought to be. She was in that picture with him, and he never did get that picture out of his mind."

I have rarely been able to describe her, the way she was then. I guess all boys have trouble with that. I said she looked like a movie star, but she was prettier than that, than that blowsy, made-up prettiness. Her face had peace in it then, serenity. It may be, after the way his life had passed, that was what he found to be most lovely of all.

She was raised in the foothills. When she came to town as a young woman, it was to keep other people's babies and mop their floors. Then here comes my father, all dressed up and slicked down and pool-hall cool, with the mountains in his own bloodline and the mill village on his driver's license, but posing as something different, something more. He was quick and sharp as a serpent's tooth in that white suit, but not sharp enough to see he did not need to pose for her. "Oh, he sure did priss around," she said. "I just liked his teeth."

———

M Y FATHER NEVER REALLY LIVED ANYWHERE but here, in the town where he was born. He was stationed overseas and in Georgia, incarcerated for a while in Virginia and found body and fender work in Texas, but mostly his life passed within the city limits of the northeast Alabama town of Jacksonville. It is a lovely town, and fifty years ago, as he wooed my mother, this was a postcard in real time, its main avenue lined with white-columned mansions and three-hundred-year-old oaks, its working-class people tucked out of sight and down the hill. The through street, old Highway 21, was named for John Pelham, a handsome young artillery officer blown off his horse by an exploding shell in the battle at Kelly's Ford. General Lee wept when he received news of the death of the boy he called "my gallant Pelham." But reverence just wasn't in my father then. In '55, he drag-raced his rod-knocking Mercury from stop sign to stop sign on Pelham Road, outrunning nobody, just powerfully bored. He checked his hair in the rearview mirror, checked his side mirror for the town's one and only police car, and laid rubber all over hallowed Rebel ground.

It ran just two lanes then, north to south. To the west was the mill village and its identical tract houses, each with its one, company-approved tree facing alphabet streets paved in ash, smut and cinders from the mill's coal-fired power plant. The Pentecostals lived here, displaced mountain people. The mill people climbed the hill to go to town, and hard drinkers from the village liked to joke that if police let them out before they were sober, they could roll down A Street right into their beds. Here, freight cars backed up a half mile, hauling in whole counties of cotton and hauling out the earth itself, from hills of red soil piled at Dixie Clay. The East Side was the fashionable part of town, but the West Side bent its back to the place, powered it, made it run.

The East Side wore a lace of dogwoods, azaleas and wild plums. Here were the college professors, the merchants and professionals, the landlords and the necktie men, prominent First Baptists and Episcopalians. The nice streets were paved with asphalt and clean, white gravel. "The East Side people dranked about as much as we did," said Carlos, "but did keep it better hid." Also to the east, but a discreet distance away, was Eastwood, which most people called Needmore. It was a black community of small, well-tended houses. On weekends, world-class baseball players, held here by color, played in epic games as concessionaires fried fish in big, smoking pots and served it on white bread with a single daub of catsup in the middle, like a bullet wound.

To the north was the college, a beautiful landscape of brick buildings, tree-shaded and immaculate, a teachers' school that grew into something more, and a small college football powerhouse. The mascot was a fighting gamecock, and when the marching band played Dixie, the East Siders and West Siders rose together, and roared.

To the south was commerce, what people even now just call the Highway. You could see two drive-in movies in a five-mile stretch, visit a bootlegger who hid in plain sight, eat the best foot-long hotdog in the known universe and buy a pistol with no questions asked, and still not be more than seven miles out of town.

In the middle of it all was the square—not really a square at all but a circle. Off to one side squatted City Hall, not an antebellum showpiece, but a yellow fortress pieced from natural rock. For my people, it was just "the jail," and we knew it the way some people know their church or a Mason's Lodge. It was an old-time jail with iron bars and iron bunks and white beans seven days a week, but the worst thing about being locked inside was the constant sound of motion outside its iron doors, as the bored young people circled, circled in their cars.

It was there, in that orbit of Hudsons, Packards and Chevrolets, that my father fell in love, betrayed a buddy, and third-wheeled his way into my mother's heart. But it's not like he snuck around about it.

Lit in the cool neon wash of the lovely old Princess Theater, he wooed my mother while she was on a date with one of his best friends. We have always been the kind of men who do not regard a woman as all that unattainable just because she is attached to somebody else by class ring, engagement ring or wedding band, but as backstabbings go, this one was remarkable, diabolical, and complete.

It was a Saturday, we believe. Underage roughnecks slouched dejectedly in front of the pool hall as, inside, decorated World War II veteran Homer Barnwell watched over the tables. "I never could play," he would tell the boys, but he took a lot of money off the ones who said they could. The theater marquee spelled out Johnny Mack Brown for the main event, but promised werewolves for the midnight show. Officer Walter Rollins, who worked days in Hoyt Fair's sawmill, circled the square in his faded black patrol car. The chief, Whitey Whiteside, had been shot to death in the mill village just months before by a drunken man named Robert Dentmon, a few days before the two men had planned to go fishing. His widow, Mary, took money for the show in her booth under the marquee. Lorrene West sold fresh popcorn.

Across the square, the Boozer brothers, buzzing clippers in their hands, shaved flattops so close it was a wonder they didn't draw blood. Ed Johnson cashed paychecks at the IGA, and Alfred Roebuck welcomed both the hopeful and bereaved into his furniture store, selling sofas in front and coffins in the back. Little boys counted pennies on the soda counter at West Side Drug Store as, in the nearby Creamery, crew-cut college boys in skinny ties chatted up flowers of the Deep South over cones of black walnut, pistachio and butter pecan. A Greek man named George turned big steaks and seared fat hamburgers at the Ladiga Grill, as redheaded Louise Treadaway welcomed travelers off the bus from Anniston at her family's bus stop café. Old men told lies in decrepit vinyl chairs at Mathis Cab, and a black cat glared from the window at Reid's shoe shop. Some nights there was gunfire and heartache and car crashes, but most nights, slow nights like this, you could have cut the whole town out of the air and hung it on the wall.

The young man my mother was seeing then, a tall, black-haired, green-eyed boy, was a good-looking rake just like my father. They were just hanging out, killing time, when the boy told his buddy Charles that he wanted to take that Bundrum girl out on a proper date. But he had just had his prized '48 Ford painted a sharper battleship gray, and any fool knows that if you drive a car before the paint dries good, every speck of highway dust in four counties will adhere to the hood. Still, he was anxious. He was pretty sure that if he didn't take her out, some sweet-talker would.

"That's that pretty girl?" my father asked.

He knew good and damn well who she was. The boy had introduced them some time ago, and my father even asked if he might write her from where he was stationed, somewhere far off and probably dangerous, and just wanted to read a friendly voice from home.

The boy said yes, she was pretty.

My father was willing to help a buddy out.

"You can take my car," he said.

The boy was apparently not eager to date my mother in a car that was liable to choke her to death with smut, but he had little choice here. He said, Thank you, buddy, and reached for the keys. My father dangled them but didn't let go.

"Do you mind," he asked, "if I go with y'all?"

When the boy went to pick up my mother, my father was sitting in the backseat, his suit pressed, a carnation in his lapel. It was cool weather, and all the flower pots and beds were just dead sticks, and she has always wondered if he crawled in a hothouse, or a bedroom window. He did not buy flowers. It was against his religion.

He just nodded hello as she climbed in the car. The other boy touched the gas pedal, and they left in a black, reeking cloud. The gears were out of sync, so my father, as the engine began to whine, would fling himself forward from the backseat, shout at the boy to press the clutch, and, leaning between the boy and my mother, shove the gearshift up or down or sideways with a horrible, grinding sound, and then settle back into the backseat, till he had to shift again.

They hadn't gone a mile when my father began talking to the backs of their heads.

"I reckon you're the most beautiful thing in this whole town," my father said.

My mother, and the boy, too, didn't know what to do.

"I reckon you're the most beautiful thing I ever seen," he said.

She just stared out the windshield, embarrassed.

"In the whole world," he said.

Whiskey can make men talk like that. But there was not one trace, one sniff, on his breath.

Then he leaned forward and tapped the boy on the shoulder.

"I'm gonna take her away from you," he said.

He did not sound like he was joking.

The boy could have fought for her, but the world is full of brave boys who limp home with their lips split and still no kiss good night. He was a rough fist-fighter himself and, my mother said, "could be mean as a scorpion." But my father's reputation, and his family's reputation, prevented a lot of violence in those days. A family that so routinely pulled knives on each other was not one you engaged without at least weighing the consequences. The boy was seething, though, and steered the oil-burning hulk to his own house, took my mother by the hand and tugged her away. He opened the door of his still-moist Ford so my mother could slide in, then drove off mad as hell, flinching at every puff of sand or flying leaf that brushed his quarter panels, leaving my father on the sidewalk, grinning like a devil in the lingering smoke.

That is what she saw, those white, perfect teeth in that devil's grin, as the other boy told her good night.

My father took her out himself the next weekend, and the next, and if any other boy even expressed an interest he paid them a visit, and the suitors began to peel away. He told my mother, all the time, that she was just by God beautiful, as pretty as Rita Hayworth. He said these things in a voice that sounded like it was coming from the bottom of a well. You could feel it, not just hear it, feel his whole chest vibrate from that deep voice, as if, like a little car with an engine that's just too big, the voice could shake that pretty little man apart. Anyway, it is the kind of voice you believe.

They got to know each other in that wretched car, just riding around; once you saw the movies, and if there was nothing happening at the convention hall, there was nowhere else to go for a month or two. She was a little bit ashamed to ride in it, but only a little. She had the beauty, the currency, to marry outside her class, but the truth was she would have been uncomfortable with a richer boy, with a people who might have looked down on her, or worse, on her people.

His family was legend in the mill village. The Bragg men drank corn whiskey, played poker, rolled dice and settled arguments with fists and knives and sometimes just acted a little peculiar, but worked hard in the mill, never refused a plea for help, gave away truckloads of food from gardens and hog killings, and asked only to be left alone, at least until the sound of glass breaking and women crying. Their women were long-suffering, loyal unto death, and lost in love, and if they had not been, their men would have rotted in jail.

"They was respected people," Carlos said, "with a few vices."

My mother's own daddy made whiskey, but drank and laughed, drank and sang, never took a sip in front of her, never let it change him from a good man into something else. Why on earth, she wished with all her heart, could it not be that way again?

She remembers a smell of citrus the first time he took her to meet his mother and father. "He had been down to Florida, and their house was full of the biggest grapefruits, oranges and lemons I ever seen," she said. She knew better than to ask how he got them. A man who could not drive past a rosebush or window box without committing larceny could not be expected to pass a thousand acres of citrus growing at the side of the road.

His mother and father, little people like him, greeted her at the door. She noticed, with some embarrassment, that she was the tallest person in the room. Bobby, his father, was ironed so stiff he seemed to be all sharp angles and flat planes, like a paper doll with a little, round, white-topped head perched on top. He wore a starched white shirt buttoned to the neck, overalls so new and stiff they made a racket like plywood rubbing together when he walked, and immaculate, black, wing-tip shoes.

Velma was tiny like her man, and had the kindest face my mother had ever seen. She was already gray-haired, a slightly stooped little woman who worked a full shift at the cotton mill, cleaned houses, helped raise other people's children and spent every other free moment trying to keep her husband, a rapscallion and brawler when he was well-oiled, from harm at the hands of police, card players, drinking buddies, his own sons, and himself. My father was her baby, the pride of her life. He called her Momma, and called his daddy Bob.

My mother noticed a tension in them, sitting there knee to knee, and when she looked closer she noticed that Bob was quite drunk. It seemed that he had gotten lit and picked a fight with Velma, and had not sobered up enough to tell her he was sorry. "He got real, real red-faced when he drank, and he was red-faced then," my mother said.

"What's wrong, Bob?" my father said.

"She's got a man hid in the house," he said.

Velma rolled her eyes.

"She ain't got no man in the house, Bob," my father said.

"I tell you she does," Bobby said.

Here my father was, trying to impress his new girl, while his daddy was having a delusion. My mother just sat, staring at her lap, and whispered: "My, them lemons sure do smell—"

"I heard him, goddammit," Bobby said.

"—nice," she squeaked.

My father vaulted to his feet.

"Come on, Bob, we'll find him."

He went from room to room, looking in closets.

"Not here," he shouted.

He ran to the kitchen, and jerked open the refrigerator door.

"Reckon he's in here, Bob," he said.

His father sat, his face redder.

My mother wanted to laugh, but just sat, politely.

It was like the circus to her, with midgets and everything.

The one thing that worried her was the way his mother looked at her. "I thought she didn't like me, 'cause she just sat there, and looked at me so sad," my mother said. As they left, Velma reached as high as she could and hugged her neck, fiercely. Years later, she would tell her what she wanted to say, but dared not, with the men in the room.

She wanted to tell her to run.

But there seemed no need to be afraid, then.

"I never saw him drink then," my mother said. "He drank coffee. I never even remember seeing him with a beer. I had heard all them people who went off in the military was social drinkers, but we would sit for hours and hours, him sipping coffee, smoking cigarettes, acting like a real gentleman."

He told my mother he had prospects, told her he might be in the Marines for life, or might work with his brothers in a body and fender shop. But he told her he would starve before he would work in a cotton mill, choking on cotton dust in a place where blades and gears chewed up people, taking their fingers, hands and arms. He had grown up seeing coughing, maimed, broken-down men pass the caskets of their brothers and sisters through the windows of houses too small and tight to fit the coffins through the halls and front door. He was not afraid of anything, usually, but that was his terror, to be passed around like that. But he told her not to worry, that he would give her and their children a better life than that. He told her, holding her hand, she could depend on him.

He was kind to her mother, who didn't like his fancy looks, and respectful to her father, who was almost a folk hero in these hills, a tall, gaunt moonshiner and hammer swinger who had never in his life lost a stand-up fight with another man, or any two men. My father took work with him on the weekends, roofing a house with him, and spent his paycheck on a suit for her, in the style the women called "sweater suits." Before he had a chance to give it to her, my grandfather took my mother aside. "Now, that boy thinks he's done somethin' real big, and you act proud, now, when he gives it to you." She told him yes, she would, but it had not been necessary. It was the first dress she ever had that was not homemade or cast-off, given to her by the rich ladies whose floors she swept.

He made her other promises, crossed his heart and hoped to die.

He gave her a silver dollar as seed corn, for money they would save.

He gave her a cedar hope chest, to hold their future.

"For when we get us a house," he told her.

When he heard she had never had a doll, growing up poor in the foothills of the Appalachians, he went to a doll maker in Jacksonville, an old woman famous for her fancy needlework, and had her make his new wife a ballerina, what my mother called a dancing doll. It cost twenty-five dollars, about half a month of a Marine's pay.

He gave her flowers all the time.

"But they didn't cost him nothin'," she said.

He would strain to stand as tall as he could when they had their picture made, so he would be almost as tall as her. It never worked. His feet were so small he could wear her shoes, and he did sometimes, puttering around the house in her little flat shoes, to make her laugh.

They spent every waking minute together, and would have spent more, but her daddy would have killed him. He disappeared on Sunday night, to go back to the base in Macon in time for duty on Monday morning. Every Sunday, he stayed with her until the last minute, then roared off into the night, sliding around the twisting roads, racing the sun.

The old car took too long to get there, and cut into his time with her. So he saved up and got a machine that would move. It was a 1954 Hudson, and had a chromed, winged hood ornament that made it look like a silver eagle was flying just ahead of it on the highway. It rolled on gangster whitewalls and four perfectly matched factory hubcaps, and had a "Big Six" six-cylinder motor, three-speed on the column, fender skirts on the rear wheels and six little-bitty chrome letters that spelled out "Hornet" on the side. On Sundays, they rode and listened to the radio and talked about the sons they would have. They would all be sons, he figured. They would have to be. They decided to name the first one Samuel, after his grandfather. With a big name like that, their kin kidded them, the boy would probably come into the world, dust himself off, and walk home.

After midnight, he would lift his uniform out of the closet, kiss her goodbye, and disappear at the corner of D Street and Alexandria Road, leaving a little skid mark there, showing off.

But every late night, in the stillness of the barracks, he wrote her a letter.

Dear Mark, he wrote. He called her that, for short.

How are you?
I am fine.

He beat his letters home, sometimes, but she ran to the mailbox anyway, six days a week.

He never wrote anything special, at least nothing she remembers.

It was how he signed them that mattered.

Goodnight
Sweet dreams
I miss you
Honey

She read every one a dozen times, then put them, in perfect order, in a cardboard box. One letter, in the fourth month, was a little different from the rest. At the bottom, he wrote:

"Look under the stamp."

She painstakingly peeled it off. Underneath, in tiny letters, he had written:

I
Love
You

She ran to the box where she had saved them, and, stamp by stamp, peeled the stamps away.

He had written it every time.

———

A T THE SPRING, people were staring at them.
The boy on his knees seemed about to implode into his little self.

The tall blonde woman, prettier than Rita Hayworth, giggled and shook.

"Are you serious?" she said.

"Yes, dammit to hell," he said.

"Well," she said, "okay."

They drove to a little town south of Chattanooga, to a justice of the peace. His sister Ruby and brother-in-law Herman, who lived in Ringgold, waited in the car.

"Your momma was so pretty," Ruby said.

She borrowed a pink sweater suit from Ruby, and wore white loafers.

He had on blue Levi's, a blue long-sleeved shirt, and black penny loafers with Mercury dimes.

She was so nervous, she stumbled over the vows.

He was so nervous he kissed her too quickly, with things still unsaid.

They ran out happy, but then she realized what she had done.

"Charles," she told him in the yard, "I forgot to say 'I do.' "

He grabbed her hand to drag her back inside, but she was too embarrassed.

She never did get it said.

———·—·———

SHE LIVED IT AGAIN, as a favor to me. She did not mind the story too much, because it was the happiest one she had. But as she talked, the man she re-created had no heart in him, no coursing blood, as if she was quoting from some book she had read. As she talked, I had in my mind a pretty rag doll sprawled on a shelf, a half-stitched hole where his heart and guts would be. I think she was still afraid, scared that if she gave him heat, or feeling, she could not stop him coming true again. But he was too much man, even as a bad one, to lie that way for too long in anyone's mind, and almost against her will he came to life, for at least a little while.

The Boy

—·—

I GOT THE BOY a sweet tea at Cecil's café, waved at Shirley behind the grill, and took him on a tour of our town. We saw mansions and monuments, its painted face. Then, at the dead end of A Street, I showed him its still, silent heart.

"Is it really haunted?" the boy asked.

I glanced at the high, red-brick walls.

"As much as a place can be."

The machines shut down five years ago. The roar that shook this village across a century shushed to a hateful quiet, and a blizzard of cotton fell through dead air to lie like dirty snow on scarred hardwood planks. The last to leave said they heard a rustling, as if generations still moved in the vast rooms that killed them one cut, one cough at a time.

That morning, I told him I would show him the place my father's people worked and lived. As I slid into the truck I tossed his travel blanket into the back, out of reach.

"You won't need it today," I said.

The truth is I didn't want to be seen with a blanky, or with a boy who needed one. We rolled through the village of sold-off houses to the mill itself. Logging chains sealed its doors, locking out two hundred people who lost paychecks and health insurance when it closed. "It ain't when it's running it's scary," a man had told me. "It's when it ain't." I wanted the boy to see it, but it was like showing him the dark side of the moon.

It was our first year together. Still hopeful for my improvement, the woman made me go to church. She made me put on a jacket and sit in a pew in one of those big, sedate churches where no one shouts much. Children lit candles and sang hymns, and after the excitement we retired to a foyer for Bundt cake. The boy grew up in it. His grandfather was a deacon and his grandmother was, too. His mother taught Sunday school. He went to church camp, and swam in a baptismal lake. He liked church, he said. What boy says that?

The boy's school was a gentle place, too, where teachers knew his mother by her first name, called him a sweet boy, well-behaved, and served ice cream with strawberries at show-and-tell. He did not ride the bus. The woman dropped him off in the morning and picked him up in the afternoon, with a suitable bribe. When you are ten, sugar is your opiate, and if he had sorrows, which is unlikely, he drowned them in root beer.

It was the same at home. At supper, his mother asked him "What would you like?" knowing damn well it was tall Dr Peppers and chicken nuggets and sundaes swimming with crushed-up M&Ms. The house was his shrine, full of kindergarten paintings and art-class abominations. His friends came over for playdates, in a bedroom buried under an avalanche of toys. At night, after prayers, his mother rubbed his back as he floated into pleasant dreams. She made sure of it. He was not allowed to watch TV news, to see the world on fire. He dreamed of ice cream, as his braces twinkled in the night-light. He had never had a cavity, and not a single curse had ever slipped from his expensive teeth.

Mine, mine were filled with lead and mercury, courtesy of the welfare. I could have had them redone in gold, but I had come to like the taste in my mouth.

I wanted the boy to see the mill, and know how lucky he was.

We idled over a ditch that might have been a creek in wet weather. Beer bottles littered the bottom and not much thrived in it but snakes.

In my father's time little boys caught them with snares made of wire and pipe and boiled them alive in pickle jars. Ragweed smothered it now, but it was a great chasm in 1942.

"My daddy jumped it when he was a boy," I said.

The boy saw a ditch.

"He was the best at it, everybody said," I said.

The boy popped sugar-free gum and fondled his Game Boy, his first love. He was not insolent, just disconnected, immune.

"Do you know what they call that creek?" I asked.

"What?" he said, to be polite.

"Shit Creek," I said.

He laughed out loud. You don't hear much cussing when everybody at supper is a deacon.

I had his attention, for a while.

I showed him the village church.

"They spoke in unknown tongues, and got slain in the spirit," I said.

His eyes opened wide.

"They didn't actually die," I said.

We passed a patch of weeds.

"There's where Robert Dentmon killed the police chief."

"Why?" the boy said.

"They said it was over a water line."

We made a right turn onto D Street, and there it was, 117.

People here call it Frogtown. My father was the prince of Frogtown.

"They fought in the street," I said, as much to myself as the boy.

"Who?" he asked.

"My daddy and his brothers," I said.

"Why?" he said.

I shook my head.

"They liked to," I said.

"Why?"

"They drank a good bit," I said.

But he had never smelled it on a man's breath, or seen it burn wicked blue. Like always, when I thought of it, I could see them again, the men of my father's house. I was a boy, too, the last time, but will never forget the just-checked violence in them, laughing, cursing at a kitchen table, cigarettes burning in their lips. They held jelly glasses sloshing with moonshine, and I wonder still why they did not blow themselves to kingdom come. As a boy, I believed they were what men were supposed to look like, handsome, unafraid, black knights with tire irons instead of swords. They toasted sunset and sunrise, and broke a thousand cups. "I'd never seen nothing like 'em in my life," my mother liked to say, "and I never will." It was their place that created them, too, but grinding, like a whetrock.

The boy asked if we could rent a movie.

"Sure," I said.

CHAPTER TWO

The Village

———·———

I WAS STILL a little boy when I saw that first sacrifice, that first empty sleeve. I was rich then. A pocketful of birthday nickels weighed me down as I chased after imaginary Indians from the saddle of my dime-store pony. It was stuck hard in the cement in front of the A&P, but I was gaining on them, one nickel at a time, when the one-armed man walked by. I was barefoot in town on a weekday, so it had to be a payday, and it had to be summer. The linoleum was cold beneath my feet as I followed the man inside, curious and staring. He was thin, his pants billowing from his waist, his face gaunt and grooved and sad, so sad that one of us, surely, had to cry. He had on a long-sleeved, checkered shirt with one sleeve hanging loose and empty, not pinned up and final but swinging ever so slightly with every step, as if that missing arm was something he expected to get back anytime now. But his face told me different, told me that lost is just lost. It was even beyond the power of the miracles in which my people believed. No one ever prayed an arm back on—we would have heard about it if they had. I had been taught better than to stare and conditioned not to cry, by my older brother, by a dozen mean girl cousins. But there was something awful about that swaying, flat piece of cloth, and I just stood there, my eyes hot, my feet turning to ice in that unnatural cold. "Was it the war?" I asked my mother, but she told me to hush, it wasn't our business. So I asked her again. She shook her head. "The mill," was all she said.

His name was Charles Hardy, and he had been about the best guitar picker in our town. A touring country music promoter saw him play one night in a convention hall, and told him, "Boy, you're too good to be workin' for a livin'." He told him to hop on the bus and try his luck in Nashville, 'cause there was magic in those hands. But he would have gotten fired if he laid out even one day at the cotton mill, and knew his wife would holler at him if he ran off to Music Row. So he put the dream in a box to keep it clean, and told himself he could always drive to Tennessee and show out with all those Nashville cats. But one day, a little hungover, he lost his concentration on the floor of the Marvel Mill and stumbled into the teeth of a machine that shredded sheets of polyester. He fought it like it was something alive as it mangled his arm to the elbow and tried to pull his body into its teeth. He finally jammed it, killed it, with a broken broom handle.

Everything you need to know about a mill village, a smart man told me once, is in that empty sleeve.

But as a boy I wondered why anyone would work inside a place that could keep a part of you at quittin' time. My mother told me only that it was work, "and people was glad to get it." I heard that all the time, in conversations of blood, bandages and bad pay. The arm was an offering to the timekeepers, to the machines, in places like Leesburg, Blue Mountain, Piedmont and a dozen other towns in the foothills of the Appalachians. My mother took us from my father's people and broke our connection to the mill village in Jacksonville before I got to know that world, before I understood how there are things you hate and things you thank God for, and things that are both.

Half my history was fashioned here, between rows of spinning steel. Like the hill people who saw their lives replanted in the mill village, I am descended from two races on my father's side, but one class. They spilled blood over a paradise neither one could own, and saw it mingle to create a people whose single greatest value would be their own expendability. Here, from the Creek wars to the Civil War to a cold-blooded industrialization of these hills, is a history of my father's people, the people of the mills.

———·———

IT WAS MAGIC masquerading as nature. The round summits of the highlands seldom stood stark and clear, but were softened by hot, yellow haze in summer and gray, cool mist in winter. Even in their shrouds, they were beautiful. Poison ivy veined the trees, blistering even the lightest touch. Persimmons hung fat, yellow and inviting, but hexed your mouth into a whistling knot if you bit into them even a day too soon. Tornadoes tore through both springtime and the turning leaves, winter trees filled with a million keening blackbirds, and the summer ground lay red in wild strawberries. Water moccasins, fat as a rolled-up newspaper, rode rivers the color of English tea, bullfrogs beat the air like bass drums, and panthers, black as the inside of a box, watched from the branches of ancient trees.

De Soto rode through it searching for treasure, massacring its people, demanding at every village to know where he could find gold. "To the west," the people always said, to keep him on the march, to get rid of him, till he died disappointed on the Mississippi.

But the whites kept coming, for timber, for bottomland, for coal and ore buried in the hills. By the first decade of the nineteenth century, the land west of the state of Georgia and east of the Choctaw lands of Mississippi was known as the Alabama frontier. Some of these men, too, had dreams of empire, but most of them had nothing at all.

They were bony and callused and their clothing fit them like feed sacks tied to crossed broom handles. They had carrot-colored and sandy hair and fair skin that burned red in summer, and looked out from blue eyes that swam with suffering and suspicion. Their only birthright was stoop labor, and their class was stitched like patches across the generations, in Scotland, Ireland, the poorhouses of England, and the ever-crowding land in the American East. Most of them had never been inside a school, but they told stories of famine, leaky ships, selfish lords and debtors' prison, quoted a Bible they had never read, and were raised from birth to believe that black is the true color of a rich man's heart.

At night, they beat Irish drums, tooted tin whistles and plucked dulcimers as they danced across dirt floors, and sang in lilting, tragic voice of lost homes, lost love and lost wars. They served crowns and toffs and top hats who ordered them into cannon fire for a few pieces of silver, and barely set foot in the red dirt before they marched off to fight for Andy Jackson and the land speculators in the Indian wars. No one told them that, once all the red men were gone, they still could not afford what the land would cost at federal auction.

The gentry called them clay eaters behind their backs, free men without property in a time of human bondage, of less value than a slave. But they cleaved to their cracked, flawed democracy, voted for the populists who told the sweetest lies, and danced on the air, legs kicking, when the deprivations of class forced them to take a respectable man's hog, cow or purse. There is little photographic record of them and they left few letters or diaries, but look into the faces of the people of the mill villages, and you will find them there.

Look even deeper, and you will see the ghosts of a people who were here before.

I have done the white people all the harm I could.

—CHIEF RED EAGLE OF THE CREEK NATION
(from *Inside Alabama* by Harvey H. Jackson III)

The men were called Red Sticks, from the paint on their war clubs. They carried iron-forged tomahawks and muskets, wore flowing capes and parson-like coats over soft buckskin and wrapped their hair in turbans. The women, regal cheekbones framing eyes like slivers of coal, wore their lustrous black hair loose to the waist. Part of a confederacy of tribes that coexisted with whites for a generation, they were not nomads. They built cabins and hoped to live in them a lifetime, and for twenty years they signed treaties, trading land for lies. As British warships set sail for America in what would be the War of 1812, the Red Sticks declared their own war on the United States.

A bloody saga played out in places like Burnt Corn and Holy Ground. The Creeks left settlers dead in squalid, smoking cabins and on muddy trails, as white militia killed whole villages. Enraged by the massacres, Chief Red Eagle and 700 warriors surrounded Fort Mims, a settlement on the Alabama River, and killed 340 militia, women and children. In the North, newspapers ran lurid accounts, and the destruction of a people was begun.

In Tennessee, Jackson raised an army and rode south into the frontier, collecting fighting men along the way, resting awhile at a trading post called Drayton, on the edge of hostile land. It was a beautiful place, a green place with good water in the foothills of the Appalachians, and some of the men said they would come back here to farm, once the Indians were killed.

From there Jackson pushed south into the heart of Creek land, fighting as he went, and backed the last Red Sticks into a crook of the Tallapoosa called Horseshoe Bend. On March 27, 1814, he attacked 1,000 warriors with 2,600 white soldiers, 500 Cherokee and 100 friendly Creeks. His Indian allies swam the river and stole the Red Sticks' canoes, loaded them with troops and set a torch to the village, burning men, women and children alive. As it burned, Jackson ordered a drumroll and sent his force on a direct assault of the breastwork that guarded land access to the stronghold. This, according to a National Parks Service account of the battle, is what happened next:

A slaughter. European American soldiers and their Creek allies killed as many Red Sticks as possible. They set fire to a heap of timber the peninsula's defenders had hidden behind; when the Red Sticks emerged, they were immediately shot down. The bloodshed continued until dark; the next morning another 16 Creek, found hidden under the banks, were killed. In the end, 557 warriors died on the battlefield, and an estimated 250 to 300 more drowned or were shot trying to cross the river.

The river ran red for a mile.

The genocide of a nation all but complete, Red Eagle rode into Jackson's camp.

"How dare you?" Jackson said.

"General Jackson, I am not afraid of you," Red Eagle answered. "You can kill me if you wish. I have come to beg you to send for the women and children, who are starving in the woods. I am now through fighting." (From *Know Alabama: An Elementary History* by Frank Lawrence Owsley, Jr., John Craig Stewart, and Gordon T. Chappell.)

Jackson rode his military victories into the presidency. He ignored treaties that set aside land for Southern tribes, and ordered the removal of the tribes—even many of his Creek and Cherokee allies. Starving, freezing, dying on the way, they walked to Indian Territory in Oklahoma, on the Trail of Tears.

In 1832, an old chief named Ladiga signed away the last of the Creek land at the Treaty of Cusseta in Washington, but was given title to his homestead, which included Jackson's old camp on the campaign south, the picturesque Drayton. In 1833, Ladiga sold it to a land speculator for $2,000, and left. The little trading post of Drayton would become a cultural and business center on the frontier. In 1834, to honor the man who opened the land to expansion, a grateful citizenry changed the hamlet's name to Jacksonville.

But even after Horseshoe Bend and the Trail of Tears, enough of a beaten people remained, drop by red drop, to color the heritage of this place, and the imaginations of little boys who ran whooping through pines with chicken feathers in their hair. If you ask old people in the mill village if they have Indian blood in them, they will tell you they are an eighth Indian, or a sixteenth, and show you faded photographs of their great-great-grandmothers or -grandfathers, of high cheekbones, hooked noses, hair like ink, and say with great pride that "she was almost full" or "he was pure, I believe." I always thought the Indian blood in us was Cherokee, but that was unlikely, said my father's kin. More likely, on his side at least, it was Creek, from a far-back place in the mountains called Pinhook. But even if there was no other evidence, it is there, in my father's face, a blue-eyed white man in the county ledger, but as much war whoop as Rebel yell.

I pledge you my word. I've never heard such a cry for bread in my life. If anything can be done, for God's sake, do it quickly . . . This is no panic, but real hunger that punishes the people.

—W. B. COOPER, a prominent citizen in Jacksonville during the Civil War, writing to Governor Lewis E. Parsons for help for women who roamed the streets of the town to beg for food (from *Poor but Proud* by historian Wayne Flynt)

The next war, the rich man's war, starved them. In Jacksonville, the citizens were split over the idea of secession, but a majority, urged on by the increasingly affluent planter class, would favor it. In the prewar excitement, the name of the county was even changed to erase the shame of being named for antisecessionist senator Thomas Hart Benton. It was renamed Calhoun, to honor John C. Calhoun of South Carolina, who had threatened to cane a colleague in Washington who opposed a state's right to choose its destiny.

When the war was still new, the Tenth Alabama Regiment gathered on the steps of the brick courthouse in Jacksonville, where ladies of the town presented officers with a hand-sewn standard they would carry into battle. "It was made of blue satin," wrote one of the ladies, Carolyn Woodward, in her diary, reprinted in a history of Jacksonville commissioned by the First National Bank. "On one side was painted a cotton plant bearing fifteen bolls. At its topmost branch was a crown." They chose the cotton boll because they believed the town's future was bound to it, the sovereign under which they all served. The share-croppers marched away to hurrahs in one of the true oddities of Southern history, to die to preserve a way of life closed to them. It is hard to explain that to Northerners, hard to explain why, a century and a half later, poor men still fly the Confederate battle flag from rusted pickup trucks. It is hard to explain that, for some men, the fight, not the cause, is what they have.

The cannon and the dysentery took the men who worked the fields, so crops failed and farms failed, and the state sold the farms at auction, sometimes for just a few dollars in back taxes. In 1864, four years in, the families of Confederate soldiers were starving. Troops, many fighting a hopeless war without shoes, began to desert.

The upper classes were still fighting it, across teacups, as the centuries changed. The Confederate on our square was erected forty-five years after the war ended, paid for by the General John H. Forney Chapter of the United Daughters of the Confederacy. The inscription reads:

> *Times change, men often change with them, principles, never. Let none of the Survivors of These men offer in their behalf the Penitential Plea, "They believed they were right." Be it ours to Transmit to Posterity our Unequivocal Confidence in the Righteousness of the Cause for which these men died.*

For destitute and landless farmers, jobless laborers and wandering freedmen, the war would never end. Between Lee's surrender and the turn of a new century, they would endure unrelenting poverty that left them reliant on government doles of corn, meal and salt until they surrendered to a life as day laborers who owned no property and had no future. They sent letters to the capitol in Montgomery begging for seed corn. As poor whites and blacks fought over the scraps, hatefulness grew. It was always blamed on color but just as surely was a by-product of a desperate competition for a place in society, any place except last.

The term "one-crop mule" came into use. It meant that tenant farmers could not afford a mule that was expected to live more than a season. Starved, blind or staggering, the mules wobbled down the rows, a whole family's hopes resting on whether they could stay upright long enough to break ground in one essential field. When they went down, desperate men cussed them up again, whipped them with chains, built fires against their bellies, or just pulled at the reins, man against dying brute, until the leather snapped in their hands.

It was about then that my father's father emerged from the mountains as if from some bleak fairy tale. In the mountain enclave of Pinhook, at the turn of the twentieth century, time had stood still. The farmers, loggers and cotton pickers of the valleys were tame and gentle people compared to the ones who lived higher up and deeper back, in squalid one-room shacks and lean-tos surrounded by families dressed in smut and rags. They wore loaded pistols down the front of their greasy britches and loaded shotguns with bent nails. They came to town once or twice a year to buy sugar, yeast and meal and packed bust-head liquor down the hillsides on mules. They lived in poverty but independence, a community of half-breeds, poor whites, poachers, hog farmers, fatherless children, wanted men, and unwanted women.

One of them, a woman named Frankie Bragg, dragged fallen logs into the clearing around her windowless cabin and piled them into massive, popping bonfires, to scare the panthers away. There was no man, only rumors of one. Frankie grubbed out a living with a hoe, and raised her children, Bobby, Arthur, Joe and baby girl Eldora. "Somewhere down through the kinfolks, there'd been an Indian," and the children all had black or dark red hair, said Carlos Slaght. Eldora was his mother. Bobby, his uncle, was my grandfather.

What few, precious things Frankie owned, she carried "tucked in her buzzom," he said. "An aspirin box, Bull Durham sack, chewing gum . . . She was thirteen, when she had Uncle Bobby." They ate poke salad, highland watercress and May Pop, till Bobby was old enough to be the man. He saved them, pure and simple. "Uncle Bobby was the provider," Carlos said. He hired himself out when he was still a little boy to farmers, and carried his mother and siblings with him. He never went to school, just sweated for another man's profit when he should have been rolling marbles.

It was then, when Bobby was still a boy, that the red-brick walls began to reach into the sky, and locomotives dragged in machines big enough to swallow a man whole. It was salvation. The cost would be terrible, but it was salvation just the same.

> If a horse had been killed, I would have lost $200.
> I can get more men, anytime.
>
> —Attributed in a family history to JAMES EVERELL HENRY,
> a Northern timber baron and principal investor in the Jacksonville
> cotton mill, after one of his loggers was killed in an accident

In the mountains around Jacksonville, it was Yankee money that saved them, that, and a rich man's delicate nose.

In faraway St. Johnsbury, Vermont, the eldest son of Elmore T. Ide, the handsome and charming George Peabody Ide, was expected to assume the presidency of his father's gristmill in 1887. But the dust from pulverized grain, drifting up from the grinding wheel, caused a severe allergic reaction in young Ide. "This created a serious problem," wrote his nephew Knox Ide, in his memoirs. It was decided by the family that George sell his interest in the gristmill back to the company, and he joined his uncle, diplomat Henry C. Ide, on a voyage by locomotive, steamboat and horse and buggy to the Deep South. They chased the promise of unlimited natural resources to a place called Jacksonville. "George thrived and became very popular with the 'natives,' especially the ladies, many of whom set their caps for him ... a handsome dashing figure when behind two full-blooded carriage horses," wrote his nephew Knox. These were the men—visionaries, in recorded history—who held the fate of a people, a people who could be used up and discarded, with more, always more, to take their place.

From the beginning, it was more than industry. The mill, formed from 1.5 million red clay bricks, seemed to grow out of the earth instead of just being built upon it, and in a way it did. The clay was dug from the ground at the construction site, and fired in ovens, right there, into hard, brittle permanence. The bricks rose around a skeleton of massive beams and round, hardwood pillars, all of them hacked and smoothed from giant, ancient trees. It was the single biggest man-made thing most of them had ever seen, three stories of vast, echoing rooms and towering ceilings, a battleship long, and so wide a man could not throw a silver dollar across it. The windows glowed even at midnight, lit by a coal-fired, crackling generator that must have seemed like alchemy in a town still lit by kerosene.

When it ran wide-open, when workers fed trainloads of cotton into its massive, gnashing machines, the mill seemed to take on some malevolent spirit, to come alive. The hardwood floors, built to last a hundred years, trembled and popped under tons and tons of vibrating steel, as billions of tiny scraps of cotton spun off the machines and flew like clouds of gnats through giant, stifling rooms. The separators, designed to rip and tear a 500-pound bale of cotton, were just the start of it. Stretching across the floor were eleven thousand spindles, bolted to the hardwood with iron screws as long as railroad spikes. They did the work of a million old women at a million looms, but screaming, shuddering, cutting and biting. The machines would do the spinning, but had to be fed, fixed, and unclogged when the yarn broke or fouled, and for that, the company needed people brave enough to reach into the spinning, whirring gears. If you were careless, even for a second, it would get you. Over the years, the machines and the people mingled, not in a silly philosophical sense but in a real one, as it took their fingers, hands and arms and pumped their lungs full of cotton dust, until they were each part of the other, metal, cotton, flesh and bone.

The company knew where to fish for such men and women, and knew what bait to use.

Beside the mill, a village took shape, a community of small, solid, decent houses, every one exactly the same. The streets were named just A Street, B Street, and so on, as if these plain people did not require anything else. There would be 136 houses in all, a town within the town. Made of cheap but sturdy weatherboard and roofed with wooden shingles, they were designed by George P. Ide's new bride, Margaret Rosa Borden, a true Southern belle. She insisted that the roof lines of the little millhouses be designed to mirror the roof lines of their elegant home in Jacksonville—the antebellum Boxwood. In this way, she explained, every worker would share in its beauty.

But inside the red-brick walls of the mill was a netherworld. Women marched home, stunned and ashamed, after the machines ripped the hair from their heads or stripped off their clothes. One man died smoking on one of the mill's walls after the bosses refused to stop production even as he worked on the power lines. Barefoot children slaved there for next to nothing, prized by the mill owners because their smaller, delicate fingers could flutter over the tiniest gears without getting caught in the machines. As people toiled, a man in a necktie—the Southern man's mantle of power—walked the floor with a rattling lockbox under his arm. A man or woman could ask to be paid for the time they had put in, right up to that minute, so they could eat. The man in the tie dispensed not money but cheap metal disks called clinkers, named from the sound the box made. The clinkers could be redeemed for a sandwich, or a cold Coca-Cola. People drank and ate the fruit of their labor at the machine, and went back to work, still poor but not hungry. Paychecks for grown men, after deductions for food, rent and more, routinely read $0.00, so it was hard to tell, sometimes, where the exploitation ended and salvation began.

The mill bosses insisted on men with families. A man with four or five paychecks linked to the mill was a man beholden to it, a man who didn't complain. A man with a bunch of dirty-faced kids running around his legs, who knew he would be tossed out of his house if he even breathed the word "union," would keep his mind right when blood was shed, and serve his master.

The first bunch went down in '05, and every year more and more men and women in faded overalls and homemade flower-print dresses trickled down, babies in their arms and barefoot children pulling on their hands. They lined up at the gate, waiting for injury or impertinence to make a place for them. They accepted the keys to the company houses, ran up a tab at the company store, and prayed at the company church. They held their tongue, or else, and the bosses never let them forget their place. One superintendent, W. I. Greenleaf, bought a panel truck and put a bed in the back so that his pregnant wife could be driven north as her time drew near, so that his baby would not be born on Southern soil.

I do not know the details of why Officer Bob Ferguson attempted to place John under arrest. Would guess it to be for imbibing too much moonshine at one time. Anyhow, I knew it led to a confrontation of blazing guns in the very late hours of a Saturday night on the sidewalk of A Street between Houses 21 and 22. I think John received more than one wound. Possible hand, arm and shoulder. I do not recall how many times Mr. Ferguson was hit. I did hear he almost died from loss of blood before he received medical help.

—CARL SMITH, of 21 A Street, in a written statement describing an altercation between mill worker John Barnwell and the Jacksonville police

They absorbed degradation at work, and took it out on each other when the hated whistle blew. But in this community of violence and suffering were some of the finest people who have ever lived, who scraped a few handfuls of flour into a brown paper bag, house by house, until a full bag could be delivered to a family whose provider was sick, shot, cut or hurt in the machines. The choking dust took a lot of them, and some just never got over the fact that they left their mist-shrouded mountains for this, and died sorry. But they met their quotas and punched their time cards and went home to sleep under quilts dyed with roots and berries, a people neither town nor country, but something in between.

Twice a shift, the women would come out onto a cement platform, where a line of older children waited with babies in their arms. The women nursed their babies not till they were full, but till the whistle blew, then handed them off to the older children and filed back inside. Shotguns and deer rifles rusted under beds as beautifully bred coon and rabbit dogs pulled at chains in cramped little yards, waiting for a hunt that never came. Women walked five, ten miles to find blackberry bushes and plum trees for jelly and preserves, and cut their peaches out of a can.

People with no experience beyond the limitless pines were squeezed into a single, limited space. When men felt hemmed up, they reacted in unusual ways. It was common then for a man to get drunk and ride his horse or mule into a café in town. "There was lots of odd things that happened back then," said Homer Barnwell, who grew up in the mill village, a child of its first generation of workers, and would become its historian. He cites the time in '38 someone dynamited the brush arbor, and the time a man named Joe Pierce got drunk at Toughy Griffin's blacksmith shop and pulled Slut Luttrel's teeth— "and by the time he got done, he'd even pulled the right ones," Homer said.

The gentler townspeople of Jacksonville contemplated them at a safe distance, in awe, and fear.

With the books of science and logic closed to them, they believed in things, in signs and warnings that had no foundation in the wider world. They planned their days in the morning, "turning the cup," when they would empty the coffee grounds into a saucer and examine the patterns on the porcelain. A teardrop shape meant sorrow. A streak represented a road, and meant that you would travel, or that someone would travel to you. A series of specks meant rain. They divined more of the future in cards. A jack of clubs meant a brown-eyed, handsome man would come to your door. A king of hearts meant a wise, older man, of fair complexion, would affect your life. The ace of spades meant death. They believed that a swarm of gnats heralded violent storms, that they could cure a sty in their eye if they stood in the middle of a darkened crossroads and chanted:

> *Sty, sty*
> *Leave my eye*
> *Catch the next*
> *Who passes by*

They believed it was an invitation to murder to bring an ax into a house, and the only way to undo it was to turn around three times and back out the door. They believed that a snapping turtle, if it bit their finger, would not let go until it thundered, that a coach whip snake could form itself into a circle, like a wheel, and roll down the trails after them until it caught them, and whip them to death. They believed if they killed a dove they would be punished by God, because the dove had been a sign of hope in a world drowned for its sins. They believed that the granddaddy longlegs, a delicate spider that moved on legs thinner than the finest wire, was good luck, and they would chant . . .

> *Granddaddy, Granddaddy,*
> *Which way is your cow?*

. . . until the spider would lift one threadlike leg, and point.

They believed that the presence of dragonflies, which they called snake doctors, meant a serpent lay nearby. They believed that they could cure warts by pretending to wash their hands over an empty washpot, and that old women could murmur worms out of the ground. They believed it was bad luck if a woman gave her man a knife, because it would cut their love in two.

The village had its own witch, an old woman who could breathe the fire out of a burned child's wound, and simple-minded children wandered into houses two blocks away and climbed into chairs at the dinner table, expecting to be fed. Faith healers blew rabbit tobacco smoke into the ears of squalling babies, and pressed scraps of Scripture to the chests of dying men.

If you did not have faith, you trusted to luck. The men bet on gamecocks, cards, and which way a bird would fly off a wire when someone let fly with a chunk of coal or an empty bottle of booze. Between shifts, they pitched pennies in the bathroom, and gathered in a circle on the railroad switchback to roll dice. It was there, in the 1920s, that an unlucky man named Charlie Tune made the strangest bet of all. "Charlie Tune needed to roll a four, and he said, 'If I don't make this four with two deuces before I crap out, I'll leave this town and you won't ever see me again,' " Homer said. He cannot recall what it was Charlie Tune rolled, but it wasn't a pair of deuces. "He got up, threw his coat over his shoulder and walked away, and nobody ever saw him again. Had a boy named Luther. We called his boy 'Two-Deucey,' on account of his daddy."

They brought more than their customs to town. They brought their livestock. Every house had a cow lot in the backyard, and when your cow went dry your neighbor gave you some of their milk, to help you get by. There was a sprawling, communal hogpen, and tiny gardens, mostly tomatoes, squash, rattlesnake beans, pepper, cucumber, a few stalks of sweet corn, collards, turnip greens and pumpkins. Chickens roamed the streets. No one stole, because the ambrosia of a frying pullet could not be contained by such thin walls. Likewise, no argument was private, no betrayal secret. If a man hollered at his wife, you heard it three doors down.

"They were good, moral people," said Homer Barnwell.

"But," he said, "pretty much ever'body carried a pistol."

A police officer was more likely to get hit with a brick and have his gun taken than serve a warrant. The hillbillies would kill you—that was a natural fact—so police usually left them alone to settle their arguments. When they did come, they came shooting.

Donald Garmon, who is seventy-two now, grew up in the village. "When you got up in the morning and put your shoes on, you was pretty sure you was going to fight somebody, before the sun went down," said Garmon. "Somebody was going to hit you, and you was going to fight. I hate to say it, but it was one of the meanest places I ever been in."

Shot five times by the police, mill hand John Barnwell—Homer Barnwell's father—was still drafted in '16, and fought in France, across no-man's-land. In the trenches, the mustard gas ruined his lungs, and he came home to work again, coughing, smothering, in the cotton mill. A world war had changed nothing here. It was still either the mill, the backbreaking uncertainty of the fields, or surrender.

They tried to unionize over time, to better themselves, and poor men burned rich men in effigy and fought each other at picket lines with pistols, knives and ax handles. But the mill bosses finally just locked all the doors, stopped taking credit at the store, and waited them out. It is hard to walk a picket line when the company owns your house.

The rich people bought them, really, for pocket change, but in their hearts they were still in the mountains, still up high. As the cotton mill used up its first generation of workers, new handbills fluttered from barns and fence posts in the foothills outside town.

WORKERS WANTED

MEN WITH FAMILIES

GOOD WAGES

GOOD WORKING CONDITIONS

GOOD HOUSING

ELECTRICITY

FREE COAL

Bobby Bragg rode past them on his mule, oblivious to the promises and the lies. He never learned to read. He was a young man by then, still sharecropping in the bleak economy after the First World War. Finally, the lure of year-round money and a ready-made house wicked out and found him, too. He rode his mule into town, to try and get on. That's how they said it, "gettin' on," like it was a boat, or a train, and if you didn't get on, you got left behind.

"You don't drink, do you?" the mill boss asked him.

"Just on Christmas," Bobby said.

The Boy

———

"RICK," THE BOY ASKED, "how do you punch somebody?"
We were supposed to be taking a walk.

"You never punched anybody?" I asked.

"No," he said.

I did not know what to say.

"Will you show me?" he asked.

I guess I should have told him there is rarely a good reason to punch someone, that it is better to turn the other cheek. I should have evoked Gandhi and King. I should have told him that the meek inherit the earth and all that razzmatazz.

"Make a fist," I said.

I tapped the bridge of my nose.

"You hit here, one time, hard, and it's over," I said.

"Why?"

" 'Cause it hurts real bad," I said. "Their eyes will water, and they will cry."

"Then what?" he said.

"Then they will run to their mommies," I said, "and tell on you."

"What if they don't run away?" he asked.

"They won't be able to see good after you thump 'em good that first time, right?"

He said he supposed so.

"Well, thump 'em again."

He was named, this boy, for a man who wrestled an angel, but had lived a life free of contention, free of consequence. I wished I could tell him it would always be that way, but all I could do was teach him how to bloody another little boy's nose.

"Repeat after me," I said.

"Hurt 'em quick.

"Make 'em cry.

"Go home."

Father of the Year.

"What if they try to step back when you swing?" he asked.

"You try," I said, as I reached out to tap him on the head.

He lurched back but could not move.

I was standing on his foot.

"Oh," he said.

I told him most little boys swing wild, from the side, and don't connect with much of anything. I lost as many boyhood fights as I won, but I learned. I tried to show how to block, jab. "You punch straight ahead, like driving a nail," I said.

I could hear my father's voice in my head.

"Is it okay to cry?" he asked.

It's not even okay to ask that question, I thought.

"Try not to," I said.

I am not, usually, an idiot. I knew I was being a little careless with the boy, the way I was with everything else. It is easy to teach someone to throw a punch in abstract, hard to explain the sick feeling that precedes any violence, even playground violence.

So I told him to walk away when he could.

"Is that what you would do?" he asked.

"Not on your damn life," I said.

He was confused now.

"I have run," I explained, when I knew I couldn't win, and the cause didn't seem worth the pain. But I was always sick, after. You choose the sick feeling you can stand most, the one before you fight, or the one after you run away. But that was complicated, for a ten-year-old.

"Son," I said, "I once ran away in a Mustang."

I told him that the rules of conduct, from the school, the church, his beloved mom, didn't matter much in the dirt, if you were getting hurt.

"You bite," I said.

He looked amazed.

"It's fine to gouge," I said.

Then his mother walked up, and I was in trouble again.

She would raise a gentle boy if she had to lock me in a shed.

"He doesn't need to know," she told me.

I nodded my head, hoping that might spare me.

It never has.

"He's ten years old," she hissed.

I told her, yes, he was getting started late.

"You are twelve," she said.

Still, I tried to modulate my behavior around the boy. Once, he asked me how to defend himself against a bigger boy.

"Kick him in the . . ." and I searched my mind for a Baptist word.

"Kick him in the scrotum," I said.

"What's a scrotum?" he asked.

He walked around giggling for an hour and a half.

So, when his mother was not looking, we boxed in the living room, and sparred in the yard. But the boy wanted to be a fighter like I wanted to be a fat Italian opera singer. He smiled when he punched, he giggled, and I knew he might live his whole life, a complete life, and never strike another man in anger.

"How did you learn?" he asked me.

I told him it was in my blood.

I saw my father fight. He barely took time to cuss a man before hitting him in the face. I remember he fought moving forward, almost dancing. At every reappearance, he schooled me. He baby-tapped me in my shoulders and gut as I swung so hard I fell. By the time I was six years old he smacked me upside the head, harder, when I dropped my guard. It was still just a tap, but it was like being hit with the end of a post. "The boy likes it," he said, as my mother snatched me up and put a stop to it. I know I will never forget feeling like a big boy, fists clenched in front of my face.

I was six, in my last fight he knew about, on the playground at Spring Garden Elementary. A boy shook loose of the hold I had on his neck and punched me in the eye. The teacher sent me home on the big yellow bus with a note folded in my coat pocket.

My father read it, and tossed it in the trash.

"Who whupped?" he said.

I told him we didn't finish.

"Finish it tomorrow," he said.

I tried to tell him it was Friday, that we didn't have school the next day. I waited, miserable, sad and nervous, to pick a fight with that little boy.

The woman tells me I am a throwback, that children settle differences now with lawyers, guns and money.

But you can't do right all the time.

A boy needs to know how to make a fist.

You know that, being stuck on twelve.

CHAPTER THREE

Bob

————·—————

BOB NEVER MET a man he wouldn't fight at least twice, if insulted, and he intended to slap all the pretty off Handsome Bill Lively's face. It happened in a weed-strewn clearing at the corner of Alexandria Road and D Street, around the time of the Second Great War. The village gamblers liked to gather there, where the thick hedges, honeysuckle and possum grapevines screened them from their wives, the rare police car, and the Congregational Holiness Church. A man named Doug Smith got cut across the eyes there, "and there was always somebody fightin', cuttin'," said Jimmy Hamilton, who grew up in the mill village with his friend Homer Barnwell, and was just a boy then. "I remember Bill Lively as a nice-looking man, dark-haired," said Jimmy. "If he'd had one of those pencil-thin mustaches, ain't no tellin' how far he could have gone. Well, Bill liked to pick at Bob when Bob was drinkin', and that day, Bob come down to the poker game, drunk. Him and Bobby got to fightin', and he worked Bob over a little bit."

Bob limped home, beaten.

"Well, about fifteen or twenty minutes later, here come Bobby back," Jimmy said.

Bob was naked.

"For God's sake, Bob," said Handsome Bill.

"You whupped me with my clothes on," Bob told him. "Now let's see if you can whup me nekkid."

I would give a gold monkey to know what Bill Lively thought, standing there looking at Bob's little-bitty, sweat-slicked, naked body, everything pretty much fish-belly white except the red on his arms and face and neck. Where do you grab a solid hold of a naked man? We just know that Bob balled up his little fists and flung himself on Bill Lively for revenge I guess, because I am not sure if you can fight for your honor with your parts exposed.

What a wonderful story it might have been.

What if he had somehow beaten down the bigger man, and gone home with his head high and posterior in the breeze?

Instead, Lively worked him over again, snatched a pine sapling from the ground, and whipped Bobby's bare behind down D Street.

Velma was there—she was always there—on the stoop, standing as Bob climbed the steps, not ducking inside to hide her face and leave him to walk the last few steps alone. She glared out the door to let any busybodies know they could all go straight to hell, and stomped off to get the salve. "I ought to knock you in the damn head, Bob," she always said to him, in times like these.

There are some people in the world who are not necessarily good at life if you see it as a completed work, but who are excellent at it one daub of bright color at a time. Bob, when drinking, lived in the twitch. He might never be respectable, in a Methodist kind of way. But the way he saw it, and raised his sons to see it, he could be free as a bird on a bunk in the city jail, as long as he showed some guts and left some blood on the ground—his, or somebody's. Bob, with a bottle, would wreak mayhem in disproportion to his size, and go find his angel, to hear his story, and bind his wounds.

He was kind to her, when sober, but would forget to be kind when he was not. She just took it, and walked miles to bail him out of jail with money she made in that stifling mill. People recall that his dark red hair went white early in his life, as if he wanted it that way, because she had loved it so.

The nature of their story, really, is that you laugh at Bob and cry for her, for her goodness and long suffering. But it is the nature of men that it is easier for us to laugh at Bob than cry for Velma, which is why women loathe us so.

I laughed as Jimmy told that story, burnishing one more legend of a tin-pot god. There have been a hundred drinking stories told on Bob, more, if you count the lies. But it wasn't always that way for my grandfather. Once, he was just a citizen, just a fella, of regular behavior, and reasonable dreams.

As a young man, Bobby was sober, ramrod straight. He was a man who could sense promise in the dirt, who could sift it through his hands and feel good things, feel the potential of okra, squash, tomatoes, and make it come true. He worked his shift in the cotton mill and sharecropped, too, and grew an oasis in his little village garden.

He could not just stand by and watch another man work. He reached for the pick. When other men sat around to drink or gossip, he slept, resting his body for the next day. There wasn't any foolishness in him, and he would only go so far into the twentieth century. He built traps and snares and walked the streets loaded with heavy stringers of fish and carcasses of squirrels and rabbits. He greatly distrusted automobiles and would not even sit behind the wheel of one, and if he needed to travel, he saddled a horse.

In his twenties, he still took care of his momma, Frankie, and his siblings, and people believe he lived a lifetime without being mean to her. In a time when most people had to stay inside on wash day because they had one pair of underwear, Bob's two full-time jobs gave him a largesse, enough to save a dollar or two most months in a coffee can, for his one dream. He liked to tell it to people, tell how much cotton he could bring in, how many mules he would stable, when he finally bought his own land. He lived for it, and nothing would distract him. If a man approached him with a bottle when he was a young man he would just tell them, No thank you, Slim, but I'll catch you in December.

Then, working a corn crop for a man named Sam Whistenant in 1919, he saw his angel. He stopped for a sip of cool water, and as he tipped the dipper to his lips there she was, hair black as the bottom of a well and so long it almost brushed the red ground. It was poetry that he found her there, next to a field, a girl with the gentlest heart in the world, a selfless, lovely, patient girl, with rows of green corn framing her beautiful face.

And like that, he was dreaming again.

"Velma's mother and father didn't want her to marry Bobby," said Velma's niece, Shirley Brown. "They were hoping for an officer in the cavalry."

They had a picture of a dashing young cadet on the mantel, and assumed it was only a matter of time before their daughter married the man. They knew she was sneaking off to see him. She climbed up behind him on his government-issue horse and they would ride, thundering through the pines, her hair trailing behind her. The young officer must have felt like the luckiest man in the world, till he found what she really loved was the horse.

The same day Bob's heart fluttered at the edge of that field, she noticed him, too, by the well. She was about seventeen, and she did not fall in love with the boy so much as with the hair on top of his little head. It was kind of auburn, but darker than that, and shined.

Why, she thought, it looks just like syrup candy. Back then, women made candy by heating a greased skillet and pouring in dollops of dark, reddish sorghum. As it cooled, they pulled it, like taffy, till it glowed, and when it cooled it set up hard as rubies. He was a little runty, true, but "he was the prettiest little man I ever seen," she said.

She told her mother, Emma, she liked the boy. It was like she walked into a party and flung dirt on the birthday cake. Emma was heartbroken, and forbade it. How could the foolish girl swap an officer and a gentleman for that little dirtdauber? Her father, Samuel Hampton Whistenant, told her she would die a wretched spinster before she would marry a sharecropper, and they kept a close eye on her, to keep her from running off. They were from Switzerland, the Whistenants, and men in their line had fought in the Revolutionary War and Civil War. Samuel Whistenant was not rich but he was proud. He farmed his own land and ran a little café in the mill village community of Blue Mountain, south of Jacksonville.

To keep her close, he put Velma to work in the café, as a waitress. She was still single when she turned nineteen, old to be waiting for a husband, a beautiful, lovelorn girl.

It was there in the café that Bobby got to see her. He came in and ate a thousand hamburgers, drank a bathtub of coffee, just to see her fill his cup. Sam always ran him off if he even tried to hold her hand. So he sat on the counter stool, stiff-backed, the starch in his overalls and shirt quietly rustling as he stared at the back of her.

A year passed, more. On June 4, 1920, for the first time in as long as anyone could even recall, his stool was empty. For the kin who followed this forbidden love story, it looked like the boy had finally taken more than he could stand.

In the afternoon, a horn sounded on the street outside.

Sam peered out the window.

A Chevrolet idled at the curb. FOR HIRE was stenciled on the door.

Bob could not drive, so he had come to get her in a taxi.

She snatched off her apron and was out the door. They raced south to the Oxanna Church, where a preacher named Williams pronounced them man and wife.

"He stole her from her parents, and the cavalry," said Shirley. It is a pattern in my family. Velma, who could have been the wife of an officer, chose the village. My other grandmother, Ava, married a roofer and a whiskey maker and lived in the dark woods. My mother married the man who once stole the keys to the county jail. Some people would say they didn't pick well, that they gave up a chance to move up in their class, or even move out of it. How wasteful, to marry for love.

———·•·———

THE MILL WHISTLE BLEW in the pitch black of four-thirty to get Bobby and Velma up. It blew again at five forty-five to start them walking, and again at six, to restart the machines. There were no clocks on the bedside tables in the mill village. There was no need. If you laid out, the hiring boss gave your job to one of the new arrivals who lined up outside the office. Bobby and Velma never laid out. They worked sick, and she worked when she was with child. Velma worked in the spinning room, Bobby in the carding room. They breathed white air, and at the end of the day, when the machines finally slowed and died and the teeth-clacking vibration finally ceased, they walked home arm in arm.

They saved as much as they could in one-dollar bills and pocket change, working for the day they could walk out of that smothering heat and noise for good, and be something more than a set of expendable hands. It took longer than he expected. His farm was still just that, a dream, when the children came in the twenties and early thirties, the boys Troy and Roy, and the girls Clara, Fairy Mae and Ruby, and then the Great Depression sank its teeth deep into the village and mountains. People struggled to hold to what little bit they had as the mills slowed and finally closed, but Bob even outworked the Crash. "They were not some raggedy Depression family," said Shirley Brown. "Bobby killed hogs, and there was pickled pig's feet, beef tripe, beef stew, chili, fried chicken." He butchered livestock for halves or the parts other people didn't want, and pushed a plow in ground that others gave up on, to grow food.

He sent visitors home with sacks of tomatoes, baskets of okra. "I reckon Bobby never did sell nothin'," said Carlos. "He gave it away."

But some of Velma's people did suffer. Store owners had no customers, and the farmers had no market. Cash was short.

Some men, in that bleakness, drank up their families' groceries, but not Bob. He was a man who rigidly controlled his appetites. The bootleggers sold a half-pint of corn whiskey for fifty cents, and Bob allowed himself exactly one half-pint, once a year, on the birth of our Savior. The liquor came in a thin, clear bottle, and was enough for two good, mellow intoxications or one pure, long, skull-popping drunk. The bootleggers called it a scant because it was so small, and it would last Bob the Yuletide. On Christmas Eve, every Christmas, he walked up to Velma and asked for his drinking money. "Velma, honey, gimme fifty cents. I'm gonna get me a scant." She felt inside the coffee can, and gave it to him.

It was sometime before the start of World War II, maybe a few years in, when he asked the last time.

She sat down and covered her face.

"What?" he said.

"We don't have it," she said.

"Why not?" he said.

"I give it away," she said.

She had given it, a little at a time, to people who needed it worse than they did, to people suffering. Her heart was too soft, too good, to say no to people in real need. She planned to make it back by sewing, cleaning houses, but Christmas just came early for a change. No one knows, really, how much it was. It may have been fifty dollars, less, but it was a lot to them.

"I'm sorry, Bob," she said.

He walked out.

He was a renter the rest of his life.

It would be wrong, and unfair, to say that Bob stopped trying after he gave up on his dream. He continued to work hard, and when he was sober he remained the most polite, decent and responsible man. That was the best part of Bob, that unbending sense of responsibility to people who depended on him, and he would have been ashamed to see his house dark or icebox empty. There would be meat at supper and sweets at breakfast in his house, and he didn't give a damn if syrup went to fifty cents a sop.

But as he grew older, more and more, he was willing to go when men came to lure him out with a jar of clear whiskey. It was a surrender, in a way. He bought his own whiskey by the gallon now, fought for the fun of it, and did odd things. Once, he hitched his horse to a wagon and rode through the mill village dressed only in his long underwear, whooping. He was Bobby Bragg, and every payday was Christmas Day.

When you're all alone and blue
No one to tell your troubles to
Remember me, I'm the one who loves you

"He'd get to drinking, and come over to my Grandmother Whistenant's house," said Shirley Brown. "I was still just a girl then. We had an old wood heater, with a pan for the ashes underneath, and he would sit in there by that heater and cry. Uncle Bobby dipped snuff, and he would spit in the ashes and cry and the tears would roll down his cheeks and the snuff would run down his chin, and he would sing . . ."

When this world has turned you down
And not a true friend can be found
Remember me, I'm the one who loves you

He did not sing well, and liked to linger on the *"Remember meeeeeeee"* part, which sounded like someone strangling a cat with a nylon cord. "Some people would run and shut the door if they thought a drunk was coming, but not Momma. We all just thought the world of him." So they all sat around, being polite, and waited for Bobby to stitch his heart back together one verse at a time.

Once, staggering home, Bob made a misstep on the footlog and plunged into the creek. Instead of getting out, he lay on his back and sang curses at the log. Far away, at his own house, his two oldest sons heard, faintly, their father's voice.

"Damn," said Roy.

"What?" said Troy.

"Bob's fell in the branch," Roy said.

His sons went to get him. As they walked, they saw his little hat bobbing down the stream.

———

TOUGHY GRIFFIN was Bobby's friend. He was not the meanest man in Jacksonville, but he could absorb pain and whiskey in a volume few have ever seen. Being kicked by a grown, neck-high mule is comparable to being run over by a small car, and he had been kicked, butted and bit. "But there was not a mule or a horse he couldn't shoe," said Jimmy Hamilton. "He was usually so drunk he couldn't walk, but he could flat out shoe. He'd get about half lit, and before it was over . . . well, I've seen him bleedin' and the mule, too."

He and Homer would go sit under the Indian cigar tree in front of Toughy's barn, for the same reason they went to the theater. If you sat there long enough, some kind of entertainment would occur. It was even better than the poker game for violence, cussing, drinking and all the manly arts. "I never knew if Toughy ever took a bath, because he always looked the same," Jimmy said. He was covered in snuff, mud, blood, manure and smut, from his bellows, but never whiskey, because Toughy never let a drop go awry. He was one of the legendary figures in Jacksonville's history, though his name appears on no documents except maybe a few old police reports. Bob liked to visit Toughy in the cool of the late afternoon, especially if he had a bottle to share.

This day, Toughy had just used the nose twisters to bring a large mule down to the ground, so it could be trussed up and shod. The nose twisters worked just like the name implies—the smithy attached them, like a big set of pliers, to the nose, and twisted them around until the animal buckled. Mules do not like this, none of it, and they lie quivering in pain and terror on the ground, until the ropes are undone and it can explode up, kicking insanely at anything close. Toughy had just tied the mule down, straddled the leg, and was driving nails into the hoof when Bobby walked up.

"Bobby had some whiskey," Jimmy said. "That was out of the ordinary."

He told Toughy to quit what he was doing and have a little drink of liquor.

"Toughy would have dropped his hammer in mid-swing," Jimmy said, "if someone came up with a bottle . . ."

. . . so Toughy dropped his hammer on the backswing, and sat down.

"So there they are, Toughy and Bobby, sitting on a rock drinking whiskey," Jimmy said.

The mule's owner, a big farmer, stared in disbelief.

His prize mule lay kicking, one leg sticking straight up in the air, as Toughy took several long pulls on the whiskey.

He walked over to the two men and ordered Toughy to get up and finish his job.

"Toughy had to kind of wall his eye around on the man, till he could focus good," Jimmy said.

He nodded, staggered up, reeled over to the mule, sighted unsteadily on his next nail and, missing the bony part of the hoof altogether, drove the nail straight into the fleshy quick of the animal's foot. Blood flew, the mule screamed and the farmer stood in disbelief. He was a respected man, a landowner, and these drunk men, these white-trash hooligans, had crippled his animal.

He decided to blame Bob, who did not have a hammer in his hand. He walked over and started cussing him. Bob dropped his bottle in the dirt—it was empty, of course—balled his fists and raised them in front of his face as if he was planning to box the big farmer by Marquis of Queensberry rules. Then, as a bell sounded that only he could hear, he pranced toward the man, swung twice, missed twice, and fell face-down in the gravel.

———

IN A VILLAGE where so many people just broke themselves against the machines and disappeared, there are more stories than there are people left to tell them. Homer Barnwell and Jimmy Hamilton have known each other since they were boys in a time between wars, when a passing car, any car, would make them stop and stare. Bob would be more than a hundred now, if he had lived, so the only witnesses to his misadventures are old men who were boys then, who peeked into every condemned corner of the village, which was their universe, to watch men drink, lie, scratch and roar. The meek and well-behaved always seem to fade, which has always made me doubt that "inherit the earth" part. It is the Bobs who live forever.

I am proud to have Bob's blood in me. In it is at least part of the reason for what decency there is in me, in any sense of responsibility to my people. But in it, too, is the answer to every time I argued from spite, all those times I fought dirty when I was in the dead, pure-positive wrong. Rules? Who ever had any damn fun with those shackles on your feet? Meekness? Who wants to inherit the earth, in such company? Once, as a boy, I repeatedly slapped a boy on a baseball field, trying to goad him into swinging at me. He wanted to hit me back but he didn't do it, maybe because he was afraid, maybe because he didn't want to hurt me. Either way, he stood there and took it. I slapped him till my arm got tired, till I finally just walked off in defeat. But I know what Bob would have done. Bob would have switched hands.

———

THE LAST CHILD of Bob and Velma came into the world on January 10, 1935. The boy, named Charles Samuel after his grandfather, was allergic to some types of milk, so Velma mixed a formula from sweet canned milk even as, in the hills around town, babies perished from simple dehydration. Born into that cycle of breadlines, layoffs and lockouts, he was wrapped in soft blankets, and raised in a house of love and whiskey.

The Boy

—·—

I WILL NEVER FORGET the first time I saw him. He was still just a roly-poly little kid, playing in the white sand with his cousins on the Alabama coast.

"Hey," was all I said to him, but I thought: You're going to be my boy. I'm going to have a boy, after all this time.

"Hey," he said, with just half a glance, and went back to burying his cousin in the sand. I watched him awhile, then went to the souvenir shop and bought him a shovel.

If you're going to bury somebody, bury 'em.

"We buried my brother once, in Pensacola," I told him. "We left him there, up to his neck, hollering, and didn't dig him out until right before the tide came in."

He grinned and said, Naw you didn't, but I was telling the truth.

The woman said she never truly worried what kind of stepfather I would be, but I did. Everything I knew about being a father, almost everything, was wrong, twisted.

"You will spend time with him," she said. "That's all you have to do."

But I didn't recognize this kind of boy.

"He's not different, he's just little," said the woman. "You never were that little, were you?"

I hate conversation like this. Am I twelve now, but I wasn't twelve then? Hell, I can't keep up.

"You never got to be," she said. "When you were his age, you broke rocks. Your momma carried you on a cotton sack. It's a different world, for him."

This woman protected her son from everything sharp. She even cut up his apples, lest he come into contact with a paring knife.

He had never lit a firecracker, and run away.

He had never fired a BB gun at a tin can.

She still ran his bathwater, lest he be chilled, or scorched.

She sat on the edge of the tub and talked to him, so he would not be alone.

"He likes it when I talk to him," she said.

"Well I hope he gets tired of it before he goes to college," I said.

I have read of boys in plastic bubbles who had more adventure.

The woman and boy lived on a dead-end street, what suburban people call a cove. The boy was only allowed to ride his bicycle on that street, never out of sight. I would watch him, circling, circling.

I thought of a hamster on a wheel.

I had believed that being a boy was about getting away with things, just short of murder, and if you got lucky, you could still be a boy when they lowered you into the red clay. What troubled me most was not that he was bound, but that he did not seem to mind it.

I was born into a people who could cuss the horns off a bull, before revival and after dinner on the ground, but he lived in a world rated G, with candy sprinkles on top. Once, in the car, I let slip a "damn" or "hell" or some other entry-level curse, and the boy puffed up like a toad and said his mother would not allow me to speak in such a vulgar fashion.

"Well," I said, and looked up, down, left and right.

"Is she here?" I said.

He told on me.

He asked for me at bedtime to tell him a story, but I never felt comfortable. Even though I made a living telling them, I knew few suitable for children. Most bedtime stories I told involved loose women and began with "And she was so damn drunk . . ." I told him finally he was too big to be tucked in. The woman cornered me, breathing fire. "If he tells me he does not want me to tuck him in, if I lose that, because of you . . ." she said, and left the rest unsaid. I thought she was going to cry, or punch me in the nose.

We battled like that, good and evil, for the boy's immortal soul.

I had always loved speed, and as I turned forty I bought myself one last rocket ship. It was low and sleek and the color of a silver bullet, and James Dean died in one like it. The first time we were alone together, the boy and me, I put the top down, told the boy to buckle in tight, and we left that safe, middle-class neighborhood behind in a hot wind. I let the engine roar before shifting, and as I popped the clutch it felt like we were riding on a pulled-tight rubber band that had been let go. A boy who doesn't thrill to speed could never be a boy of mine, and as we flashed over the asphalt he oddly raised both hands heavenward, as if pleading for deliverance, or a soft landing.

I wanted to twist that engine up to a hundred, to show him how it felt to fly, but it seemed wrong to torture a boy who was calling to the Lord, so I eased off. I knew that if I hurt the boy the woman would kill me and drag my bones behind a minivan, so I eased off some more.

He looked like he had something to say, so I asked him what was on his mind.

"Rick," he said, "why am I here?"

I had just started seeing his mother. I wanted to tell him the bald truth: 'Cause I'm after your momma, son. But I didn't.

" 'Cause your momma is my friend," I said. "So, I want to be your friend, too."

He didn't say anything to that, but I could almost smell the smoke from the gears spinning in his head as we swooped off the four-lane and geared down, growling into a turn.

He raised his arms again, as if in surrender.

I told the woman about it, how he raised his hands, like he was giving himself to God.

That wasn't it, the woman said.

When he rides in a convertible, she said, he likes to shut his eyes and pretend he's on a roller coaster.

He raises his arms, she said, to show her how brave he is.

CHAPTER FOUR

Fearless

———

H E CRESTED THE HILL on his red tricycle, two RC bottles
full of canned milk corked and holstered, one in each side
pocket of his little blue overalls. Charles Bragg, five years
old, pedaled hard to make the summit, pushing when he needed to,
then stopped to stare contemptuously down the long, sweeping grade
that sliced through mean blackberry bushes and creaking, flexing
pines. If the breeze whispered, Caution, child, caution, it failed to fil-
ter through his dark red curls. He rocked back and forth, once, twice,
and he was gone, pumping furiously to keep up with a front tire that
spun like a sawmill blade, the spokes a blur. He couldn't keep his feet
on those whirling pedals, so he stuck his legs straight out and rode it
down, teeth clenched, knuckles bone-white on the handlebars, every
rock and rut bouncing him off the seat, threatening to pitch him into
those murderous trees or fishhook thorns. He was almost down,
almost safe when he lost it, when he bounced high and came down
wrong, tilting, careening right into a few thousand stickers, because
tricycles never will wreck in a straight line. He did not cry as he extri-
cated himself, but it took a while, since anyone who has ever been
caught in blackberry bushes knows that two barbs stick you for every
one you pull free. He had time to think about the foolishness of what

he'd done, as pinpricks of blood popped up on his arms and the milk leaked down his leg. Finally, he righted his chariot, took the bottles from his pockets and set them on the ground, and went back up the hill to do it again.

"He was my hero," said Shirley Brown, his first cousin. "I was always so afraid and he was so brave, and I thought he could do everything. He was short and cute and his hair was curly, and in colder weather he wore one of those little aviator caps, the ones with the earflaps. He would strap that little hat on and ride a cardboard box down a hill, and light firecrackers in his hand and throw them, at the last second. Even when he was little he walked everywhere by himself, looking to get into some adventure. Velma worked a twelve-hour shift at the cotton mill, so he stayed with us and played with me, the 'fraidy cat. And I guess I thought he was the grandest thing in all the world."

Shirley's father was a wandering man who wandered away. "He always had on a brand-new suit and drove a big shiny car, and he would blow in and leave so quickly, just a beautiful, shining light that I always knew was out there, but could never quite touch," she said. When she was just a little girl she went to Jacksonville to live with her mother's people, the Whistenants, in an unpainted house. She needed a friend.

"Let me tell you about your daddy," she said, and it was like she broke the lock on some dust-covered toy box and scattered its contents—decommissioned lead soldiers, rode-hard wooden horses and a bottomless bag of cracked, flecked marbles—across the floor.

She told me how they played in the red mud until Velma scrubbed them raw with Octagon soap in a big washpot by the elephant ears, how they walked the footlog like it was a high wire, then snuck into the house to watch Troy and his fiancée Dinky make out on the couch. When he was beginning elementary school and her a little younger, they climbed trees until her nerve gave out and she tried to pray herself down. "The preacher on the radio told us if you've got faith enough you can do anything. I got up in the apple tree and lost my faith." But he climbed till he ran out of tree, till the limbs were just twigs and the treetops bent and swayed beneath his weight. Even then there was no fear in him, only disappointment in the flimsy, insubstantial chemistry of clouds.

"Velma whipped him," Shirley said.

But how do you whip a boy out of the sky?

She told me they sneaked fried chicken legs off the big table in Velma's kitchen, and painted their faces with illegal pie. She told me he was so fierce that the big boys ran away from him when he picked up a rock, but was never mean to her, never pinched or made fun of her because she was afraid of the same world he stood master of in his doll-sized shoes. But mostly, she told me how he stood by her when she needed to be more than she was, how he still clutches at places in her heart even though they drifted apart after just a few years, when he reached that bubble of time in a boy's life when he is ashamed to be in the company of blonde-haired little girls.

———

IT SEEMS LIKE two separate universes, sometimes.

In one universe, three sisters, Velma, Odell and Eva, stand in almost-matching flower-print dresses, purses clutched in front of them, waiting for a nurse at the reception desk to notice they are alive. It is the 1940s, and the nurse, reigning over a doctor's office in Anniston, the Calhoun County seat, knows these women, or knows women like them, just timid country people. She pushes a physician's sign-in form across the counter and turns away. Shirley and my father, scrubbed bright pink and suffocating in their dress-up clothes, hold to their mothers' hems, watching.

The three sisters just stand there. Velma has worked in pain for days, standing at her machine. She needs a doctor to look at her feet, and right now wants nothing more than to just sit down. Odell and Eva, Shirley's mother, came in solidarity, as was custom then. You rarely saw just one working-class woman in the doctor's office. When they went among the swells, they went together. The nurse showed them her back for a few long minutes, then turned to look at them with cool superiority.

"Have you signed in?" she said.

The three ladies shook their heads.

"Why not?" she said.

The three ladies stood silent.

Every eye in the waiting room bored into their backs.

"Well?" the nurse said.

"I can't," Velma said.

She could write her name, but she could not decipher the form.

In the other universe stands a big, white house on Glenwood Terrace, the most fashionable street in the city of Anniston. The two-story house, where Shirley lives now with her husband Charles, is filled with antiques, with dark-wood furniture, with china and crystal and knickknacks without end. She is a beautiful woman, still, and he is a successful, retired businessman. She recently hosted an English tea for her book club, and sometimes meets the ladies for lunch at the club. Not a speck of red mud shows on her now.

But she is not one of those people who pretend they were born this way. She would lose too much if she did, and lose my father altogether. She remembers how the red earth would steam after the violent summer thunderstorms, and Grandfather Sam Whistenant would sneak ahead of Shirley and my father as they walked the trail through the dripping pines. Old Sam would bend down, scoop a handful of the wet clay in his hands, and craft little mud people from the warm, red muck. He would place his sculptures along the trail where the children were sure to find them. She would walk in the gloom and rustle of the deep trees, holding hands with her little hero so that his courage, like electric current, could flow through them, back and forth. And, around every bend, they would find those tokens, as if the raindrops were seeds and these mud people sprouted up along the dark trail after every storm. Old Sam, who had an old man's license to lie to children at will, denied any involvement in it, so haunts or fairies, he told them, it had to be.

There had to be witches, too, in a forest like that. She would walk through it on one condition.

"I was safe with your daddy," she said.

———

THE BOY CHARLES may have been brave because he was protected by the talismans he carried in his pockets, a gris-gris of charms and nonsense, like his homemade rabbit's foot, gristle sticking out of the skin, half a pocket comb, a lead sinker, and interesting rocks. He carried a knotted mile of monofilament and a bream hook sunk in a piece of cork, in case he should come across a promising ditch, a broken-handled pocketknife with one and one-half blades, and an unspeakable mess of what had once been two graham crackers sandwiched around a daub of commodity peanut butter. One whole pocket bulged with marbles, just marbles. He would have carried more treasure, certainly, if he hadn't already been weighed down like Balaam's ass with all that sloshing milk.

Velma petted the child, but as soon as he was able to walk she made him, because there was little room for clingy, dependent children in a place where you nursed your baby to a punch clock, and got docked good money if the line didn't start because you were still buttoning your blouse. He never crawled much, just stood up one day and went. Velma seldom let him out of the house without those two bottles of thick, sweet milk. She liked the RC bottles because the glass was thicker than store-bought junk and less likely to break in the rough-and-tumble that was just a given with little boys. He had no playmates in the house, so Velma corked his bottles, gave him the admonishment that generations of mothers have given their children in the age of the automobile—"Now, don't you get run't over"—and sent him through the pines, to his cousins.

Shirley can still remember the first time she ever saw him, striding up over the hill and into the yard in his old-fashioned high-top shoes. She had been a pudgy baby, so one of her uncles nicknamed her "Fatty," and still called her "Fat" for short.

"You ain't fat," he said, puzzled.

"I know," she said.

"He ort not call you that," he said.

She noticed his bottles.

"Why you bringin' your own milk?" she asked him.

" 'Cause I can't drank reg'lar," he said.

She did not laugh.

Friendships are sealed, tight and forever, in a minute like that.

Being so small and burdened with the milk bottles, he would have been doomed, sacrificed to children's cruelties, if he had been even the slightest bit meek. He would have never come out of the cotton mill village alive, would have been called nipple head and momma's boy and beaten half to death. Instead, it was like the midwife clipped his nerves when she cut the cord, and he answered every jeer and cat-call the same way. He picked up a rock, and threw it. Some little boys throw rocks and run away, but he ran at his target, closer and closer, till he was right on them, till he couldn't miss.

He led Shirley across days of danger. Her heart wasn't in it, but she went because she loved being with him, and wondered how any-one so small could be so unafraid. He was not wild-eyed and crazy-acting, but serious-faced and confident, till he got to the top of a tree or the bottom of a hill. Then, she believes, he was in pure joy. As he said then, "Doin' somethin' was always better'n talkin' 'bout doin' somethin'."

He showed up one day with a whole pack of Black Cat–brand firecrackers—sometimes, being Bobby's boy had real advantages. They crept off into the woods, far enough so that the blast would have been just an innocent pop in Grandma Whistenant's failing ears, and set to work blowing up dirt, anthills, tin cans but not frogs, because that was sadistic and stupid. "He was rough, but not mean," Shirley said. But he soon tired of blowing up things from a distance and began to play a game with himself, a kind of child-sized Russian roulette. He lit the Black Cat with a Blue Diamond kitchen match and held it, sizzling, as the fuse burned shorter, shorter . . .

"Throw it, throw it, throw it," Shirley begged.

. . . till he flicked it away, to explode in the air.

He was miserable under the eyes of grownups, his wardens. He would stare out a rain-streaked window, waiting, and then the screen door would be snatched half off its hinges, and she was racing to keep up.

He remains, to this day, the undisputed lightweight champion of the sewage-ditch pole vault. He would cut a thin pole as long as he could find and as heavy as he could lift and swing around. He would hold it in front of him, the far end waggling and wavering, because he was so small he could barely hold it up, and start to run. When he got to the edge of the ditch, he would gouge the end into the bottom near the other bank and heave himself upward, then turn loose of the pole, and fly. "He could go further out and higher up than any of the other little boys," Shirley said. The first time she tried it, she set the pole, soared upward and fell straight into the snake-infested, questionable water below.

It was a time in their lives when a discarded box was a covered wagon, a castle, a tank. But mostly, he turned them into sleds. In a world without snow, he discovered that pine straw can keep you going at a pretty slick clip. She remembers walking with him up the hill and, against her better judgment, climbing inside the box.

"It's so high," she said.

"No it ain't," he said.

"Uh-huh," she said.

She decided she would just sit awhile.

No one ever broke a leg sitting in a box.

"It'll be fun," he said.

"It won't," she said.

"It will," he said, and pushed.

She went the last few yards sideways.

He ran down the hill, jumping into the air every few steps.

"You done good," he said.

He liked to wear his aviator cap on his turn. It was just a box sliding on the pine straw or slick spring grass, but if you believe for a second he was not airborne, that he was not throttling through the clouds in his Sopwith Camel, machine-gun bullets clipping the guide wires with a sound like snapping guitar strings, well, you didn't see what Shirley saw.

He led her on spying missions, crawling behind furniture, through closets, under the kitchen table. One day they crept from under the porch, through the darkened house and toward the sounds of, well, something odd, in the middle room. There was a couch there, and further back in the boxcar-like house sat an unused rollaway bed on which Velma had piled mountains of folded quilts, sheets and other clean laundry. They crawled belly-down through the rooms, climbed the rollaway bed, cringing when the springs squealed, and burrowed under the laundry. From there they could see Troy and Dinky on the couch. It was the first smooching either of them ever witnessed that actually made a noise.

"Why do you reckon they do that?" he whispered.

"Don't know," she hissed.

"By God," he whispered, "I won't never."

It was all backflips and giggles, a cycle of washtub swimming pools, fatback and biscuits and eternal sunshine, till they almost killed Grandmother Whistenant.

The old house, made of batten board, was built into the side of a hill. It stood on pillars of natural rock, and the front porch was so high a child could stand under it. The porch was the center of life. Women rocked and snapped beans and cut okra and Uncle Carl Whistenant would lean his straight-backed chair against the wall of the house, and doze. It was mostly Braggs and Whistenants, the clans. There was no television, just a dust-covered radio, so they told stories, and gossiped. World War II raged in the Pacific and Europe, and in window after window in the village was taped a cardboard star, to show that house had given a son to the war. Word of their fate trickled through the streets, the church, the weekly paper, and made its way to the high porch. Louis H. Harris, of 111 D Street, had been captured in the

Philippines after the fall of Corregidor, and died of starvation in a Japanese prison camp on October 1, 1942. James E. Johnston, of 36 A Street, was killed on his ship. Olin L. McCurry, of 69 C Street, and Renay W. Webb, of 98 D Street, died in combat. George Robinson Jr., of 73 C Street, was killed when his ammunition ship blew up off Marcos Island. But the hardest news was of Everett Slaght, my father's cousin, who was blown from his gun turret on the *Iowa* and disappeared in the waves.

The war news baffled the children, who were too young to grasp it. The gossip was just as hard.

"Well, poor ol' so-and-so's with child again."

"She don't tell nobody."

"Bless her heart."

"Don't know who she's foolin'."

"Um."

"Ain't nobody come forward."

"Um."

"Bad, ain't it."

"Bad."

"It's a shame."

"Bless her heart."

Big, fist-sized chunks of ice, chipped off a twenty-pound block with an ice pick black from rust and time, knocked against the side of jelly glasses and Mason jars filled with iced tea. Snuff, which they ladled into their mouths with the tiny little paddles you get with tubs of ice cream, would lift off on the breeze in mid-dip and sift down through the planks to the gloom below. If they listened, they could hear a small child sneeze.

"I guess you know poor ol' mister and missus so-and-so's having trouble again?"

"Lord, no."

"Mm-hmm."

"Came home drunk."

"Well."

"She called the law."

"She ort to have."

"Bless her heart."

The children could hear but not see much, since the house was built tight in a time when carpenters never said things like "Just let that do." The boards of the porch joined just right, so children could lurk unseen for hours. There was, though, a single knothole, and the bravest children would press an eye against it like it was a telescope, and spy.

"I think it's where I learned my morals," said Shirley, who sat there a thousand days and nights with my father, eavesdropping. One evening, Grandmother Whistenant, who had finally forgiven her oldest daughter for not marrying into the officer corps, half dozed in her chair as kin gossiped around her. Under the porch, the children noticed that the old woman's chair was positioned perfectly over the knothole. Shirley cannot remember whose idea it was, but they took a curvy stick with a small knot on the end and poked it through the hole, and touched Grandmother Whistenant, ever so gently, on the leg.

Grandmother Whistenant looked down just in time to see the knobby end of the stick withdraw back into the hole.

Her face turned white and her breath died in her throat.

"Lordy, Lordy, mercy on me," she wailed. "A snake has bit me."

She sank to the planks and prepared to die.

She prayed, the words tumbling from her lips.

"Oh Lord, though I walk . . ."

The children ran from under the porch.

"We got scared," Shirley said. "She was so worked up, we thought she really was going to die."

Her kin helped her to her feet and made her stand, so they could check her for the fang marks. After as effective a search as could be made with decorum under the long skirt, slips and apron, it was determined there were none.

"You ain't dying," her kin assured her, one by one.

"Yes I am," Grandmother Whistenant avowed.

She insisted on dying, but had to wait quite some time.

The men looked for the snake, and my father, grinning, helped. Their search failed, but as was the custom in such things, they killed innocents for the entire summer, black snakes and rat snakes and the rare copperhead and baby ground rattlers. Fence rails and tree limbs hung with them, and the birds feasted. But the children slept easy, because there is nothing in the Bible that sends you to hell for killing snakes.

Shirley does not recall being afraid of them then, when she and my father ran barefoot in the weeds. But she found, when she first came to live with her mother's people, something that did frighten her. With fine-tuned cruelty, children in Jacksonville quickly picked up on the things that most hurt Shirley Vasser, the new girl in town.

One little girl, a preacher's kid, climbed to the top of a sliding board and stared down at Shirley, pious and accusing.

"My momma says your momma is going to hell, 'cause she got a divorce," she told Shirley.

"She ain't," Shirley said.

"She is," the little girl said.

"Well . . ." Shirley worked her brain. "Well . . ."

The little girl waited up high on the slide, triumphant.

"Well, you're ugly," Shirley said.

The little girl's mouth fell open.

She looked at my father, standing there.

He nodded.

The little girl slid down with her lips trembling, and ran off crying.

Another snooty little girl asked Shirley why she lived in an unpainted house with so many relatives.

"Well," Shirley said, "this is just our extra house. We've got another house."

"You do?" the girl said.

"Yep," Shirley said.

My father just watched, complicit.

"It's got a 'frigerator," Shirley said.

"It don't," the girl said.

"It does," Shirley said.

Every house for blocks around just had an icebox, an apparatus dependent on the whims and health of a man named Lanky Snyder, who showed twice a week with a twenty-pound block of ice.

But this new girl, this Shirley, not only had a 'frigerator, she had a summer house, too.

The little girl walked away to spread the news.

"I know the Good Lord doesn't want us to say such things, but it felt so good," Shirley said.

My father, if she asked, would have hit them with a rock.

———•——

HE WAS NOT completely unafraid. No little boy is. He dreamed about coffins that glided through the windows of the little houses, dreamed of old men in overalls and faded black coats lifting, pushing. He dreamed of machines, and in his bed he could hear them pounding through the walls. It was no wonder ghost stories did not impress him much.

Every root cellar, every closet was haunted then. Every dirt road ended in murder, every rope dangling from every limb was a hangman's tree instead of a rotted-off tire swing. "A witch lived in the cedar tree, and would grab you if you walked too close," Shirley said. She would draw you into her thick green, and let the birds peck out your eyes.

My father squatted at the base of the haunted tree, daring her to show herself.

"Come out," he called.

The witch withdrew into her needles, and waited for a different boy.

In the old cemetery, the restless dead of Rebel campaigns whistled from stones marked with LOVING HUSBAND, whispered from behind cement angels. The children ran past it, but he prowled inside, his slingshot loaded with a cat's-eye marble, because any fool knows there's magic in that. The dead just hunkered down in the rustling leaves, and let him pass.

"I wanted to be like him," Shirley said.

She told me a lot of stories. Then she told me she wished I had talked to her, if only for a minute, before I had dismissed him, in my words, as a mean drunk and tragic figure.

But it doesn't fix anything, I thought. *He changed, between her time and mine.*

I told her I wished I had, too.

The Boy

———

THE ONLY GENTLENESS the boy got, I gave him by accident.
The woman and boy lived in Memphis most of our first year together, and I commuted from Alabama. He met me at the door.

One night, near Christmas, he was on the couch, trying to figure out how many apples Johnny would have if he gave five-eighths of them to Sue, who gave four-fifths of them to Jimmy, who gave two-thirds of them back to Johnny, who I am pretty sure would have never gotten in the apple business to start with if he knew he was going to have to figure out this mess.

I was in the kitchen, wrapping presents. It was bitter cold outside—if you look at a map, Memphis is damn near as close to the Great Lakes as it is to the Gulf of Mexico—and the kitchen smelled warm and fine. There was nutmeg, cinnamon, evergreen. The big tree was covered in handmade ornaments from three little boys' lives.

I love Christmas, and have since my big brother used to wake me, standing all serious with a big flashlight in his hand.

"Has he done come?" I always asked, the light blinding me.

"He done was," he said.

My baby brother was too small to fool with. We let him sleep.

What did he know about Santy Claus?

We had to sneak to the tree, past my mother sleeping on the couch. It was forbidden, to peek before dawn.

We never waited on dawn in our lives.

The simple act of wrapping a present always pulled me back in time, shut out everything else, and sometimes, if I forgot myself long enough, even made me sing.

> *Old toy trains, little toy tracks*
> *Little toy drums, coming from a sack*
> *Carried by a man, dressed in white and red*
> *Little one don't you think it's time you were in bed*

It probably sounded pretty bad. I sing like an angel drunk, but do not drink anymore.

I looked up to see the woman smiling.

She walked over and whispered.

"He's in there on the couch, just grinning."

"Why?" I said.

"Because he thinks you're singing to him."

My father believed it was wrong to treat a boy, even a boy just five years old, as a helpless thing, so he rarely held my hand. He would carry us sometimes, Sam and me both, like a carnival ride, but when we walked he walked at his pace, and now and then he would wheel around, grin, and tell us, Come on, boys, come on. I remember a sidewalk in the mid-1960s, remember running to keep up when I was four or five years old. Sam, never helpless, matched him step for step. He would have killed himself, had his heart burst, rather than let him know he had won. Me, he had come back to retrieve, his face red.

But my legs were shorter.

We don't talk about him a lot, Sam and me.

I went home to see him later that Christmas season. The ring still felt hot on my finger then, and I pulled it on and off as cars passed us on Highway 21.

We were driving to Anniston, the county seat, to look at a used truck. You look at a million over your lifetime, and buy four. It's just good, somehow, to go look. There might be a magic truck out there.

We walked round and round one that day but it was just a truck, and on the way home we stopped for a barbecue at a place called Dad's.

"Tell me one good thing about our daddy," I said.

"I don't remember one," he said.

"There had to be something," I said.

"He didn't even buy no groceries," he said.

We left there in a cold rain, so he drove slowly—even slower than usual. He says I drive too fast, but most people who drive like him are wearing pillbox hats and pearls. I hope when we are old he does not drive me to the hospital when my heart begins to fail. I would have to get right with God as I crawled in the cab, because I would never see the emergency room.

"There has to be one good memory," I said.

Four red lights and an eternity later, he nodded.

"One," he said.

"Well?"

"It was that Christmas he got me that red wagon, and bought you that big tricycle," he said.

"Daddy never bought me a damn tricycle," I said.

"He did. He got drunk, and when him and some others left they run over it in the driveway," he said. "Momma took it in the house, and hid it in the closet. We moved, it was still there."

CHAPTER FIVE

The Bootlegger's Rhythm

———

THE DITCH CLEAVED FROGTOWN into two realms, and two powerful spirits held sway, one on each side. One was old, old as the Cross, and the other had aged only a few days in a gallon can. Both had the power to change men's lives. On one side of the ditch, a packed-in, pleading faithful fell hard to their knees and called the Holy Ghost into their jerking bodies in unknown tongues. On the other side, two boys, too much alike to be anything but brothers, flung open the doors of a black Chevrolet and lurched into the yard of 117 D Street, hallelujahs falling dead around them in the weeds. In the house, a sad-eyed little woman looked out, afraid it might be the law. When your boys are gone you're always afraid it might be the law. But it was just her two oldest sons, Roy and Troy, floating home inside the bubble of her prayer, still in crumpled, cattin'-around clothes from Saturday night, still a little drunk on Sunday morning. They were fine boys, though, beautiful boys. They were just steps away now, a few steps. She would fry eggs by the platterful and pour black coffee, and be glad they were not in a smoking hulk wrapped around a tree, or at the mercy of the police. She thought sometimes of walking over to the church to see it all, to hear the lovely music, but that would leave her boys and man unsupervised for too long. Her third son was eleven or so then. He could hear the piano ring across the ditch, even hear people shout, but he could smell the liquor that was always in the house on a Sunday and even steal a taste of it when no one was looking, so it was more real.

THE HOLY GHOST MOVED INVISIBLE, but they could feel it in the rafters, sense it racing inside the walls. It was as real as a jag of lightning, or an electrical fire.

The preacher stood on a humble, foot-high dais, to show that he did not believe he was better than them. "Do you believe in the Holy Ghost?" he asked, and they said they did. He preached then of the end of the world, and it was beautiful.

They were still a new denomination then, but had spread rapidly in the last fifty years around a nation of exploited factory workers, coal miners, and rural and inner-city poor. Here, it was a church of lint-heads, pulpwooders and sharecroppers, shoutin' people, who said amen like they were throwing a mule shoe. Biblical scholars turned their noses up, calling it hysteria, theatrics, a faith of the illiterate. But in a place where machines ate people alive, faith had to pour even hotter than blood.

It had no steeple, no stained glass, no bell tower, but it was the house of Abraham and Isaac, of Moses and Joshua, of the Lord thy God. People tithed in Mercury dimes and buffalo nickels, and pews filled with old men who wore ancient black suit coats over overalls, and young men in short-sleeved dress shirts and clip-on ties. Women sat plain, not one smear of lipstick or daub of makeup on their faces, and not one scrap of lace at their wrists or necks. Their hair was long, because Paul wrote that "if a woman have long hair, it is a glory to her, for her hair is given her for a covering." Their hair and long dresses were always getting caught in the machines, but it was in the Scripture, so they obeyed. Some wore it pinned up for church, because of the heat, but before it was over hairpins would litter the floor.

They listened as the preacher laid down a list of sins so complete it left a person no place to go but down.

"They preached it hard, so hard a feller couldn't live it," said Homer Barnwell, who went there as a boy.

The people, some gasping from the brown lung, ignored the weakness in their wind and pain in their chests and sang "I'll Fly Away" and "Kneel at the Cross" and "That Good Ol' Gospel Ship." A woman named Cora Lee Garmon, famous for her range, used to hit the high notes so hard "the leaders would stand out in her neck," Homer said.

Then, with the unstoppable momentum of a train going down a grade, the service picked up speed. The Reverend evoked a harsh God, who turned Lot's wife into a pillar of salt, and condemned the Children of Israel, who gave their golden earrings to Aaron to fashion Baal, the false god. "I have seen this people," God told Moses, "and behold, it is a stiff-necked people. Now therefore let me alone, so that my wrath may wax hot against them."

As children looked with misery on a service without end, the preacher read chapter 2 of the Acts of the Apostles:

And when the day of Pentecost was fully come, they were all with one accord in one place. And suddenly there came a sound from heaven as of a rushing mighty wind, and it filled all the house where they were sitting. And there appeared unto them cloven tongues like as of fire, and it sat upon each of them. And they were all filled with the Holy Ghost, and began to speak with other tongues . . .

The congregants' eyes were shut tight.

"Do you feel the Spirit?" the Reverend shouted.

Their hands reached high.

"Can you feel the Holy Ghost?"

They answered one by one, in the light of the full Gospel.

"Yeeeeesssss."

Then, as if they had reached for a sizzling clothesline in the middle of an electrical storm, one by one they began to jerk, convulsing in the grip of unseen power. Others threw their arms open wide, and the Holy Ghost touched them soul by soul.

Some just stood and shivered.

Some danced, spinning.

Some leapt high in the air.

Some wept.

Some of the women shook their heads so violently that their hair came free and whipped through the air, three feet long. Hairpins flew.

The Ghost was in them now.

They began to speak in tongues.

The older church people interpreted, and the congregation leaned in, to hear the miracle. It sounded like ancient Hebrew, maybe, a little, and other times it sounded like nothing they had heard or imagined. They rushed to the front of the church and knelt in a line, facing the altar, so the preacher could lay his hands on them, and—through the Father, in the presence of the Holy Ghost—make them whole.

One by one, they were slain in the Spirit, and fell backward, some of them, fainting on the floor. The services could last for hours, till the congregants' stomachs growled. "If it's goin' good," Homer said, "why switch it off?"

———

As STRONG AS IT WAS, as close, it was as if sounding brass or a tinkling cymbal, across that ditch.

"We could have by God stayed longer if you'd have brought some damn money," griped Roy, as they meandered toward the house. It is unclear where they had been that weekend, but apparently they had a real good time. Roy, the prettiest of all of them, leaned against the car for balance, and cussed his older brother a little more. Roy's eyes were just like my father's, a bright blue, and his hair was black. He was tall for a Bragg, and the meanest when he drank. He was not a dandy and just threw on his clothes, but was one of those men who would have looked elegant standing in a mudhole.

Troy cussed him back, but cheerfully. He always wore snow-white T-shirts, black pants and black penny loafer shoes, and as he blithely dog-cussed his brother he bent over, took off one loafer and dumped several neatly folded bills into his hand. Then, hopping around on one foot, he waved the bills in his brother's face.

"You lying son of a bitch," Roy said.

Troy, his shoe still in his hand, just hopped and grinned, trying not to get his white sock dirty.

He sniffed the money, like it was flowers.

"I'll kill you," Roy said.

But they were always threatening to kill somebody.

Troy, in a wobbly pirouette, laughed out loud.

In seconds, they were in the dirt, tearing at clothes and screaming curses, and rolled clear into the middle of D Street, in a whirl of blood and cinders.

The commotion drew first Velma and then Bobby from inside the house. Velma, unheard and ignored, pleaded for them to stop. Bobby, on a binge and still dressed only in his long-handles, cackled, hopped, and did a do-si-do.

My father banged through the door and into the yard, and, like a pair of long underwear sucked off a clothesline by a tornado, was carried away by the melee.

In the rising dust, they clubbed each other about the head with their fists, split lips and blacked eyes and bruised ribs. My father, smaller than his brothers, was knocked down and almost out. Velma bent over my father, to make sure he was breathing, and yelled at the older two: "I'll call the law." Then she left walking, to find a telephone.

How many times did Velma make that walk to a borrowed telephone, having to choose between her sons' freedom and their safety? My Aunt Juanita, driving through the village, remembers seeing her walking fast down the street. "Her heels was just a'clickin' on the road," she said.

She stopped and, through the window, asked Velma if she was all right.

"The boys is killing each other," she said.

In the yard, the boys were staggering now, about used-up. The neighbors watched from their porches, but no one got in the way. The distant scream of a police siren drifted into the yard. Velma had found a telephone.

By the time the police came, the street was empty and quiet in front of 117, the brothers inside, ruining Velma's washrags with their blood. Bobby had enjoyed himself immensely, and gone a half day without pants of any kind. Velma walked back, her flat shoes clicking slowly now. But her boys were safe, and nothing mattered next to that.

In the aftermath, she cooked a five-pound block of meat loaf, a mountain of fried potatoes, a cauldron of pinto beans, and dishpans of squash and okra—nothing special, just the usual supper for the kin that, every Sunday, trickled in to eat.

It was nothing special, either, that fight, nothing to get all worked up about. The brothers regularly fought in the middle of D Street. "I watched 'em fight," said Charles Parker, who lived next door.

Or, as Carlos put it: "You didn't never ask about that big fight Roy and Troy had, you asked about which one. It happened regular." It was just part of the rhythm of the week, the rhythm of their lives.

Most lives move to one kind or another. On the coast, they move to tides, and in a factory town they move to an assembly line. For Carlos, a body and fender man and wrecker driver, life moved to the rhythms of the highway, to the voice of the dispatcher on the radio. In the week he cruised slow and easy, but on Friday nights, when drinkers hit the roads, the dispatcher's voice crackled with possibility. He stomped the accelerator and raced from ditch to ditch, his winch cable whining, yellow lights spinning, mommas crying, ambulances screaming away or, if it was a bad one, not screaming at all.

For his cousins on D Street, it was the bootlegger's rhythm. "The boys and Uncle Bobby all worked, and only dranked on weekends. They'd get goin' real good on Friday and still be goin' on a Sunday. Of course, sometimes they could still be going on a Tuesday, depending on how much liquor they had. They were the best people in the world, gentle people, when they were all right. But all your daddy's life, on a weekend, there was liquor there in that house."

In the calm of a Monday, the nights had a warmth and peace in Velma's house. After work, her extended family gathered in her kitchen, eating, talking, babies riding on their knees. But mostly, in that quiet, she cooked. "Oh my," said Carlos, "did she cook." She cooked showpiece meals, meals most people only got on Thanksgiving or Christmas Day, and Carlos loved to go see his Aunt Velma in the calm. "It didn't matter what time of night or day it was, or even if she had to get out of bed, when you went to Aunt Velma's house the first thing she did was ask you, 'Y'all boys had something to eat?' It didn't matter if you'd done eat, 'cause Velma was gonna feed you anyway."

The iron stove had a cast-iron warmer on the top, and in that warmer would be pork roasts and pork chops and fried chicken, two-gallon pots of butter beans with salt pork, navy beans with ham bone, rattlesnake beans glistening with bacon fat, pans of chicken and dressing, macaroni and cheese, cornbread and cathead biscuits, mounds of mashed potatoes and sweet potatoes, skillets of fried green tomatoes. She made meat loaf in a washtub, working loaf bread into the meat, onions and spices with her hands. There would be fried pies, apple and peach, in the warmer, and a banana puddin' in the icebox. She cooked her pies in a pan the size of a Western Flyer, and she did not cut you a piece but scooped out a mound, a solid pound of pie.

It was not just food. There was a richness in it, of cream and butter and bacon fat. Her dishes were chipped and her forks were worn, pitted steel, but when people were done the utensils looked like they had been licked clean, and sometimes they were. She taught generations of women to cook, including my own mother, who thinks of her with every shaker of salt. Generations of men, like Carlos, get teary-eyed when they think of her supper table on a random Monday, because they know it will never be that good again.

In the calm of a Tuesday, the mercurial Roy lay on the couch in the living room with a baby asleep on his chest. He would fight an army when he was drinking, fight laughing, bleeding, but sober he was a gentle man. "Whose baby are you?" he always asked, as the infants opened their eyes. "Roy rocked the babies in the rocking chairs, when he was all right," my mother said. "He would sing, and hum to them, and he would even diaper them—I guarantee you that your daddy never got nowhere near a diaper." Roy was not married then, and had no children of his own. He just loved babies, and would rock Troy's children and sing, and hum the part where the bough breaks, and the baby falls.

He was a mechanic, a good one, with a set of paid-for tools. Women chased him. He had everything to live for, on a Tuesday, and no reason to dull his life with liquor, no reason to hide in a whiskey haze.

In the quiet of a Wednesday, Troy walked home from his job at the mill, to tend his birds. In that time and place, it was as noble a job as being a horse breeder. He opened the coop and stuck his hand in toward the fierce creature inside, eyes yellow, beak sharp as a cat's claw, trilling a warning so low it was almost a growl. But it did not draw blood as he reached in and lifted it out.

He would sit on the porch, a cup of Red Diamond coffee on the rail, and stroke its beak, cooing to it, as if he wanted it to understand the awful sacrifice he was asking it to make. He had one bird that had won seven fights, a remarkable feat in a death sport, and he would run his fingers through its feathers, looking for parasites. He would treat it with Mercurochrome, like a child with a skinned knee, and let it peck corn from his palm. He fed them a mix of vitamins and racing pigeon feed, to make them strong and fast, and spiked their diet with pickling lime, to stanch the bleeding when they were cut.

He had to get drunk to fight them, to drop them in that pit on the weekends, had to be good and drunk to watch them die. But on a Wednesday he just loved on them, then went into the house to help his mother snap beans, like any good son.

On a Thursday, Bob helped his wife sweep the floors, helped her wash the dishes. They would stand side by side, her washing, him drying. He would pick her a gallon of blackberries, just to see her smile. He raised a perfectly matched pair of redbone hounds, and would chase them for hours and hours through the mountains, listening to them sing. He knew the mountains and never got lost, when he was all right. Some evenings he would saddle his riding horse, pull up a child or two, and walk them gently through the streets. The mothers who handed their babies up to my grandfather never fretted about it, because it was just a Thursday.

———

In the mountains, they cooked, too. Joe Godwin made liquor in Muscadine. Moe Shealey made it in Mineral Springs. Junior McMahan had a still in Ragland. Fred and Alton Dryden made liquor in Tallapoosa, and Eulis Parker made it on Terrapin Creek. Wayne Glass knew their faces because he drove it, and made more money hauling liquor than he ever made at the cotton mill. He loaded the gallon cans into his car in the deep woods and dodged sheriffs and federal men to get it to men like Robert Kilgore, the bootlegger who sold whiskey from a house in Weaver, about ten minutes south of Jacksonville. "I could haul a hundred and fifty gallons in a Flathead Ford, at thirty-five dollars a load," he said. Wayne lost the end of one finger in the mill, but he was bulletproof when he was running liquor, and only did time once, for conspiracy. "They couldn't catch me haulin' liquor," he said, "so they got me for thinkin' about it."

It was business, not art. He remembers driving for an old man who calmly told him: "Now, boy, if you steal my liquor, I'll blow your heart out." He did not race around like a Hollywood fool, but rode with the traffic, to blend in. He was coming through the county with a carload of liquor when he saw Sheriff Roy Snead blocking the road. "I jumped through the hog lot, jumped a five-strand barbed-wire fence, him shootin' at me."

He lost that load, but liquor always got through somehow.

"I remember one time, around Christmas, there wadn't no liquor," said Wayne. "Got some in Ragland, finally. Liquor had a blue color."

On Friday, Bob would give one of the boys some cash and say: "Go get us some liquor," and the calm drowned in the squeal of a metal lid. The men, Bob, Troy, Roy, others, gathered at the table and drank. Their belligerence was a weed that grew in the stuff, and they argued chickens, dogs, horses, the words to a song, the meaning of a look, the heart of women, the soul of man.

This was my father's boyhood.

Sober, Bob bought pigs from Roy.

Drunk, Roy came in the night and stole them back.

Sober, Bob could walk the mountains with an unerring sense of direction.

Drunk, he went off with other drunk men, cussed them out, got put out of the car and wandered lost in the woods of Whites Gap for two days.

Sober, her boys treated Velma with respect, love.

Drunk, she would vanish, cease to matter, except as a medic or bondsman.

But it all faded, that chaotic rhythm, on a Sunday night. "Everybody was always all right after a few days," Carlos said. Bob or one of the older boys would thump the can and it would boom, hollow, and it was over. In a few hours they were begging Velma for coffee. Their stomachs, which could not hold food and liquor, would gradually rumble in a more natural way. "Cook us somethin', Momma," they would say.

I don't know, truthfully, when my father took his first drink. I don't know what he thought about growing up that way, if he wanted to be just like them, or if he even had a choice, trapped the way a bug is trapped inside the windows of a speeding car. The only thing I know for sure is something he told my mother when they were together. He said that when he was small, and the drinking and fighting and yelling started and grew and grew, he would go sit in the outhouse, and hide.

The Boy

———

IT WAS ALMOST SCIENCE FICTION, the way he could change. One minute he was a brat, who pretended to be ill when we were out at supper so he could go immediately home to watch cartoons. Then, as if he changed in a phone booth, he could transform into a sweet, noble boy.

I saw it the first time in a thunderstorm.

He loved to go to Alabama to visit my mother—or maybe he just loved biscuits—but even if it was an overnight trip he packed five bags, all jammed with toys, electronics, movies, his blanket, pillows and, for God's sake, fuzzy slippers. He took slippers, for the car ride. "That's not how a boy packs," I said, but I guess boys have changed.

I didn't care if he rode bulls or danced ballet, and that's the truth. But what made me crazy was the idea that he was the kind of boy I used to despise, the kind who looked down his nose on the boy I was. That was it, I realized, as I drove the silver car alone on a windswept highway between Birmingham and Memphis. That was what needled me. My mother cleaned their houses, cooked for them, diapered them. I would not have a boy like that.

The woman and boy followed behind me, the truck loaded with things we ferried from her Memphis home to the University of Alabama, where I was Professor of Writing. I guess one of these days I'll get a title fancy enough to cover up everything else. The boy loved to ride with me but I was mad at him for whining, and exiled him to the Chevrolet. Besides, with his accoutrements, I would not have had room to shift gears.

I rarely listened to the radio as I drove—the flat, six-cylinder engine, more like a jet plane than a car, made its own music—and I was feeling guilty but free as I roared ahead, then sank back, till the storm hit. Lightning ran sideways across the sky in electric pink, as other jags stabbed the ground. Ahead of me, burning even in that rain, a roadside store or barn blazed up yellow and red, a casualty of the storm. Behind me, the rain wiped out everything beyond a few feet. My family disappeared behind that curtain of rain, as if the headlights just winked out, and I panicked a little. I jabbed the phone, useless, over and over, till I finally found her.

We pulled off at the first exit, a combination McDonald's and convenience store, crowded with old pickups and ragged work cars, the kind of cars that flood out in a storm like that. I slid in between them, and walked over to the woman and boy.

The boy was sullen, pouty. The excitement of the storm had not erased the fact that he had not had his way about something neither one of us, now, can even recall.

"Can I have a quarter?" was all he said.

A few arcade games stood in a corner. I fished out a handful of change and put in our order at the counter. The woman and I sat at one of the hard plastic tables, not saying all that much. A large family sat just a few tables over, sheltering as we were from the storm.

I knew them, not their names but their lives, or thought I did. They were working people, mill or day laborers, a woman in dollar-store clothes, a man with grease embedded in his hands, pants pocked by battery acid, cheap boots, vinyl maybe, cracked and run-down. Women know shoes. Men see boots. They had five or six small children, and even in McDonald's that can put a dent in a poor man's paycheck, at suppertime. A little blonde girl, smaller than my boy, was asking for money, too, but the woman shook her head and the man didn't acknowledge her at all, not being mean, just unwilling to pay good money for a few seconds of bright, blipping lights. The little girl did not cry or whine, just walked over to stand in front of one of those games, the kind where you pay your quarter and then try to snatch a stuffed animal with a dangling claw. It was full of bears, cats, dogs, cartoon characters. She just stood there, looking inside.

My boy stepped in front of her as if she was invisible.

I went cold.

I didn't yell or put my hands on him. I never felt it was my right. I just called to him, and for the life of me I can't recall what I said. But I can still see his cheeks go red, like I had slapped them. If he had been a man, I would have. I would have knocked him to the floor.

He didn't say anything, just walked away. Then, as if it was his way of telling me to go to hell, he circled around to the game and dropped in his quarter.

So it was true, I thought.

I had one of them.

He is at home in an arcade, in a life where the quarters run in a silver, tinkling, never-ending stream. On his first try, the boy deftly snagged a stuffed animal, a blue and yellow dog.

Then he walked over and handed it to the little girl.

"Thank you," the girl's mother said to us.

The man nodded his thanks, too.

I sat there ashamed of myself, till the last cold French fry was dragged through a puddle of red.

The boy walked a little apart from me as we left, but I walked over, quick, and threw my arm around his shoulders.

"You are a noble boy," I said, and squeezed him till he yelped.

"What's that?" he said.

I told him it didn't matter, but it was good.

We walked into the parking lot, the storm not over, just gone someplace else.

"Ride with me, the rest of the way," I told him.

I unlocked the doors, but he ran toward his mother's car.

"Where you goin'?" I shouted.

"To get my blanky," he said.

CHAPTER SIX

Flying Jenny

THE BOYS PULLED ON their most raggedy garments, because something unspeakable could splash on them, especially if there was a big girl inside. It happened in the season of the witch, pumpkins aglow on every porch. My father and the rest gathered quietly in the backyards of A, B, C or D Street, to skulk and whisper in the weeds. Before long, a screen door would bang, a flashlight beam would jiggle across dying grass, and footsteps would rustle through fallen leaves. A creak of hinges followed by a soft thud, the closing of the outhouse door, would sound in the darkness, telling the boys it was safe to creep closer, closer. Sometimes one of the delinquents would giggle and the girl inside, a big girl usually, would freeze, Sears, Roebuck in her fingers, drawers to her knees. The outhouse door would crash open and the flashlight would stab the dark, accusing, till she finally gave up, muttering. As soon as the door shut, the boys rose like Lazarus from the dark, mouthed "one . . . two . . . *three*" and swarmed. They rocked the structure once, twice and heaved, the occupant snatching at her clothes, yelling curses as she rode her outhouse down. The boys scattered, laughing, as porch lights winked on up and down the street and old women screamed what they have screamed over generations: "I see you, you little half-raised idiots." The next morning, the victims would raise their outhouses up again, but it was like rebuilding in the known trajectory of a hurricane. In the village, boredom would build into imagination, swirl into mischief, and blow them down again.

Billy Measles was twelve, maybe thirteen, when his father got on at the mill and moved his family to D Street, three doors from the Braggs. My father, about the same age, introduced himself with a hard, hooking left to the new boy's head, and as soon as lights stopped twinkling around Billy's skull he saw, instead of an enemy, a tight new circle of friends.

"We run with Bill Raines. He was short, redheaded, had freckles. He had a good heart. There was Leeman Bragg. Leeman was hairy as a monkey and stocky-built, loved horses more'n anything. And there was Garfield Bragg, darkish, a loverboy, always after women. Whistled and hollered at 'em, all the time. Alfred Davis was lanky, slender, and black-headed. He smoked cigarettes and played marbles. You'd try to bum a cigarette off Alfred and he'd say the same thing. 'These got to do me all week.' Say it in this grown-up voice, 'Boys, I'd like to, but these got to do me . . .' Bill Joe Chaney was there. He turned over the outhouse with that big Shuttles gal in it. And Dave and Jake Strickland, short and stocky, both of 'em, and black-headed. Billy Joe Champion. He was a talker, and liked to build big bonfires, and he'd sit by 'em all night. Wallace Key had blond streaks in brown hair, and he could buck-dance. His daddy taught him. Little Carl Bragg was with us. Carl wouldn't go to bed by himself. And me. I think I weighed ninety pounds. And there was your dad. He was left-handed. Did you know that? Well, I didn't. I thought the world of him, but I won't never forget that hard left hand . . ."

Billy Measles is seventy-two years old now. He is a smallish man, like my father was.

"I guess," he said, "it was the time of our lives."

Their club had no name, no treehouse, no secret handshake. Their leader was not elected. He took power, through a series of tests. Who could build the most lethal weapon from scrap wood, chinaberries, and cut-up inner tube? Who could jump the widest ditch with a night watchman on his tail, talk to a live girl without sounding like a dumb-ass, or pick up a softball soaked in kerosene and, bare-handed, throw a comet across the evening sky?

Who could ride Flying Jenny and not throw up?

Who could drink a gallon of water and pee over a Studebaker?

Who could beat up everybody else?

"He was the best, your daddy was," Billy said, "at all that stuff."

But he remembers the fighting best. It seemed like my father always had his fists up. "Your dad just didn't know how to take nothin' off nobody," said Billy. He fought big boys and town boys—when they were foolish enough to stray into the alphabet streets—and won, always won. He could have been a great painter, or a captain of indus-try, and not mattered as much to people here as he did for that.

Child labor laws had given them a childhood, and banished the shame of eleven- and twelve-year-old mill hands. But the boys in the mill village, and the girls, still didn't have as much time left as the chil-dren in town. The law said you had to be sixteen to quit school in the state of Alabama, but could quit at fourteen if your mother or father would sign for you. You had to be sixteen to take full-time work in the cotton mill, but your people could sign for you there, too, sign away the last days of your life barefoot and buck-wild. But for now there was still time, time to rattle down the suicidal corkscrew of the mill fire escape on a sled made from a Coke crate, time to spy on the high school girls at the swimming pool, gasp, choke, fall to the grass, clutch your heart and pretend to die.

It was an exclusive club. You could be stingy like Alfred, redheaded like Bill or hairy like Leeman, but could not win a place in their circle till you had the guts to look another boy in the eye and fight him, win, lose or draw. You could even be afraid of the dark like Carl, as long as you did not run away in the morning.

The boy Billy had to fight, the one they all had to, was my father.

Billy's father was a sharecropper who followed the promise of the mill into town, like everyone else. Billy was waif-thin and short but he wanted to belong, so he raised his fists and waited for the dark-haired boy to step into a ring formed from the bodies of all the rest. He did not expect to win. "Nobody ever whipped your daddy," Billy said.

The other boys did not whoop or holler.

This was too serious.

Would the new boy run, or cry?

Or would he take it.

"Well," Billy said, "we didn't even get started good."

My father walked into the circle in a pair of neatly ironed bib overalls—Velma even ironed their underwear—and set himself in a classic, right-handed fighter's stance. The boys might not have known much about the outside world, but they were students of violence. They watched newsreels of Joe Louis, and listened to prizefights that hissed from the single speaker of big, waist-high radios. When they fought, they did not swing wild but jabbed, jabbed, then came in quick with hard overhand rights or undercuts that could make you bite your tongue off, if you happened to be waggling it at the time. The boys in the circle smiled as my father set himself, his left hand leading, his right held back, for the big punch, the tooth-rattler. They had seen this secret weapon before.

"I didn't know he was really left-handed, or maybe I forgot," Billy said.

My father jabbed with his left, almost gently, but Billy kept his eyes locked on the right hand, the punishing hand.

He didn't see my father shuffle his feet, shift his balance. He jabbed with his right and Billy automatically ducked away—right into the path of a wicked, hooking left.

Oh Lord, he thought, as the world came apart into twinkling lights.

Purty, he thought.

My father didn't hit him again. The new boy seemed lost.

"I wobbled around and just sat down," Billy said.

After a while, he saw my father kneeling in front of him.

"I didn't mean to hurt you," he said.

"Yeah you did," Billy said.

But now he understands that, among boys who had so little apparent gentleness in them, he was seeing them at their most gentle. My father could have beaten him half to death that day for sport, but that was not the point. He and the other boys knew all they needed to know. Billy Measles, all ninety pounds of him, was a member with all privileges in a club that had just one. For the rest of his fleeting time as a boy, no one would get to knock him down except one of his best friends.

———

THEY HAD NEVER SEEN a roller coaster. There was just a lumbering Ferris wheel and a mamby-pamby merry-go-round, which came once a year in ragged caravans of poo-flinging monkeys, scarred, crippled elephants, and hucksters who charged people a dear nickel to gaze on a two-headed pig in a jar, or bounce softballs against milk bottles filled with lead. Men stuck their heads into the yawns of toothless lions and walked a wire no higher than a clothesline, and still had the gall to shout "Ta-da!" My father might have run off to join the circus if one had ever come by that was worth his time.

"Your daddy was a real daredevil," Billy said, and the village was his big top. He led his troupe into local history, if history means old men will one day shake their heads and wonder how, in the foolishness of it all, they did not die.

In the summers, some of them took part-time work in the mill, sweeping up mountains of lint, but as soon as they had a little silver they were gone, standing barefoot at the little clapboard stores to buy ice-slicked RCs, then running wide-open to the banks of Shit Creek. Sometimes, their heartless mommas kept them in bondage a few awful hours more, toting wood or scraping dried egg off plates and stainless steel, "but not Charles, 'cause you sure wouldn't never catch Charles washing no dishes," Billy said.

The boys were amazed by Bob, but careful what they said. Young Charles would blaze up like a match dragged across a cement block, and bloody their nose and black their eyes. He did not respect Bob always—that is why, as he grew older, he called him Bob—but he loved him, my mother always said.

Once, when my father was just twelve, Bob got into an argument with his middle son, Roy, that escalated into a bloody fistfight and threats of more bloodshed. Afraid that his brother would, in his rage, hurt or even kill his father, my father hustled Bob down the road and into the woods. My father slipped back into the house in the dark and took a .22 rifle, an ax, a knife, and an old piece of tarp. He built a shelter, kept a fire, and hunted for rabbits and squirrels. They stayed there for days as Bob sobered up, as the hot-blooded Roy calmed. "It's that damn Indian in you," Bob told his son, "that made you able to do this." When the other boys asked him where he had been, he told them he had to smuggle Bob out of town. Knowing Bob, the others nodded their heads, but said nothing.

But most days, when Billy knocked on the door, my father just pushed through with a cold tater biscuit in one hand, and together they picked up more boys as they ran through the streets. Some days they would go to the baseball field or city pool, but most days they wound up on the creek, to fish and to lie. They fished village-style with old circular saw blades discarded from the mill. They stood on the banks, waiting for a fish to wiggle by. Then they would throw, and cut the fish in two. It was a cruelty, but in that place, among those boys, it was only a small violence, one to grow on.

They cobbled their day together that way, from scrap. But while others built treehouses and soapbox racers, they built flying machines.

The Flying Jenny was about the most dangerous thing in Alabama except for the electric chair. The boys found a fresh-cut stump, about waist-high, and drilled or burned a dime-sized hole in the center. They stole a two-by-six or a two-by-nine board, at least six feet long, then drilled a hole in the center of that. They greased the top of the stump—little boys can always locate grease, the same way a dog can always find a tick—and lined up the holes. They slipped a long, greased bolt through the hole in the board, into the stump, to create something much like a propeller on a plane. Finally, they fixed a rope to one end of the board, so they would have something to pull on. My father always went first. The other boys took their places on the rope, grinning, as he climbed onto the other end, got a grip on the board and told them: "Let 'er go." The boys ran in a circle, pulling till the board spun faster than they could run, spun till the bolt began to smoke in the hole. If you fell, it would knock out your brains. He flew, flew till he was sick, green, and flew off, then staggered around like a drunk man as the other boys whooped and hollered like it was the grandest thing they'd ever seen. He flew a hundred miles, a thousand, and once the scenery itself finally stopped spinning around him, he saw it had not changed.

"He couldn't scare hisself enough," Billy said.

It was the same on the cotton mill corkscrew run. Cotton mills were death traps in fires, because even the air burned in the swirling lint. In Jacksonville, the company built a fire escape ramp on one wall, a massive corkscrew with a slick, stainless steel slide. For generations, village boys sneaked into the mill, and rode it down, for fun. But for real speed, you needed a sled. Billy Measles remembers how happy my father was the day they liberated a wooden Coke crate from the back of a grocery store and lugged it to the mill. The watchman, a man named Duck Ford, tried to catch them, but Duck was old and they evaded him, and stood at the top of the corkscrew, looking down. My father rode the Coke crate down, banging into the walls, leaving skin on the screwheads and metal seams, hollering "Wahoo!" till he shot out the bottom onto a concrete pad, grinding to a stop. Later, he would tote up a bucket of water and pour it down, to make it slicker, but it was never slick enough, or fast enough, to take you anywhere but down.

Karl Wallenda, the great-grandfather of daredevils, said life is the wire, and the rest is waiting.

My father couldn't scare himself, but he could scare the rest of them.

"I guarantee you, we wasn't never bored for long," Billy said.

Some of the town boys had BB guns, but that was an impossible dream, here. So, they sawed the rough shape of a rifle from a scrap board, fixed a short nail at the front, where a front sight would be, another where the rear sight would be, and stretched a long, thin circle of inner tube around the nails. They loaded them with chinaberries, which flew straighter than a rock but hurt just as bad, and went to war. It was just a wicked slingshot, really, but it would break a beer bottle. "Your daddy's would raise a blister, when he hit you," Billy said. His had to be stronger, had to pull tighter.

At one o'clock, on the days she was off, Velma called him in to eat, and the rest came, too, the screen door rattling as a small army of boys rushed through. There they would have to wait in line with cousins and other kin, but no one was turned away. Later, full as ticks, the boys lay in the shade, trying unsuccessfully to beg a cigarette off stingy Alfred, as the ones who had money for the cowboy matinees filled in the ones who didn't have money on what had happened a Saturday before. "Well, you see, Red Ryder got Little Beaver from them Indians, and was raisin' 'im . . ." They spent a lot of time talking pure nonsense, like who could hold their breath the longest, or kill the most Germans.

"But mostly," Billy said, "we talked about girls.

"There was Mary Ellen Coker. Black hair. Purty. And Joyce Phillips. Dishwater blonde. Had these big brown eyes, hazel eyes. Lord, I loved them hazel eyes," and all the breathtaking rest. They would pass and a boy would whistle—it was Garfield, usually—taking his life in his hands. If you whistled at a village girl, she might walk over and punch you in the mouth, or her papa might kill you—in the village, romance could make a black widow seem like a sweet deal. "Most of us was still scared of girls," said Billy. If a live girl had stopped to talk to them, they would not have known what to say, and some of them would have turned and run. "Except Garfield. Garfield never run from a woman in his life. He run toward a bunch of 'em, though. He was a booger.

"But we didn't know nothin' really, about girls. One day I had to go to the bathroom real bad out behind the mill, where they had all these outhouses set up, and I snatched a door open and there sat Missus Edna Allen. And she just looked at me. 'I will be out in just a little bit,' she said. But I was already tearing out of there at a dead run. That ain't the way you want to find out about girls."

My father loved girls, but there was no girl he was in love with, not that Billy knew. He was in love with the idea of girls, all girls, and he would sit in the circle of lies at the bonfires they built in the middle of dark fields and talk about a shape, a look, a sound, long before he had firsthand knowledge. Even Garfield claimed more knowledge than he had, unless getting your face slapped on the square is considered second base.

The bonfire, made from pine and trash and whatever they could find, would pop and shoot sparks till it singed someone, and then they would laugh about that. They talked for hours, till their mommas' calls drifted in from distant porch lights. Billy cannot remember one story they told. It was being there, he said, that was worth remembering.

Some nights, walking home, the gaggle of boys would see what seemed to be a meteor arc through the night, a ball of fire with an orange tail six feet long. It would land in the wet grass with a hiss and splatter of flames and roll smoking across the field. It was kind of beautiful, on a slow night, burning red and orange in the air. But when one of them, the bravest, rushed over to pick it up, it was just a softball soaked in kerosene. He threw it to the bigger boys, who chased it back and forth across the night sky until it just consumed itself, and winked out.

"Daddy got a job a couple years later up in Albertville, sharecropping, and got free rent on a house," Billy said. "We left the village, and I lost track of your dad. I came back when I was seventeen to work in the mill, but your daddy was done gone."

I asked him if he kept up with any of the other boys.

He heard Bill Raines was still alive.

"But I think most of 'em's dead, son," he said.

I heard one or two of the others might still be alive, and tried to track them down. I found a Wallace Key in the Anniston phone book, and dialed the number. An ancient voice answered the phone.

"I been lookin' for you," I said.

"Who?" he said.

"Wallace Key."

"Who?" he said.

"WALLACE KEY."

"I'm him," he said.

"I think you played with my daddy, Charles Bragg . . ."

"Who?" he said.

"CHARLES BRAGG."

"No," he said, "I don't recall."

My heart sank.

I asked him, twice, if he remembered Billy Measles.

"No," he said, "I don't recall him, either."

I guess a bonfire only burns so long, too.

"Could be," the old man said, "you got the wrong Wallace Key."

In the background, I could hear a television roar.

"Wallace Key," I said, my voice ratcheted up. "Lived in Jacksonville in '45. Liked to buck-dance."

"No," the old man said, "I never did."

He said there were about five of them, around, with that name.

"I know that Wallace Key. He died."

He told me he was sorry he was the wrong one, and hung up.

But I wasn't sorry.

I am sorry dancing Wallace Key is gone, but in a way I was relieved. I had started to count on the notion my father the boy was someone people remembered, and I didn't like the idea that he could be forgotten like everything else.

"I won't never forget your dad," Billy said, looking at his boots.

His trailer on the Alexandria Road is spotless, his yard immaculate. There is a wagon wheel by the front gate, and a permanent porch. Living here, you realize that just because a house is dragged in by a truck, it doesn't mean it will ever be dragged back out again. No college men, not a one, remember my father's name, but they will never forget him in the mill village, or mobile homes.

As for those outhouses, I remember how my father used to laugh every time he saw one upright. They had been a refuge once, when he was small, but that wasn't how he remembered them. They were trophies.

The statute of limitations, surely, has long run out, but the last living princes of Frogtown will not inform, not turn, not rat each other out even when so many of them have escaped into their graves.

"I guess I turned over that Shuttles gal's outhouse every time I seen her in it. I didn't wait for Halloween," said Bill Joe Chaney. "She was about three hundred pounds, but once you got 'er to rockin', well, she just had to go. But I do not believe your daddy was with me when I did that, and if someone else was to say different, well, that's their business. I'm sayin' he was innocent, of that."

Then, looking me right in the face, he winked.

To escape detection, some of the boys would turn over their own outhouses. Then, the next morning, they would go around the neighborhood to help the other people set their outhouses upright. What good boys, the people said, and sometimes they pulled out a change purse and gave them a buffalo nickel.

"Oh, we was innocent back then," said Billy Measles. "We was innocent all the time."

The Boy

———

S HE WAS HAPPY with a gentle, helpless boy, because a boy like that would need her forever.

"That one will love you forever," I told her, certain of that.

Some boys just have Peter Pan in them.

But sometimes there is a sadness in mommas so deep you are afraid to get close to it, lest you fall in.

She had a door frame in her house in Memphis marked with her boys' names, ages and their heights, year after year. She would have ripped it off the wall and broken it in two, to stop time, to keep them all needing her forever, and loving her the way little boys do.

I destroyed one of her memories, by accident. Throwing a football in the front yard with the middle boy and the little boy, I threw a pass with less than pinpoint accuracy, barely missed the head of the woman who was sitting on the front porch, and shattered an old clay pot. At least, I thought that's what it was.

She just stood there, looking at the pieces.

"It had the handprints of all my boys in it, in the clay," she said.

Some days, you wish you had never left Alabama.

"I'll glue it back," I said, and never did.

She saved the pieces.

I tried to make it up to her, with another keepsake. The woman had a tiny wooden table and chair in the living room, in front of the television. All three boys had sat there, eating breakfast, mesmerized by cartoons. It was made for a five-year-old but at ten the last little boy sat there still, ridiculous, like an elephant on a motor scooter, till the wood split under his weight.

"He looks kind of silly, doesn't he?" I asked her.

"No," she said.

I glued it back together for her, the best I could.

It may be I am jealous of this boy.

I watch him sometimes and I try to put myself behind his eyes, but there is just too much distance between that boy and the boy I was. I wonder sometimes what would have happened if we had met on a playground, in a neutral time, both of us just ten years old.

I think I would have beaten him up.

I did pick and shovel work when I was his age. I ached to grow up, to get away. I watched my mother break herself on her responsibility to us, to lift us a few inches off bottom. You love her for that, but you always wonder why it had to be you, and her, that way.

"My dad's house," the boy told me once, "has four TVs."

He has all the love in the world. He has everything. What did he get from me, from being around me?

I told the woman once that I should have found a poor woman, with a poor child. Then, at least, I would have had something, something solid and concrete, to give to them. And it would have mattered to them, those things. It would have made their life better. I would have made their life better no matter how badly I messed up at everything else.

I grew up in my grandmother's house, a Jim Walter Home, a small wooden box. You lived elbow to elbow with people, knee to knee, but there was a room in the back, a tiny bedroom that was all mine. My mother made it possible by sleeping, all her young life, on a living room couch. There was no door, no privacy. You passed through my room to go to the bathroom. There was no light fixture, just the naked bulb on a bright orange drop cord. It doubled as a storeroom. Clothes, boxes, everything we owned, leaned against the walls. Mice and rats and chicken snakes lived in the maze of boxes, and skittered and rustled in the dark.

Long before I had a boy, I thought of the room I would give him.

I gave him two.

In our Tuscaloosa house he has a flat-screen television, a desk and bookshelves, an ergonomic chair, file cabinets for his schoolwork, all on a gleaming hardwood floor. On the walls I gave him the adventures I thought were missing from his world. Paintings promised him travel by sea, air and train. In a big poster, a seaplane dropped from a tropical sky as a beautiful girl in a grass skirt, flowers in her hair, waited by a blue lagoon. Dolphins jumped across the waves on one wall, and pirates—I always wanted to be a pirate—leered down from the shelf. You have to walk through his room to get to a bathroom, too, but it is all his. A grown-up guitar leans against one wall. When I was done with it, done nailing, decorating, I found a chair and just sat there, wishing it was mine.

On the Alabama coast, in a house I always wanted not far from Mobile Bay, a sign in his room welcomes you to a TROPICAL PARA-DISE. He has a papasan chair, another television, and a floor plan big enough for Frisbee-throwing, or a football game. Marlin leap from the walls, and he has a chart with pictures of every game fish in the Gulf of Mexico. There are boogie boards leaning on the wall, diving masks and flippers on the floor. His room has a view of the pool.

I used to daydream myself away from my room.

I want the boy to do that too.

I just don't want him to have to.

CHAPTER SEVEN

My Fair Orvalene

MY FATHER THOUGHT no girl would resist him, at thirteen, and if he had kept his eyes from wandering outside the village he might have been correct. But he didn't figure on Orvalene. She had blonde hair that was darkening to brown, fair skin, and made her own clothes. "I would not say that I was beautiful," she said, fifty-six years later. But she was. She had to be. My father, so full of his little self, would not have looked twice if he had not seen a beauty there. They went to school together at Cedar Springs Junior High School just outside town, "but I don't remember him being very diligent, as to school." She believes the first time she ever really had any interaction with him was in the summer of her eighth-grade year. "We lived in Angel Station, close to the railroad tracks. As I remember, I was sitting on the porch, hemming a dress I had made, and I saw this horse and rider coming up the road. As they got closer I saw it was Charles, and I don't know if he was coming to see me or if he just saw me on the porch and decided to stop and talk to me. I remember he had dark hair—long and slicked back—and dark skin. And . . . tell me, did your father have really pretty teeth? When I tried to remember him, I kept seeing those pretty teeth. I didn't have pretty teeth, and it was the first thing I looked at. I guess I'd have to say that he was being a little bit flirty," and might have been sweet. "He was just so bold, so much bolder than the other boys, and he just seemed older and wiser than the other guys. He said, 'Why don't we go for a ride?' Well, my daddy was Baptist. We went to Angel Grove Baptist Church. And you know how Baptists can be."

He did not say, as he swaggered up: "Would you like to go for a ride?"

He said: "Let's go for a ride."

"No, I can't do that," she said.

He asked again before she even had a chance to explain herself.

Her father, an auto mechanic, and mother, a seamstress, had rules. "When we were here by ourselves, we were not allowed to go off, and we were never allowed to bring people in the house," said Orvalene. She didn't quite know what to do about this boy who just showed up and expected her to go riding off into the sunset.

"I think he knew he was a good-looking guy—he always tried to look good, always dressed nice. I remember checkered shirts," she said. "I think he knew he had some features that were quite acceptable."

He chatted with her on the porch as the horse, his father's horse, cropped at the grass. The horse was Able Lady, a chestnut, sleek and lovely. Bob wouldn't have an ugly horse.

"Let's just go," he said again.

She told him no again.

He said, well, he reckoned he would just go, then.

"Can I have a glass of water first?" he asked.

Orvalene went inside to get his water, and when she came back he was leaning in the doorway.

"He scared me, a little bit," she remembers.

"Come on. Let's just go for a ride," he said.

She was a little scared, not of my father, really, but of the possibility her father or mother would come home and find a boy at the threshold of their home. But he just drank his water, and rode away.

"He was determined," she said. "And he was . . . confident."

"Full of himself?" I said.

· "He was that," she said.

"Would you have gone, if you could have?" I asked her.

"Oh, Daddy wouldn't have let me. The first question he would have asked me was, 'Where does he go to church?' And I don't think that your daddy went to church, did he?"

No, I said. But, I thought, if it hadn't been for a weedy ditch in Frogtown, I am pretty sure he would have fought clear into the parking lot of one.

"In that world, in that time, if you didn't go to church, there had to be something wrong," she said, and there was. My father was trouble no matter how you looked at him, and it didn't matter if you were a Baptist, Methodist, or howled at the moon.

His pride wounded, he never rode by again, and he never told about it around the bonfire because they might have kidded him, and he would have had to beat them up—two or three of them at least. He had tucked his shirt in, mounted his charger and gone to claim a princess.

It might have been the first time he realized that being a prince in Frogtown might come with a tinfoil crown.

The Boy

———

THE BOY LOVED STORIES, and after a few months, after being shushed by the woman in mid-sentence a few thousand times, I finally figured out how to tell them to a little boy. I told him about seeing crocodiles lunge out of the water to seize a wildebeest in the Masai Mara, described coming face to face with a black rhino in a forest of thorns, and how the Masai warriors jumped high into the air around a popping fire as they sang of the killing of lions. I left out the women and children I saw starving against the wall of an Ethiopian church.

I told him I had been to the great deserts to see camel trains plod across a burnt-orange horizon, and stood on the same sand as Alexander the Great. I omitted the bombs, and men who leapt through flames from burning tires to prove their love of a man named bin Laden.

I told him of voodoo priests in Haiti, of zombies and pounding drums, but never mentioned bloody coups or funeral flowers cut from tin.

"He's lived one inch from death," the boy told his mother.

She rolled her eyes.

In my office, he saw guns, a lever-action Remington, a 30.06 with a scope, 12-gauge over-and-under bird guns, the stocks gleaming, blued barrels shining—because all I did was polish them now. In my mother's house he heard us talk about being boys, tough boys, fighting boys.

It is easy to impress a ten-year-old.

That was the problem.

It happened as I tried my first real lecture. He is smart, real smart, but sloppy in his schoolwork. I was, too. I told him, sitting in the living room, he had to do well in school, that it was his job. He just smiled, because a lecture from me was just ridiculous, as if the Abominable Snowman told you to stop tracking mud in the house, or the Creature from the Black Lagoon told you to be sure and put the toilet seat down.

Still, it made me mad to be ignored.

"I'm serious," I said. "This is your world. You have to succeed in it. You are not tough enough to make it in a blue-collar world."

It stung him.

For a while, he almost killed himself, to show he was not a pampered boy.

He had been so lazy he would help his mother carry in groceries by lifting a roll of paper towels, and skipping away. Now he staggered under bags, cartons of soda, and watermelons.

He suffered greatly from allergies, and it would break your heart, sometimes, to hear him trying to breathe in his room at night. Without thinking, I asked him one late afternoon if he wanted to throw the football. I had not noticed he could barely breathe. "No, I don't think that's a good idea," the woman said. But the boy jumped off the couch, announced that he was fine, and after a half-hour search for his sneakers, ran into the yard.

He was so hopped-up on decongestant he could barely see. I threw a bullet at him in the backyard and it tore through his fingers and smacked him in the face, hard. He lay as if dead and he would have cried, he said later, but he could not feel anything above his chin.

I ran over to him, but he jumped up, pushed me away.

The welt rose on his face.

The other hurt was there long after that one faded.

He hurt me back a little, now and then.

"You're not a dad," he told me once.

Dads are responsible. Dads pose with your mother and brothers in a Christmas card.

"What am I?" I said, and even though I had done damn little to deserve better, it still bothered me, to be told outright.

He thought awhile.

"I dunno."

Sometime later, it came to him.

"Well, you call me little buddy," he said.

"I do," I said.

"So you're the big buddy."

"Well okay," I said.

I knew how to be a buddy.

He was not like me, true, had none of my blood in him at all, but there were worse boys to have. I saw them in movie theaters, screaming into their nachos as a poor, pitiful man went back to the snack counter to exchange Whoppers for Milk Duds, or Gummy Bears for Gummy Worms. I saw them hunched over video games like a crack pipe, saw them screeching like a tornado warning siren in the Target, for God knows why.

The boy was spoiled, but not yet rotten.

In time, I even got used to the nastiness. The woman was right. The boy was no nastier than other children, so I just resigned myself to eating with a boy who stuck his nose *in* a bowl to eat rice and shoved three forks of food in his mouth before beginning to chew.

"Close your mouth when you chew," the woman said.

"Why?" he asked, around a wad of something I won't even say.

" 'Cause it's what humans do," I said.

Mostly, I just lived with it. But even after I realized the boy carried no known, life-threatening disease, I still didn't hug him enough. I hugged him because he insisted I did. He was too big to hold like a baby, but the woman said he was too little to deny, to turn away.

I was still living mostly on the road our first year together, writing and talking about it. He often answered the phone when I called from the road. I automatically asked for his mother, because I had not mastered the art of talking to a child on the telephone. It takes a skill, and a vast patience. I had told myself a long time ago I would never be one of those men, one of those harried, travel-worn men in a faraway city, talking to a child on the edge of a hotel bedspread or airport seat, talking nonsense. I used to pity those henpecked fools hunched over their dainty phones, finally pleading: "Can I talk to Mommy?"

It hurt his feelings, every time. "You don't want to talk to me?" he asked, and I said of course I did, but I was running to a plane, or exhausted, or my feet or head hurt, and everything in between.

But when I came home, he almost always stood at the door.

The next talk we had, of a father-son kind, came after he committed a little boy's transgression, misplaced his pants, something, and the woman made him cry.

I was just glad it wasn't me she was after.

"Let me talk to him," I said, like a grown-up person.

I think she thought I was going to lecture him on irresponsibility—wouldn't that be a pill—but instead I just held two fingers tight together in front of his face.

"She's got to carp at you 'cause it's her job, but you and her," I said, wiggling my joined fingers, "you'll always be like this. There is no reason to cry, to get all upset about this little stuff. No matter where you go, or what you do, you and her will always be like that."

I thought it was brilliant parenting.

He just looked at me.

He waited.

He waited.

"Me and you," I said, wiggling those conjoined fingers, "we're like that, too."

But they are smart, little boys, for creatures that will run in front of cars if you don't hold their shirttail. They believe what they feel, not what you tell them.

In sixth grade, his teachers had their students write a book for English class. It was supposed to be fiction, but he wrote a real-life story and just changed the names. He wrote about a little boy (him) who went to visit an old woman on a farm in Alabama, a woman who cooked magic biscuits, and had three sons. The old woman's middle son (me) was named Fred, and he was the boy's stepfather. Fred was not unkind to the boy but sometimes treated him as an afterthought. But at THE END, as the boy and his mother got in their car to leave, Fred waved goodbye to them, "and for the first time in my life, Fred was smiling square at me, not at my mom."

CHAPTER EIGHT

The Hanging

———

FROM THE CRADLE, they had been taught that their very worth as a people was tied to their ability to labor. Their fathers told them, sometimes with a ragged Bible or a fresh-cut hickory in their hands, that a shirker was a pitiful and a sorry thing, and sloth was not only a sin but a deadly one. They would stripe the legs of a lazy child as quickly as they would a mean or mouthy one, and quote from Ecclesiastes as the stick hissed through the air.

The sleep of a labouring man is sweet . . .

And there would be the sting, and the rising welt.

. . . whether he eat little or much.

Grandparents, their lives and fingers shortened, their eyes red-streaked and hard as peppermint candy, would pull frightened grandchildren close, and whisper:

"You are as good as anybody."

But the one true thing you learned in the village, as real as the whistle that shook you from bed, was that a lot of people who lived outside the alphabet streets believed, really believed, they were better than you. Because their world was cleaner, nicer, they believed their lives held more value than Bill Joe Chaney's people, than my father's, who did the dirty, dangerous work and came home to identical rooms that smelled of snuff and bacon grease and Mentholatum. You could not make them look at you differently. You could only punish them, for the way they did look at you.

The rigid caste system, as hard-stuck then as racial segregation, had not flexed in fifty years. After a crime was committed in town or in the outlying county, investigators came to the village first, even pulled workers from their stations, lined them against the wall and questioned them or compared their faces to the police artist's sketch. Across generations, town boys in their daddies' cars egged houses in the village for sport, and yelled "Linthead!" at old women walking home from a twelve-hour shift.

In fifty years, there had not been a homecoming queen from the mill village, or a cheerleader. The people of the mill village took revenge, but it would be wrong to say they got even. In those days, a vending machine at the mill routinely cheated workers out of nickels and dimes. "It would keep your money but it wouldn't give you nothin' to eat," said retired mill worker Donald Garmon. One day, Garmon's brother Eugene and a friend, Alan McCarty, dropped nickels in the slot and the machine hung up again. It was all they could take. "They throwed the machine off the third floor," he said.

Town boys who wandered into the mill village on foot were chased and beaten. "You didn't come here if you was town," said my father's friend, Bill Joe. Even if you had a rare friend outside the village you could not side with them against your own. "We stuck together," Bill Joe said.

My father hated the swells, hated the stigma, and hated himself, a little, for his place in it. "Your daddy had a lot of false pride," my mother always said. She was not ashamed to mop other people's floors, but he was ashamed for people to know it. It is why, when he had to choose between a car that would run and one that looked good at the curb, he picked the one with the best paint job, and poured burnt motor oil into it by the bucketful.

As a boy, he picked fights every weekend in town, over a word, or a look.

"Your daddy," Bill Joe said, "was a good bit meaner than the rest of us."

———

Bill Joe Chaney swiveled his head to watch for witnesses, but the schoolyard was deserted except for the hanging party, under an elm tree. The town boy was already in the rope. Still, he did not struggle too much. "I don't think he knew how serious we was," Bill Joe said. The hanging party, none of them older than thirteen, rambled around the schoolyard in their overalls, searching for plum trees. "We were going to pull him up, and whip him with plum branches as he dangled," Bill Joe said. The condemned boy, also about thirteen, meandered around in a small circle as Bill Joe held the other end of the rope. It was surreal, as he remembers it. Even as he took up the slack, the boy did not beg for his life or even cry. He thought he was wearing the black hat in some B western, and even smiled. But as the minutes slipped by he began to understand that this was not a play. He must have done something bad to these village boys in that summer of '48, something unforgivable.

Bill Joe saw my father then, saw him saunter by the schoolyard, glance over, stop and stare, and turn and walk toward the elm. He was about thirteen then, also.

"What you doin', Bill Joe?" he asked, like he saw a hanging every day.

"We're hangin' this feller," Bill Joe said.

"I figured that," my father said.

Bill Joe was a big, tough boy. Not too many people talked smart to him.

"Why you doin' it?" my father asked.

" 'Cause he thinks he's better than us," Bill Joe said.

My father just nodded. He did not ask what the evidence was.

My father just looked at the boy.

It was insanity, and made perfect sense.

"Your daddy knew why we was doin' it," said Bill Joe, more than fifty years after that day.

"He was one of us," he said.

The condemned boy was right, though. His hangmen had gotten the idea from the westerns at the Princess Theater. "They was always hangin' somebody," Bill Joe said.

But sometimes, at the last cinematic minute, a dark, handsome hero would ride up, tell the mob they would have justice but "not like this, boys," and order the hangmen to cut the condemned man down. Then he would kiss a girl and sing a song to his horse.

My father looked the part. He was not in ragged overalls, not barefoot like the village boys tended to be. He was going to town and had dressed accordingly. He had on a checkered dress shirt and ironed dungarees and his shoes gleamed like a Birmingham lawyer's. The village boys were often shorn almost bald, because of lice and chinch bugs that lived inside the walls of the company houses. Their mommas poured scalding water in the cracks to kill them. "I remember your daddy had a full head of hair," Bill Joe said, and as they talked my father took out his pocket comb in a quick-draw and ran it through his hair. It must have been clear then to the condemned boy that this boy was not his salvation after all, just a linthead posing, with silver dimes shining in his black penny loafer shoes.

———•———

B ILL JOE IS A BIG MAN in old age, and still looks strong. He still wears overalls, but accessorizes now with a white porkpie hat, toothpicks saved inside the hatband. He is not one of those big talkers who carry you along like a current, and often leaves things half-said, as if, since he knows what comes next in the story, you should, too. It is a condition of old Southern men that they will tell you they are proud, a lifetime later, of the darkest things, and blame it on the times, or blame it on Dixie. But he is not proud of what almost happened in the schoolyard. "I'll tell it, though, 'cause of your dad, 'cause it's the least I can do."

"The boy we was hanging was a straight-A student," said Bill Joe. "He was 99 percent more educated than us, and he always thought he was superior. One day, he was running around in the classroom, acting a fool, and . . ."

Funny, he can't remember what the boy said.

It may be he didn't say a thing.

Bill Joe's father had been a top sawmill hand before he came down to work at the mill. His net worth was tabulated on how many straight boards he sawed and how much cotton he spun, and night after night Bill Joe could hear his future, like the other village children, through the thin walls of their house. It was hard for the mill hands to catch their breath even hours after the shift, because the lint tickled their throats and a bacteria that rode the cotton fibers seized their lungs. They couldn't cough it up, no matter how hard they tried.

"So we caught that boy and carried him out to them big elms. We already had the rope, and we had him pretty much hung, pretty much ready to pull up, when your daddy walked up."

Bill Joe remembers how my father looked standing there, quiet. Bill Joe wasn't worried that my father would intervene. To help the boy, my father would have had to betray his own history.

Bill Joe decided to get on with it.

"Hold it," my father said.

"What?" Bill Joe said.

"Untie him," my father said.

Bill Joe glared down at him.

"Why?"

"Turn him loose," my father said.

He balled his fists.

"I was a whole lot bigger than him, but your dad was all muscle," Bill Joe said. "I believe he would have scratched us some, if we hadn't done what he said. I turned him loose."

Bill Joe quit school not long after that, and went to work in the mill.

But first, he and my father faced each other under the elm tree.

"Why'd you do it?" Bill Joe asked him.

Of all the descriptions of my father by so many people, the one description I had never heard was "uncertain." He was deliberate, pointed. Even in his own destruction, he was that. But he didn't have an answer for Bill Joe.

His fists came undone.

He turned and walked away.

———

"WHY DID HE DO IT?" I asked Bill Joe.

"I think he did it for me," he said.

Bill Joe's great meanness never was. It never happened, he said, because of my father. It would be nice to believe my father did it from simple human kindness, to keep the boy from being hurt if not killed, but Bill Joe is convinced the life my father truly saved that afternoon was his.

"I would have gone to reform school at least. Maybe they would have sent me to prison, I don't know. I think he knew that, and I think he stopped us 'cause he wanted to save my life, not that boy's. He was just a kid like us, but he figured that. I think he changed my life."

"Would you have really hung him?" I asked.

"I guess I could say we might have just hung him a little bit," he said.

"But I believe," he said, his voice quiet, "we would have hurt that feller."

They might have cut him down, like in the westerns.

"But we would have hurt him."

He had a good life, he said. He worked in the mill on the outside crew and inside, with the machines, and worked for the city. He went in the army in '58, rolled his active service into two decades with the Army Reserve, and retired with a government pension.

He has to go to the hospital for his chemotherapy, for the cancer in his throat. "But I can still eat, thank the Lord," he said. His friends say Bill Joe might live forever, and in 2006 he was in remission.

"I got no regrets in my life," he said, then.

He says my father gave him that.

He relishes his days now. "I like to ride," he said. "I got a king cab Chevrolet truck, and me and Louie Hamilton, my buddy, we like to ride, up where it's pretty."

Old women call it loafering, and I've always loved that word. I guess it is just how we say the word "loafing," but the way we say it makes you think of loafers, of wearing out your shoe leather for no good purpose. Old women like to sniff and use it as a condemnation. "He ain't here. He's off loafering." It means you are shirking work and responsibility. To the men who loafer, it means they are free, free to waste time, to count mailboxes, and wave at other old men who, as the rear bumper vanishes in the distance, wish they were loafering, too. I plan to loafer someday. At least I hope to.

The one thing you cannot do is loafer with a heavy heart. Good intentions and bad intentions wash together, pointless over so much time. You can't get into heaven for one, and can't get sent to hell for the other. Bill Joe rolls down his window and just drives, sometimes as far as the Georgia line. The mountains and hills are at their prettiest now, in spring, as the hardwoods, the pines, even the weeds take on a luminescence that will shimmer into summer, till the heat itself will make the landscape fade. But for now it all just shines. His heart is light. His conscience is clear.

———

B ILL JOE DIED in the summer of 2006.

The Boy

———

THE BOY LOVED TO READ and read even when he was not ordered to, or threatened. He read with his nose almost in the pages, like he was sniffing out the story there instead of just taking it in with his eyes, and he had to be told twice, sometimes three times, to put his book down and turn off the bedside light, or he would have read all night.

My mother had to tell me to stop reading, too. I read by that naked, 60-watt bulb that dangled over the bed, and when she turned it off I replayed the pages in my head till she went to bed. As soon as I was certain she was asleep I took out a big flashlight and read underneath the quilt, and thought I fooled her but of course I never did. She came in, quietly, and switched it off after it tumbled from my hand. I never told the boy we had that thing in common, that reluctance to give up on a good book in the middle of the night, but I guess he'll know it now.

Having a boy was like getting to do that all over again. But instead of Frank and Joe Hardy he loved James and the Giant Peach, and the BFG. Hogwarts, I would learn, was not a disease, nor Lemony Snicket a flavor of ice cream.

He read whole books in the backseat, and if you asked him a question he didn't even hear, he was in so deep. Larry McMurtry wrote of an Indian tracker named Famous Shoes who wanted to learn to read so he could track the little black footprints across the page. The boy read like that, with such single-minded purpose we hated to make him go to sleep.

But, to me, it was the only adventure he got.

"What do you like about those stories you read?" I asked him.

"The heroes are kids," he said.

"They have adventures?" I said. "They beat the bad guys?"

"Yeah," he said.

One night he came into his mother's bedroom.

"Tuck me in," he ordered.

Instead, I grabbed him up by the neck of his shirt and seat of his pants, and threw him across the room.

I did aim him, roughly, at his mother's king-sized bed.

He was still small enough to throw, and I got a good bit of wind under him on the upswing. He didn't even have time to scream like a girl before he slid to a belly landing against the giant, poufy, totally unnecessary pillows that always covered the woman's bed.

His mother stood at the door, a brush in her hair, stunned.

"You'll throw him into the wall," she said.

"I can't throw him that far," I said.

The boy rolled off the bed and ran out of the room, into therapy I supposed.

The woman drilled me with her eyes.

My back throbbed, but I grinned.

The boy ran back into the room just a few seconds later. He had on a blue plastic spaceman's helmet, and a cape.

He struck a superhero's pose, hands on his hips.

"Do it again," he said.

We named him Captain Zoom.

Every night, before he would even consider going to bed, I had to catapult him into space onto the landing strip of his mother's bed.

"Throw me," he would say, after the evening news.

It was a start.

CHAPTER NINE

Settin' the World on Fire

J ACK ANDREWS CANNOT REMEMBER when he met my father, or how, only that they were friends forever from that forgotten moment on. They were teenagers then, fifteen or sixteen, as the 1940s slid into the 1950s. But even across all that time, Jack remembered what was in my father's mind, the things he said before they left town in uniform, the only ticket out of town for a West Side boy. Some words vanished, like silver dollars he buried in the yard and forgot where he dug the holes, but some were right where he left them.

"I remember, when we was about fourteen or fifteen, we made us a kite. We had a big ol' spool of nylon cord, a damn mile of it, and the wind was strong, and we just kept feeding and feeding that line until that kite got so high it was just a speck, plumb out of sight. I remember that we laid down on our backs in the field, to see just how high it would go. And this boy we knew, he come up on us, and Charles whispered to me, 'No matter what he says, don't say a word,' and I didn't. The boy said, 'What y'all doin' settin' in the field?' and then he saw the cord in Charles's hands. 'What y'all got on the end of that cord?' But Charles and me just let him wonder. It was killin' that boy, 'cause we wouldn't say. And finally Charles said, 'Why, hell, we're fishin'.' And the boy said naw, but we just laid there. 'Well,' he said, 'what you fishin' for?' And Charles just stared up at the sky. 'We're fishin',' he said, 'for the man in the moon.' "

Like so many people here in the foothills of the Appalachians, he is an eloquent man, a survivor from an age of storytellers in a place where such people grow wild. He does not merely tell me he loved my father, he shows me, painting pictures on the dark, like the time my father's family sent them to search for firewood in a cold spell, when the whole village was turning blue. They found instead a pile of scrap wood and tar shingles. "They'll burn," my father reasoned. He piled them into a fireplace, lit them, and they did. But the tar and creosote formed explosive gases that collected in the chimney, and "all of a sudden, there's big balls of fire shooting out the top of the chimney, into the sky," Jack said. "I looked at your daddy, and he was a'laughin' and a'jumpin' up and down."

"Look, Jack," he said, "we're settin' the world on fire."

Jack is ice-pick slim, and his soot-black hair is mostly gone. But he still sports a little pencil-thin mustache, and when he smiles you see the rascal he once was, that they both were. You get the feeling that if he came across one last damsel in his old age, he would still know how to find a railroad track, and tie a knot. He lives by himself in a trailer on a hilltop not far from Billy Measles, and walks slow and careful when he comes to the door now, so careful some people give up and go away. He has an old movie poster above the couch, *Hondo,* starring John Wayne. "We used to talk about going west, me and Charles, to be cowboys," he said, smiling. They didn't want to string wire, rope cattle or chop wood. They wanted to ride across the movies on silver-studded Mexican saddles, shoot pearl-handled revolvers, sign autographs, drive long convertibles with steer horns on the hood, and date platinum-haired starlets two at a time. "We was full of foolishness, it's a fact," Jack said. "But man, we built us some dreams."

His lips trembled then, so he covered his mouth with one bony hand.

"It's good to live to be so damn old," he said, "but it's awful lonesome."

When they were fifteen they nailed steel taps to their Steinberg shoes so pretty girls could hear them coming, and it never occurred to them that the homely ones could hear them coming, too. But at night they would slide their heels across the sidewalks, and sparks would fly. Jack carried an old guitar slung on his back, and could whup "Lovesick Blues" like it was going out of style. My father played the spoons, laughing out loud, as the girls drew close, hypnotized. "Pick it ag'in, Jack," he liked to say, and Jack picked it till the frets felt hot in his fingertips.

His glasses are thick as funhouse mirrors now. He said he'd play me a song, but his strings are broken.

I told him not to worry, he could tell me one.

He remembers a time they got drunk, or tried to, on a sample of perfume. They were giving it away at Crow Drug Store, and it was mostly alcohol. They sipped it, and waited.

"You feel anything?" my father asked.

"No. You?" Jack said.

"Reckon it's poison?" my father asked.

"Could be," Jack said.

"Be bad, to be found dead," my father said, "with perfume."

"Bad," Jack said.

My father gasped.

"What?" Jack said.

"Look at that damn monkey."

"What damn monkey?" Jack said.

"That damn monkey, climbing up that damn wall," he said.

Jack was pretty sure he was lying, but he looked, to make sure.

"Well, there wasn't no damn monkey there, but that don't mean Charles didn't see one."

People had always told me my father was quiet—even my mother told me that. But he talked to Jack.

"I knew him when he was wild as a hillside rabbit, and I was, too. People tried to bust us up. Police Chief Ross Tipton, some others, they all hated Charles even when he was a boy, 'cause of his people. They'd say, 'You might be some count, Jack Andrews, if you'd keep better company and quit hanging round with that sorry damn Charles Bragg.' And then they'd go tell your daddy, 'Charles, you might be somebody if you'd stop hanging around with that sorry damn Jack Andrews.' But there wasn't no bustin' us up. We was like magnets, you see," and he banged his fists together hard. "We had a feelin'."

He remembers fishing in a creek with my father as dark fell and the lightning bugs flickered on, phosphorescent green on the damp air. He saw my father smiling at them.

"What you thinkin', Charles?"

"I was wonderin'," my father said, pointing to the lightning bugs, "what they were thinkin'."

The meanest fist-fighter in the village, pound for pound, was mulling the secret lives of fireflies.

"Well?" my father said.

"What?" Jack said.

"What do you think they're thinkin'?"

"I don't know," Jack said.

"I mean, up yonder there's that nice, clean place, where all the lights and people are, and they're down here with us in this brush, where all these old trees and limbs and trash have washed up. I mean, why are they here and not up there. They can be anywhere they want to be."

Jack had to think about that. My father just cast, and waited.

"Well," Jack said, "maybe they're here for the same reason we are, because it's quiet and it's peaceful. This ain't no bad place. I mean, we could be up there, too."

My father just watched them dance a bit longer in the humidity.

My father loved being alive then, Jack said. So what if he quit school in sixth grade, Jack said, and painted himself into a grim corner, as they all did?

"You don't never quit dreamin', son," he said.

He was not from the village and was not part of my father's circle of friends when he was a little boy, but Jack was from working people, too, from a place on the West Side called Nine Row. His father, John, ran a service station, and his mother, Lydia, raised a houseful of children. "Kids would make their mommas and daddies pass three service stations and almost run out of gas to get to my daddy's, 'cause he gave free bubble gum," Jack said. He and my father became friends for life. They dressed the same in stiff, snug Levi's—"we liked 'em where they fit real tight, and the girls liked 'em, too"—checkered shirts and penny loafers, and when people mistook them for brothers they didn't correct them, since it was mostly true.

Most of their friends had already vanished, twelve hours at a time, into the mill, but not them. They did not want to die working in the mill, or even live that way, and just figured they were sharp enough to ride any luck that came their way straight out of town. They did sawmill work for hamburger, ice cream and movie money, and dreamed of California, but never got any further west than Birmingham.

The closest they got to a soundstage was the front row at the Princess Theater. "A quarter was as big as a wagon wheel then," Jack said. "You could go to the movies, buy a bag of popcorn and a soda, and still have a nickel left to go to the old Creamery and get yourself ice cream. What flavor? Why, vanilla. That's what me and Charles always got."

The closest they got to a convertible was the time they turned Jap Hill's little Ford over in Cub Hedgepath's cornfield. "It didn't have no motor so we had to push it up the mountain. Well, it didn't have no brakes, neither. We couldn't make the curve."

And the closest they came to a starlet was the time they saw Minnie Pearl live on the town square, that, or the time Jack drove his uncle's '40 Ford to a brush arbor meetin' just off the Cove Road, to watch a lay preacher try to bring several comely young women to the Lord in the glow of a bonfire. Jack and my father sat on the hood to watch till the sweating, angry minister ran them off, shouting, "Y'all need to get you some church," as Jack frantically tried to herd my white-hot father into the car before he waded into the congregation and gave the minister the left foot of fellowship right in his Sunday pants.

Mostly, they wasted days, and wasted none at all.

"We was over on ol' Dean Edwards' mountain. Back then, when they clear-cut a mountain, the government planted pine trees, just a few feet apart, to stop soil erosion. It was a sweet deal, because you got paid for the timber, then twenty years later you cut the pine. But the government planted the pines in a straight line, and you could stand on the ground and there would be a row of trees as far as you could see going one way, and a row as far as you could see going the other way. Your daddy got to lookin' at it, and he got that look on his face. 'I believe,' he said, 'we can go across this whole mountain and never touch the ground.' "

So they climbed a tree, and started moving, reaching from limb to limb, tree to tree. It was a gritty, nasty, gummy process, and every snapping limb seemed to fling specks of bark in their eyes. It would have been no excitement at all if they had tried it close to the earth, so they climbed as high as they could go and swayed from tree to tree. Jack can't remember how far they had gone when he lost his hold, and fell.

He grabbed for the limbs as he dropped, the pines snapping, popping in his hands, till he landed on the pine straw with a loud *whoompf.*

He heard just one cry of "Jack?" and then he heard another body crashing through the limbs as my father threw himself down his tree, and came running.

Jack lay on the ground, bruised but alive.

"I thought you killed your damn self," my father said, out of breath.

Then he looked down at his pants. The inside of the legs were covered in pine sap, from where he slid down the tree.

"Well, hell, Jack, look what you made me do to my pants," he said, and stomped off.

But it was too late. Jack had seen.

"We'd follow each other to the jumping-off place, and jump," Jack said.

He would catch my father, often, just watching clouds.

"What do you see?" he asked him once.

"Looks like a angel, don't it?" my father said, pointing.

Jack would stare up with him, and ask him, after a while, if he was ready to go.

"Naw, let's just lay here and see what it changes into next," my father said.

Another time, as they were wasting time at Germania Springs just listening to the water bubble out of rocks, he saw my father, his eyes closed, begin to grin again.

"What now?" Jack said.

"I was just thinking, what if we lived in the desert."

"What if we did?" Jack said.

"What if we lived in the desert, and owned this spring?"

"Oh," Jack said.

"We'd be millionaires," my father said.

The only time he ever regretted asking my father what was in his mind was the time he had been thinking about God.

"You really believe all that, about going to heaven," my father asked him, in the vanishing light of another wasted day. They liked to sit in the pitch dark and talk, for the privacy, but to Jack it seemed spooky this time.

"If you're good, yeah," Jack said. "You don't?"

Most people did not dare even raise the possibility, here.

The idea of hell was bad enough, but you could always change your ways and get into heaven, even the greatest sinners believed. There was time to change.

But what if this was all?

And worse, my father said, what if you were born to live in hell on earth?

"Sometimes it seems like there's somebody in me," he said.

Jack knew better than to laugh.

"You mean like spirits?"

"I mean," my father said, "suppose you've lived a life, and you was a bad person. If you come back, do you have to pay?"

"That's not what the Good Book says," Jack said.

"See, sometimes I think there's something like that in me," he told Jack. "It's like I've been here before, and I didn't do right that time."

Jack had never seen my father afraid.

He wished they would talk about something else.

"Well," my father said after a while, "I was just thinking."

I asked him if he knew when my father took his first drink, when he let that demon into his mouth. But it was impossible to tell, in a house where whiskey sat on a table like salt. He stole sips whenever he wanted, but he did not hunger for it at fifteen, Jack said. "Funny," he said, "that I don't remember us drinking that much. I mean, now and then there'd be something, like this man I knew who called us over one time and let us have a drink of white whiskey flavored in peppermint. There was whiskey all around, but we was just boys, then." He looks a little wistful when he talks about it, the way old, reformed drinkers do, like a married man thinking about majorettes.

———

THEY DECIDED, finally, to be entrepreneurs, instead of just dreaming about it. They picked something they knew—whiskey—and decided to get rich being bootleggers. It was their first business venture together, a tub whiskey operation in a five-gallon can in a holler outside town. "Take five pounds of sugar, two yeast cakes, and one can of Blue Ribbon malt syrup. Put it in warm water, and set it someplace warm, where the sun can hit it. We hid it in the honeysuckle," Jack said. "About seventy-two hours later, you've got yourself some home brew." It was not quality whiskey. "You had to be careful not to get the sediment stirred up, or you'd get a terrible headache." They made it, but wouldn't drink it on a bet.

They filled Dr Pepper, Nehi and RC bottles with the stuff, and sold it behind the pool hall.

"Twenty-five cents a bottle," Jack said, "and they'd drink it up fast."

He supposed there was some risk of poisoning.

"But it was better than stealing," Jack said.

One day he and my father walked up to their primitive still—really just a bucket full of mess allowed to sour in the heat—and saw that a possum had fallen in the swill.

"Is it dead?" my father asked.

"Yep," Jack said.

The possum seemed to be grinning at them.

"What we gonna do?" Jack said.

"Well," my father said, "we ain't gonna pour it out."

They filled their bottles and sacked them up. They were not even driving yet, and already bootlegging. They made their sales in their usual places, and watched as the boys poured it down, as usual. If their customers noticed any unusual flavor, they did not complain. A hog could have drowned in it, and not greatly affected the taste.

Walking home, my father started to laugh.

"What's so funny?" said Jack, who had just been happy no one had keeled over dead.

"I was just wondering," my father said, "if any of them boys got any hair in their teeth."

There was nothing to do but win, win over and over again, with so little to lose.

Once, they did odd jobs for a family that had a hundred cats.

"Let's kidnap one of them cats," my father said.

They would write a ransom note, and demand whatever a good cat was worth.

But the plan fell through, when they figured what that was.

"For the record, I never killed no cat," Jack said.

But he wonders, did anyone ever do a better job than they did, of squeezing the last little bit out of being a boy?

"I remember this time, up in Rich Bundrum's barn loft, we found this case of dynamite," Jack said, and then he paused and shook his head, as if realizing now what he should have then: that there are no

good endings to stories that begin with *we found this case of dynamite.*
"Well, we found the blasting caps and wire, and got this ol' flashlight battery, and went to Big Creek. But first, we took a knife, and,
real, real careful, we cut that dynamite into little pieces. We had this
ol' homemade boat, and we floated down to this place where the water
pooled . . . and, since the water was real deep in that place, we thought
it would be safe . . ." Jack fixed the cap to the dynamite and the wire to
the cap, then leaned out over the boat, to drop it in the pool. A rusty
steel cable ran across the stream there, and Jack held on to that with
one hand, for balance. He let the dynamite nubbin go and watched it
swirl down as my father touched one end of the split wire to the old
battery negative post, then touched the other end to positi—

BLAM!

Jack was blown off his feet, would have been blown into the air, but
he kept his grip on the wire, his toes pointed to heaven, till he crumpled, eyeballs bulging, ears ringing. "You all right?" my father mouthed
at him, but Jack really didn't know.

He can still see my father laughing, laughing, but with no sound.

"That might be what's wrong with me now," Jack said.

———

ONE DAY, after they turned sixteen, they were tapping down the
sidewalk side by side, *clickety-clack,* and saw their buddies on
the square, "and ever' one of 'em was all dressed up," Jack said. "A. J.
Bragg was up there, and all the Stricklands. I said, 'Where y'all goin'
all dressed up?' 'We goin' to church,' they said. 'Why?' I said. ' 'Cause
we done found a whole church full of pretty women,' they said. So we
all went. Me and your daddy walked in and, oh Lord, I never seen at
the pretty women. I don't know where all them women came from. I
never will forget it, us in the pews with our hair slicked back, singing hymns. The preacher preached it fire and brimstone, I mean he
preached it like it *was,* and me and your daddy sat and nodded our
heads." They would look left at big-eyed brunettes and right at

dime-store blondes, and if the girls looked back Jack and my father would nod, mouth a discreet "amen," and turn back to the Word. "You know, a lot of the boys got their wives there," Jack said. "I mean they *married* 'em."

But Jack and my father still had too much running around to do, so they watched some of the boys forfeit their sins at the altar call, then backslid home to Jacksonville. My father did not go to church again, but Jack did. "It's where I learned to pick the guitar," he said, and I like to believe there was God's hand in that.

"Your daddy," Jack said, "loved to hear me bend them strings."

Jack learned from every half-drunk picker who would teach him a chord. "But gospel was the first music I played," he said. He learned at the knee of J. D. Hulsey in the heat of Emmanuel Holiness. "Watch, young 'un," J.D. would say, and Jack would follow his fingers along the frets. Every church picker in the South had to know Ferlin Husky's "On the Wings of a Dove" in 1950, and J.D. could play it just like they did on the radio.

> *On the wings of a snow-white dove*
> *He sends his pure sweet love*
> *A sign from above*
> *On the wings of a dove*

It was always the three of them you saw, my father, Jack, and Jack's guitar.

He didn't even believe in the faith Jack sang of, but he loved the songs.

"I don't know, it's like it put him to rest," said Jack.

On Sunday mornings, with church music drifting from every block, my father and Jack would find a clean, green, shady place to lie down. "Pick us somethin' purty, Jack," he would say, and Jack would pick till sunset, then pick in the dark.

On Saturday nights, the two boys gathered around a radio for the

Grand Ole Opry, live from the Ryman Auditorium in downtown Nashville. Ernest Tubb sang "I'm Walkin' the Floor Over You." Through a hiss of static, they heard the place go wild over Hank.

I'm gonna find me a river, one that's cold as ice
And when I find me that river, Lord I'm gonna pay the price, Oh Lord
I'm going down in it three times, but Lord I'm only comin' up twice

They would walk miles to see a front-porch picker drink and play. James Couch tore it up on lead guitar, and Charles Hardy, of course, played flawless rhythm, and they sang with that tortured voice you cannot fake, that you can only get in a cotton mill, or a red-dirt field, or if your children call another man "Daddy." The music itself was flavored by corn whiskey that made Jim Beam taste like soda pop, and culminated in a sound as different from modern-day country music as a rattler is from a garter snake. One of the best front-porch pickers in town was in the family, my uncle Bartow Wall. His friends shortened his name to Bato, then shortened that to Bat, which we pronounced Bot, and if you ask me why I would just have to make something up. He married my aunt Clara, and if you can't marry a dentist, the next best thing would have to be a guitar man. It was like going to the Opry or the Louisiana Hayride when you walked up on their porch. Bot bootlegged a little, but there wasn't a hillbilly song on this earth that he couldn't play.

My father didn't have that rhythm in him that Jack did, so he got some spoons, so he could keep time, and beat them on his leg as Jack and the grownups picked. "He was just happy," Jack said. "As long as music was playing, your daddy was happy." The girls loved it, too, Jack said. "That guitar was a master key, for me and your dad," Jack said. "The women loved that guitar."

He got a brand-new guitar as soon as he thought he could afford it. "I didn't play but one kind . . . maybe two, if you count a Martin," he said. "I got me a Gibson." It cost $260, which was a fortune. He bought it on credit for $17 a month. "I touched the strings, and it was like they knew where to go," he said. He lived part of his dream with that guitar. Next to the John Wayne poster is a faded photograph of a genuine country and western band. All the men in it are young and straight and whole. There's young Charles Hardy, Vernon Copeland, Jimmy Roberts, Frankie Snyder, and Jack, young and handsome with a mop of jet-black hair. "We'uz playin' the convention hall in Gadsden," Jack said, and the people used to holler at them like they were true stars, like they were Hank Williams' hat. He played a big talent show in Gadsden, the parking lot swimming with tail fins and shining with baby moon hubcaps, and a whole contingent of fans—my mother and her sisters were there—came over from Jacksonville and hollered like crazy. "He done good," said my mother, who knew Jack when they were both teenagers. "He liked to have won."

My father was always there to clap for Jack, but he didn't see her, and she didn't see him. They would have remembered if they had. He would have noticed the prettiest girls, and she would have noticed he was pretty well drunk. By seventeen, he was drinking hard on weekends, fighting for fun. "I could calm him down with that guitar, but just a little bit," Jack said.

My father was still underage when he signed up for the Marines, as the war in Korea ground to a bloody tie. Velma signed a paper and cried, because he was underage, and he was gone.

Jack wound up in Korea, too, just a little later, in the army.

They never saw each other there. Jack dreamed a lot about home, since it was more real than anything there. He dreamed about music running through the streets like clear water, and the sound of spoons. *"Pick it again, Jack."*

He was afraid he would lose his buddy there.

It might have been easier if he had.

The Boy

———

I MIGHT HAVE GONE TOO FAR, too soon with the snipe hunt.
One cold night in our first year, after the snakes had gone in
their holes, I told him it was time for his rite of passage. We were at my
mother's farm in late fall and had just had supper with my family, my
mother saying how it was a sin, what they charged for KFC.

I stood and hitched up my pants in a manly fashion.

"Put your coat on, boy," I said, "and let's go get us a snipe."

"What's a snipe?" he said.

"It's a flightless bird," I said.

"I never heard of them," he said.

"Well, they're rare," I said.

"Oh," he said.

"But they're not real bright," I explained.

"How do you know?" he asked.

"You can catch them in a sack," I said.

"Oh," he said.

"You get to hold the sack," I said.

He got so excited I thought he was going to levitate.

Anything we did together, just us, made him smile. We did his
homework together, trekked with Coronado and Ponce de León,
pounded spikes on the Great Plains. I worried over logic, named off
state capitals till my lips went numb, and when he opened his math
book I did not even try. At night, on an old couch with three boys'

worth of Ninja Turtles, Power Rangers and SpongeBobs lost forever in its dark recesses, we watched men wrestle giant snakes, and ate sugarless Popsicles that tasted a little like cough medicine on a stick.

He still believed the only thing that really held me to him was the woman, so even in the middle of a belly laugh he could look a little sad.

But the snipe hunt tickled him to death. He had heard me talk about hunting, how it was something men did where I was from, something that fathers and sons did together, free from women in the dangerous, primal woods. I did not tell him it was also a tradition to take a boy on a snipe hunt and, for the sake of frivolity, abandon him in the trees.

So we got a sack and flashlight and walked into the dark, his mother again drilling holes in me as we went out, but not stopping us. A few minutes later my brother Sam slipped out the door and crept behind us, then circled behind and above us, on the hill.

The traditional snipe hunt is not too traumatizing, in itself. You just position some poor fool bent over holding a sack in the dark, and go home.

Sooner or later, bent over like a moron, he figures it out.

But we have our own twist here. As the boy and I walked in the gloom, Sam, above us in the dark, pushed a big rock down the hill.

It rolled crashing through dead leaves and dry sticks, banging into tree trunks. He aimed it away from us, of course. It would not have been funny if one of us had been knocked off the mountain by a rock the size of a five-gallon bucket.

"What's that?" the boy hissed.

"Bear," I whispered.

We hunkered down in the leaves.

"Rick?" he whispered.

"Shhhhhh," I whispered.

"Rick?" louder this time.

"What?" I said.

"What do we do?" he said.

"Well," I said, "hope it ain't hungry."

I reached over and put my hand on his shoulder.

He was shaking.

"You want to run home," I said.

"No," he said.

But I think he changed his mind when my brother began to stomp down the hill in the dry leaves.

"Rick?"

"What?"

"Should we pray?"

"Well," I said, "the bear might hear."

The woods were still now, except for the faint creaking of the trees.

"I think we're okay," I said, to give the boy a shred of hope.

"Why?"

" 'Cause he'll probably just eat one of us."

A full minute passed in silence.

"Which one?" he asked.

"The slowest one," I whispered.

I had heard that joke somewhere, about how fast a bear could run.

For dramatic effect, I slipped my pocketknife out of my jeans and opened it up, with a loud click.

"You ain't armed?" I said.

"No," he said.

"Pity," I said.

Out of sight, I eased the knife closed and put it back in my pocket.

Fun is fun until someone puts an eye out, Momma always said.

"Well, I better lead, then," I said.

We began to ease down the hillside.

"Now," I said, "if the bear attacks, don't wait for me. I'll keep him occupied."

"Okay," he said, a little too quick.

Soon we saw the warm, yellow lights of my mother's house shining through the dark, and I think the boy did say a prayer then, of thanks. When we were safe inside he told the story of his near-death experience, leaving out the part where I heroically agreed to fight the bear off while he ran home. He did not notice the smiles for a good long time.

"Son," I said, "there was no bear."

I pointed at Sam.

He waved.

The boy just looked at me.

"There's no such thing as a snipe."

I saw tears begin to form in his eyes.

Of all the boys left in the woods, I never saw one cry.

"He thought he was going to get a bird to take home," his mother told me later.

The boy always wanted a bird, she said.

"Well how in the hell would I know that?" I said.

At first, I fretted again at his fragility. But the more I thought about it, the more I realized that boy just wanted there to be a bird to catch, and even wanted there to be a bear in the trees. And he wanted to believe that, together, we were safe in the woods.

CHAPTER TEN

What You're Supposed to Do

———

T HEY TALKED ABOUT IT ONE TIME, what they saw across the ocean, and never talked of it again. They both had a story to tell, one that just wouldn't sit right in their mind, and the liquor made it easier, that's a fact. "I remember I was sittin' at the house, me and Hubert Woods and his brother Slim. We'd been out on the reservation, playing music," Jack said. "They wanted me to go out with them that night, to do some runnin' around, but then I saw Charles's car comin' up the driveway. 'Y'all go on,' I told 'em, 'I'm gonna stay here and talk to Charles.' Well, I had some beer in the house, and I had some white whiskey hid in the back, and we just set and talked a long time, like we did when we was kids. Charles said, 'Jack, you see a lot of bad things over yonder?' and I told him I did . . ." He told my father how he was an army medic at the close of the war, assigned to the minefields and the young men who cleared them. The mines went off and blew men apart, and he bandaged what was left. He came home to work in the mill, but on weekends he still pulled on his western suit, and picked every place he could find a stage. He was still whole, and if someone tossed him a dream he could still grab it with both hands. "Well, I told it, and we dranked." They drank it all, and sat in the quiet, listening dark.

Jack picked a little, to satisfy it.

As I walked down the streets of Laredo
As I walked down Laredo one day
I spied a poor cowboy all wrapped in white linen
Wrapped up in white linen and cold as the clay

"You believe I killed a feller over yonder, Jack?" my father asked.

"Why, sure I do," Jack said.

"I didn't shoot him," my father said.

"What'd you do?" Jack said.

"I drowned him," my father said.

He sounded ashamed.

"Ain't no need talkin' about it, Charles," Jack said.

"I drowned him with my own hands," my father said.

Jack took a pull on the air itself.

"You don't know anybody you shoot," my father said. "You just shoot, and you don't really see their face. Well, I know how it feels to look 'em dead in the face."

The story my father told, he told in a few sentences, the same way he told it to my mother on a sleepless night, and told to me, when I was in high school, as he finished drinking himself to death. He told of a bitter-cold night, and killing a man with his bare hands, holding his head underwater until he went still.

"You think if somebody does somethin' like that, in a place like that, it ought to bother you?" he asked.

"You didn't do nothin' wrong," Jack said.

"No?"

"You didn't do nothin' you wasn't supposed to do," Jack said.

"I see by your outfit that you are a cowboy"
These words he did say as I boldly stepped by

"Come sit down beside me and hear my sad story
I was shot in the chest and I know I must die"

"There was still killin' goin' on when I got there, and Charles got there before I did," Jack said. "He was a fighter, your daddy, but he hadn't never killed nobody."

All my life I had wanted an excuse for his drunkenness, a catalyst for the man he was, and I seized on that, when I was a teenager. Jack is sure it haunted my father. Certainly, he had to water it down with whiskey to even speak of it. "But there was a lot of things haunted your dad," Jack said. The people who loved him say what happened to him in Korea rode in his mind forever, but did not begin his alcoholism. That train had been rolling a long time. He was born on that train.

It is likely, though, that the killing made it worse somehow. I really don't know. I just know that in the early 1950s my father was still on the threshold of his adult life, and killed a man before he was old enough to buy a beer or cast a vote, or shave. If it was a ticking bomb, an unexploded mine in my father's head, it rattled round in there with other things, Jack said. "He never blamed anything that happened to him on it," Jack said. Besides, Jack said, my father would have drowned a man every night in his dreams, if he could have only done over the years to come.

That night, he just picked, and they let the liquor run through their blood, circle their heart, and soften their heads, like a pillow, without laying down. It did not matter if the lyrics were sad. It never had. He picked and my father rested. The thing that outsiders never understood about old country music, the music derived from Irish ballads and mountain folk songs, was that the sadder it was, the better it made you feel. It told you that you were not alone on this miserable rock, not fighting anything special, anything new.

"What you gonna do now, Charles?" he asked.

My father's dreams had shrunk, become more practical. He intended to romance as many pretty women as possible before he found the one he wanted, the one he could not live without, and have fat, pretty, happy children, and maybe get out of this town after all, this time for good. He was still in uniform, but there was plenty of blue-collar work out there in the big cities. Detroit, maybe? Half of Alabama had moved to Detroit, to hang bumpers on Cadillacs. He had always wanted to try on a big city, and see if it fit him all right.

Jack told him that seemed fine.

"We never did say no more of it, that other," Jack said.

Jack watched my father meander to the car. He walked with his back straight, with dignity, but his legs belonged to somebody else. He fired up the old smoker and left, the tires wandering.

Jack put his guitar away, the way a nurse puts away a hypodermic.

We beat the drum slowly and played the fife lowly
And bitterly wept as we bore him along
For we all loved our comrade so brave, young and handsome
We all loved our comrade even though he'd done wrong

The Boy

————

THE FIGURINE on the basketball trophy seemed familiar.
He was clean-cut and handsome, the boy made over, in
chrome.

The engraving read:

MOST CHRIST-LIKE

The boy has several trophies in his room, most of them for sports-
manship. He asked me if I had any, and I told him no, but I did get
whistled once for elbowing a man in the stomach on the foul line at the
YMCA, during a time-out.

"I wasn't always a good sport," I admitted.

"Why?" the boy asked.

"I just wasn't a good boy," I said. "I mean, I wasn't good."

It was painful, to watch the boy's team play. It was a church team, so
there was no cussing except for what little bit might have escaped my
lips in the bleachers, and I had to be careful myself, being as I was in
the gym of the Lord. There was a lot of running up and down the
court, but not a lot of scoring.

"Do you not ever pants anybody?" I once asked the boy, referring
to the practice of tugging down another player's shorts on the foul
line.

"No," the boy said.

"Want to?" I asked.

"No, he does not," said the woman.

They played mostly other suburban churches, with final scores of 12–6, and 7–2, till the day finally came when they played a team of inner-city children from Memphis.

The home team walked into their threadbare gym in mismatched uniforms. One of them, a fat kid, had no strings in his sneakers. There were only six of them, and two of them, the biggest two, were girls.

"This is gonna be bad," I whispered to the woman.

She looked at me, questioning.

"For us," I said.

One of the two girls scared me, and I was a spectator. She stalked the hardwood floor as if she could smell the weakness in the white-bread boys. If one of the little boys got close to her, she plowed through them, and if one tried to drive the lane, she put them on the floor.

The first little boy went down hard, curled up in a ball, and sobbed. The second, the one she put into the wall, lay in the fetal position, as if she had knocked him back in time. The third, a big kid himself, took an elbow, and lay on the floor like cast-off clothes.

So the woman was right. Our boy was not special.

The boy only got to play about half the time, and for the first time I was kind of grateful. But with so many weepers on the floor, he had to take his punishment sooner or later. He was not a great shooter, but he tried hard and played good defense. He took a carom off the board and was dribbling up-court when the big girl came at him like a locomotive.

"Oh Lord," I said out loud.

She reached for the ball with her left hand, and, still moving forward at a dead run, slashed her right elbow across his mouth.

I have never seen a finer elbow thrown, at any level.

I still don't know how he kept his feet. The ball went rolling, and as players from both sides chased after it he just stood there, hurting. Then, he came wobbling diagonally across the court, toward his mom.

No foul was awarded, no time-out was called. It was surreal, in a way. As the game continued down the court he just meandered to the bleachers.

"Go back," I said.

Then I saw his face. His lips were already swelling.

"Don't cry," I said under my breath. "Don't cry, don't cry . . ."

He didn't. He just wobbled on, till he stood before us.

"She knocked out my teef," he said, and spit them into his hand.

The girl had snapped his front teeth in two.

He handed the pieces to the woman.

Then he looked me right in the eye, and walked back on the court.

"THAT'S MY BOY," I shouted, and I thumped my chest.

CHAPTER ELEVEN

At Least a Hundred Dollars Then

———•———

I T WAS THE YEAR my mother came to dislike roses.

Their first year together was a good year, mostly, their one good year. She worked keeping house for the East Side ladies, and in the early evenings she filled her time with flowers. She spent hours, days, coaxing them to grow in cracked plastic ice cube trays, in the middle of whitewashed tires and in pots made from cut-down Purex jugs. Even when she didn't have a leftover dime, when a five-cent packet of seeds was too much luxury to lavish on herself, she would take a cutting or a bulb from her sisters' gardens, and she would have flowers. She had sweet williams, in purple and blue, and yellow marigolds, orange day lilies, and zinnias, which she called old maids, in red, pink, orange and the rare white. She found something pretty about spider plants, with blooms that looked like dangling legs, and grew them in discarded paper cups. She even grew roses, but they always seemed unfaithful, somehow. "They always stuck me," she said.

He was still stationed in Macon then, so she stayed with her momma and daddy, when he was away. But when he was home they stayed with his parents in an old house on the edge of town, not far from the mill village. The place heaved and sighed with family, wives, husbands, children, sweethearts, grandchildren, cousins, second cousins, third cousins, and people just looking to be fed. They all seemed to love her and treated her as family, and she loved them back, till the whiskey arrived, and the whole clan came to pieces for days, leaving women and men in a shaky aftermath, blinking like hurricane survivors in a landscape of blackened eyes and broken sticks.

He said it was only temporary, that life. They fled it together, and rode through town, looking at FOR SALE signs on the narrow streets of the West Side, knowing damn good and well they lived in a FOR RENT world.

He did not buy her a ring, at first. His sister Fairy Mae gave my mother one of her old wedding bands, just till he could do better. He saved money and, in that first year, gave her a plain yellow gold wedding band and an engagement ring with a tiny diamond. "They was real, and your daddy gave a whole lot," she said. "It was at least a hundred dollars, even way back then," she said. They were new, not once-tried pawnshop rings that carry the bad luck and unhappy spirits of the people who wore them before. These rings were new in the box. She was afraid to wear them, because she worked with her hands in soapy water, so she borrowed her daddy's hammer and drove a nail into the wall, and hung them on it. That way she could work, washing and ironing other people's clothes, and still look at them.

It took patience to love my father even in the best of times. He would volunteer to sweep the floors for her, because the Bragg men did things like that when they were all right, and he would sweep hard and vigorous, gouging at the corners, making the old wood floors shine. One day she noticed little humps in the rug in the middle of the floor, and in fact noticed little humps in all the rugs, on all the floors. "He would just sweep the dirt under the rug," she said. "I told him not to, and he would say he wouldn't do it no more, and then he would."

He got into fistfights and came home bloodied, and when she asked what he was fighting for, he explained with the depth and veracity of a six-year-old: " 'Cause he got me mad." He left broken glass in the yard from target practice with a .22 pistol, and locked himself in the bathroom for hours at a time to read stories like "I Battled a Giant Otter" and "The Whip-Crazy Killer of St. Paul," in magazines like *True Detective* and *Man's Life*. The outhouse was still the only place, in that roiling family, there was any peace. When my mother complained that, in her condition, she needed a little more access, he built her a little outhouse of her own. "He put a little window in it, so I could see out," she said, shaking her head. It never occurred to him that people could also see in.

He drank, of course. He had flat out lied about that. He loved to fish but would not fish sober, and would get drunk and fall in almost every single time. "Mark, that mud was slicker'n owl shit on a linoleum floor, and . . ." and he would blame it on everything except what it really was. On a road trip to Florida, he got drunk and stole an alligator, a four-footer straight from the pen at a roadside show, and stored it in the trunk, not as a prank, apparently, but as an investment. He figured there were several wallets, belts and key fobs in it, but he got pulled over in North Florida by the highway patrol and waited what seemed like an eternity for the trooper to write the ticket and disappear. He hopped out right there, opened the trunk and, using the tire iron as a prod, gave the thing its freedom.

Then, on a frog-gigging trip, he and his brother Roy had enough whiskey to make them believe they could wade all the way across Aderholt Lake. But they didn't want to get their pants wet, so they had my mother drive their shoes and pants around to the other side of the lake, as they wobbled off across the water in their boxer shorts, tridents in their hands. The bottom was mud and weed and rotted everything. "What does the bottom feel like?" my mother shouted to them. "Feels like plush carpet," Roy said, and he and my father found that so uproariously funny that they began to laugh uncontrollably and had to hold to each other to keep from falling down. Passersby, some with little children by the hand, stopped to stare at two grown men knee-deep in the lake and in their obvious underwear, giggling and clutching each other while trying not to mortally wound each other with their three-pronged spears. They couldn't have gigged a milk cow if someone held it still.

But I think the whole whiskey-drinking world knows there are good drunks and bad drunks—not the men drinking but the experience itself—and those were mostly good drunks, then. They were not binges, really, not weeks at a time, but weekends, as he held to family tradition, to the almost sacred rhythm. He would announce he was going squirrel hunting, which meant he was going to get drunk, or say he was going rabbit hunting, which meant he was going to play cards and get drunk. He never stayed gone long and he always made it home at night, and if you ask some women what they will settle for in an imperfect world, that is it, exactly.

He drank mostly as she worked, because in the beginning he did not want to waste his time with her by making her unhappy, and if a drinking man marries a teetotaling woman, there is no way to close the distance, when he is drunk. He did not get drunk in front of her at first, but she would return from a trip to town or from cleaning a house to find him so, the way a stern momma comes into the kitchen to find a child with a cookie on his breath.

But the world was backwards, or upside down, in his daddy's house. Most people come home to get sober, to get all right, but at home he did not lock the liquor out when he closed the door, he locked it in. Toward the end of that first year together, she began to lose him to the family tradition. He rejoined his father and brothers at the table, around that can.

Drinking men who remember that white whiskey say there was something special about it, something unreal. It hooked you like heroin, till it was hard to do much else with any pleasure, any real enthusiasm, except sip, swallow and pour, and as the weekends tumbled by he spent a little more time with it. On Sunday evenings, sometimes wobbling a little, he lifted his uniform out of the closet, hung it carefully on the hook over the backseat, and drove southeast to Macon, to be a Marine again.

One afternoon, just a few days after he left for the base, a friend brought her a newspaper that said Marine Charles Bragg had been badly injured on his way to the base in Macon after running his car into a bridge railing, and had suffered severe head and chest injuries. He was in the hospital for weeks and in recovery for months, and though the Marines considered him fit for duty, Carlos, who knew something about car wrecks if not broken bones, said my father hurt the rest of his life from fractures in his chest and ribs. "He walked different and moved different and you could see him shifting his weight sittin' down, because he hurt so bad," Carlos said. He ate aspirin like M&Ms, and found a new reason to love the liquor. It was a painkiller now, not as good as morphine but close, close enough.

"People said it was Korea that pushed him over the edge, but it was that wreck. That hurt him bad, and he wasn't sober much, after that," Carlos said.

This was how their first year passed, with him broken up and hurting, medicating himself. From the beginning, they had seen each other only on his weekend passes, and it occurred to her, as she began to show, as their first anniversary neared, they had known each other less than a month, if you counted up the days.

"I married a stranger," she said.

Like a few billion women before her, she believed that having the baby would settle him down. For a while, it did. He bought her a gown to wear in the hospital, and bought a tiny pair of overalls, tiny shirt, and four tiny pairs of socks, all blue. It would be a boy, he was certain. It had to be. It was his.

But the odd thing was, no matter how much she told him how much he meant to her, he never quite believed. It is not a condition unique to him, I now understand. He lived in a common insecurity some men have about women, born of the simple fact that they can never quite figure out what women think—which, in his defense, is a little like trying to map the cosmos on the back of a Juicy Fruit wrapper with a toy telescope and a piece of chalk.

It wasn't enough that she loved him.

It wasn't enough that she said so, all the time.

He had to be shown, to know it, absolutely.

He got into trouble on base—what, we're not sure—and the officers canceled his next few leaves. On his last trip home, the last time she would see him for weeks, she had to work part of the day, cleaning a lady's house. She rushed home as soon as she could, so they could have just a few moments together. But the house was quiet. She ran from room to room, calling his name. She ran through the living room and checked the kitchen, rushed from bedroom to bedroom. She remembers turning in a circle, light-headed, then sat on the edge of a bed, and cried. She noticed, then, a scrap of cardboard taped to the front of a beautiful old dark wood chifforobe.

It was a note from my father.

Mark,
I am sorry. I had to leave today. They would put me in the jail if I didn't show up on time. I will write you, and see you when I can. I love you,
Charles

"It was just a little piece of cardboard," she said. "It was three inches wide and five inches long." She sat back down on the bed, the note in her hand, and cried again. Five minutes passed, maybe more.

Then, behind her, the door of the massive old chifforobe slowly opened, and my father, resplendent in his dress uniform, tiptoed into the room.

"Hey," he said.

She spun around.

He just stood there, smiling.

She forgot to be mad, forgot the cruelty in it.

"Where you been?" she asked.

She asked it a half dozen times.

She should have balled up her fist again and punched him in his goddamn nose.

But she just wrapped her arms around him, and waited for him to go for real.

Later that day, my mother, her brother William, and his wife Louise drove my father halfway to the base in Macon, then let him out in Roanoke, to take a bus the rest of the way. She cried all the way home.

When they pulled into the yard, he was standing in the front door.

He was smiling. He had hitched a ride at the bus station, and beat them back to Jacksonville. He was AWOL by morning, and a fugitive by afternoon.

"Have you lost your mind?" she asked.

"I wanted to come home," he said, and to her, he sounded like a little boy.

"They'll come get you," she said.

But he just stayed, and stole the days. The sheriff and his deputies came for him, once, twice, more. They never looked very hard. It was federal government business, and they had enough to do. He hid in the woods, at kinfolks' houses, and in the chifforobe. "I never did figure out why he didn't want to go back," she said. "Sometimes your daddy did things that didn't make any sense because he just wanted to do them. Sometimes he didn't think things through real good."

He finally left in handcuffs.

It was irresponsible of course to risk the future on the here and now, but if he was telling the truth, and maybe he was, it was because he just couldn't stand to leave her.

He was serving a year in the stockade in Norfolk when his first child was born, on September 11, 1956.

She wrote him that it was a boy.

Again, they wrote each other every day, and it kept her sane. He wrote that he missed her, and sealed it in an envelope. He signed them the same, and left the same secret under the stamp.

His military discharge, issued February 20, 1957, reads: "other than honorable." His son Sam was five months old when he came home. My mother ran out to meet the car as it turned into the driveway, because there was still hope then, and even as he staggered out of the car she was still glad. The boy was in the house, and they walked in together, to look at him. My father bent over, to lift his son off the bed, and as he did a slim pint bottle of liquor tumbled out of a pocket and fell to the floor.

"I can still see the label," she said. "I can still see them Four Roses."

———·———

IT WAS LIKE A SIGN, the way it happened, and she believed in signs then.

Whether it was a curse or not, everything pretty much turned to dirt after that. He drank all the time, even breaking his family tradition of weekend drunks. Once a man cannot tell his Wednesdays from his Saturdays, he is well and truly lost. He would give her money, sometimes, but usually just let her make her own way, one clean floor at a time. He vanished, reappeared, robbed her purse, and vanished again.

The next few years followed a bleak pattern of separation and reconciliation. She wouldn't give up. She ran away from him and ran back to him, and he would promise to do right and break his promise by sundown. In defeat, and ashamed, she signed up for welfare, so there would be something to live on when he disappeared. For long months he just forgot about them, and lived single, as if they were not flesh and blood but something he could drag out of a closet when they crossed his mind, like a style of shoe.

She had to sell the few things she owned, to feed her and my brother.

She sold her wedding rings to her sister Edna, to pay debts. She sold the beautiful cedar chest he got her to her older brother William, for groceries. She held tight to the solid silver dollar, till her baby got sick, and she swapped it to the pharmacist for a bottle of cough medicine.

I was born in the summer of '59, in the middle of it.

Somewhere out there he was binge drinking and joyriding.

But, as the cliché goes, that is another story.

———·———

LIKE A LOT OF PEOPLE from the mountains, faith and super-stition crisscrossed in her mind. She bent her knees and prayed for deliverance, for God to touch her man's heart, or at least his conscience. But she still looked for signs in coffee cups, in the sky, in the jack of diamonds and queen of hearts. If ever a woman needed to see into the future, it was her.

She went to see Sadie.

Every mill town, pipe shop town or coal town had a fortune-teller, widow women, usually, who worked from their sewing rooms or kitchens in little houses covered with asbestos siding. They hung a homemade plywood sign from the porch or on a stick in the yard, with a name or a phone number and a FORTUNES TOLD, and always a crude drawing of an eye, the all-seeing eye. My mother never wondered why, if that eye really does see all, those women did not move the hell out of an asbestos house. But she had a lot more to worry about then, when she scrapped together her ironing money, and went to Piedmont, to have her future told.

Sadie didn't say much, for a mystic. She was neither young nor old, just a plump woman who greeted the curious adorned in her house-dress, in a tiny white cottage on a plain, working-class street in Piedmont, about fifteen minutes north of Jacksonville on Highway 21. Sadie would tell you your future, or at least tell you what she saw, flashing through her mind as she read a palm, or flipped through a deck of cards. The problem with Sadie, my mother said, "was she didn't explain it real, real good," so she often left Sadie's house as mystified as when she walked in. Sadie charged two dollars to look into the future, so it may be she figured that two dollars of the Gift was good for a hint, a peek maybe, but not enough to just fling the door open on the way that things would be.

She paid Sadie in copper and silver, and waited to find out if there was any hope, or if there was a warning, because things can always get worse. Sadie shuffled her worn cards, businesslike. She was not overly friendly, usually. She was a seer in a mill town, a prophet to working women, and you had to foretell a lot of love and prosperity to make a buck and keep 'em coming back. But she didn't tell my mother, this day, what she wanted to hear.

"I see you crossing water with the child," she said, pointing to me. "I see a lot of water."

My mother nodded.

"When?" she asked.

"When you are old."

That was all Sadie had to say about that, but it was a lot. My mother would live a long time, and see things beyond the foothills.

Sadie shuffled, and dealt the days to come.

"I see writin' in your life. I see you writin'... lots of words," she told my mother.

My mother wrote poetry, and would write it all her life.

Sadie shuffled again, and flipped the cards across the table.

"I see your life in a circle," she told my mother. "I see you doing things young, and doing them old."

"What things?" my mother asked.

But Sadie just shook her head.

"It don't say," she said.

"Tell me, please," my mother said, "about my man."

Sadie shuffled and dealt, and shuffled and dealt again.

It was nothing bad, no evil omen.

He just didn't come up in the cards.

People were waiting on the porch to see into their own future.

"She just left me hangin'," my mother said.

She went back to Sadie one more time after that, but stopped going when she got religion, "because the Bible says that nobody knows the future but the Lord. I was wrong to do that," she told me. I told her that if every fortune-teller in the world was going to hell, New Orleans could fill it up all by itself. "At least she didn't lie, and tell you we'd all live happily ever after," I said.

I do not believe Sadie was a fraud, not really. I believe she looked for the future in those cards, and told it the best she knew how, and sometimes life shuffled around to fit her vision and sometimes it didn't, but she got one thing dead-on.

She went looking for my father and she couldn't find him in our future. It is a wonder the deck did not catch fire, and burn the house down.

———

I T WAS NOT ALL BAD, of course. My first memory of him, as a tiny boy, was bright and fine. I remember my mother was hanging white sheets on the line on a hot, windy day. She sang as she hung them, but what song I cannot say, and the sheets puffed up like sails on a ship, and now and then a gust would make them snap and pop. I had a handful of something sticky, I believe it was wild strawberries, and she made me go sit in the grass, to keep me from handling and ruining the sheets. I saw a car pull up in the gravel driveway, tires crunching, and park behind a line of evergreens. The trees stand thirty feet high now, but then a man could still peek over, even a little man. Then, I saw what seemed to be the head of a large, goofy animal, a bear I believe, peer at me over the trees, and disappear. A few seconds later it rose again, slowly turned sideways, to show me a profile, and glided along, just its head showing, behind the curtain of green. I was dumbstruck. My father appeared at the edge of the trees, carrying the biggest stuffed animal I had ever seen, a bear as big as he was. It was my birthday, I believe.

But he continued to change. Wild is one thing. They make movies about wild boys. We laugh about them, and even admire them. I used to be one, myself. Even a neglectful man, you can forgive. But mean is mean, and that's how he got, the drunker he got. He had the woman of his dreams, and tore her down. My little brother Mark was born in that time, November 10, 1962, as the world around us began to grow darker.

"The thing about Charles was, he just couldn't figure out how to be a drunk and a daddy, too," said Carlos.

My mother just absorbed it.

Unlike Velma, she never called the law.

There are all kinds of darkness in this big ol' scary world. Old men in this town recall being wild boys themselves back then, recall sitting in the window of a café on the square as a big man with a pale, round face rolled by in his cruiser. They remember how the man's pasty face would turn toward them, and ruin their supper. They could be chewing on a steak, on a payday, and it would taste like their last meal.

The Boy

—·—

IT WAS FOOLISH, against all science, to expect the boy to take after me. I could dress him like me, cut his hair like mine, hide his socks, even teach him to cuss, but he would not be like me. I knew it, the first time I peeked into his room. There were robots, dragons, monsters, spacemen, and not one model car.

I see flashing blue lights in my sleep, and I had more cars than I had girlfriends. In my life, there were three Camaros, two Firebirds, three Mustangs, three thirdhand Porsches, a '56 Chevrolet and a '66 Corvair, a car deemed "unsafe at any speed." As a young man I daydreamed no more about centerfolds, of 36-24-36, than I did 289, 327, 429, and the very word "hemi" made me sweat. I would race anything with wheels then, and as an older man I twice drove the silver car to the straightaways of the Mississippi Delta, to test my own failing nerve. As a boy I rode motorcycles, even a moped, but took the muffler and pedals off, for speed.

The woman's two oldest boys did not love speed or cars—had never looked under a hood. To me, that would be like reaching puberty without ever peeking down a blouse.

But this could not be allowed in my boy. He could not be my boy and be a peddler, a pedestrian, a pilgrim with a bus pass.

He would drive.

The woman would have gutted me with a dull spoon if I had bought the boy a motorcycle, and the truth is I wouldn't have. There are too many fools on the roads now, blowing on their lattes, dialing little-bitty phones, rolling through stop signs as they text their grocery list. So I did the next best thing. I bought him a high-performance go-cart with an engine so big it could have shot a lawn mower to the moon.

The previous owner sold it to me because his wife made him, after his youngest son flipped it going wide-open and hung upside down, screaming for his momma. But really, how dangerous can something be that you start by pulling on a rope?

It looked safe to me. The driver sat in a cage of steel tubing, strapped in with a full-body harness, and wore a helmet with a full face guard to shield against low, whipping tree branches, or the errant June bug.

He buckled in, pulled on his helmet, and pressed the accelerator. He decided, in that second, that life has two speeds—"Stop" and "Whoa, Nelly"—and what fun is there put-puttering around? He made it almost one full turn around the yard, knobby rear tires sliding in the grass, before he miscalculated on a sharp turn around the tetherball pole.

It happens.

He cut her too sharp, sideswiped the pole and jumped the concrete foundation used to hold the whole apparatus upright. His machine wedged there sideways, one rear tire, the one attached to the drive chain, spinning wide-open, the motor screaming, as the boy unsnapped his harness and bailed out like he was on fire.

"What in the hell were you thinkin'?" I asked him.

"Well," he said, "I wasn't thinking that much."

The woman looked at me, in surrender.

"He's yours," she said.

CHAPTER TWELVE

Ross

IF YOU BROKE THE LAW you dealt with Ross, and dealt with him till the preacher led revival over your bones. Once Ross made up his mind you were trouble, he would fine, imprison and humiliate you with or without papers, because he didn't mind signing a judge's name to a warrant if it meant taking out the trash. If you fought him, when he was a young man, he would walk you to his police car across asphalt scattered with your own teeth. He was big and wide and white, like a Frigidaire sitting on size 12 wing-tip shoes, and wore black-framed glasses on his benign, MoonPie face. He had been a prizefighter before he served in the Pacific in World War II, and the blue steel .38 on his gun belt was just an afterthought, an unnecessary accessory, like a tie clip. Ross could point a finger at you and take everything you would ever have. He passed judgment on the Braggs soon after taking office, because they offended his sense of how the world should turn. "He hated your daddy 'cause he couldn't get him to do right," my mother said, and while that is certainly true, there was more than that between them. One day, in '58, my father and mother were helping my grandfather Charlie Bundrum roof a house in town, and looked down to see Ross, all six feet five, three hundred pounds of him, leaning against the hood of his Chevrolet. Ross didn't speak, just smiled pleasantly up at them, then cocked his thumb over a pointed finger, sighted down his knuckle on my father's face, and squeezed the invisible trigger. "Bang," he said.

Chief of police Ross Tipton lectured the Exchange Club on humane enforcement of the law, and liked to prove his humanity by giving some of my more docile, drunken kin his castoff shoes. But in my father, fresh from the Norfolk stockade, he found a poor but uppity white man he could not scare. Ross was determined to humble him, to break him, so he chained him like a dog where Pelham Road meets College Hill, and put him to work with a sling blade. That way, everyone saw what happened to people who dared strut around in Ross's town.

My aunt Jo and uncle John Couch, two of the people who helped raise me, were walking through town one summer and saw him chained there, as the whole population rolled by. He had been arrested for public drunkenness and fighting and deserved his jail time, but men who worked off fines were not routinely chained. Ross stood by, his gun belt riding high on his big belly. My aunt Jo, a little woman with a heart of glass, could not stand it. Her eyes burned behind her cat's-eye glasses, and she marched over and confronted the chief.

"You ought not do that to the boy," she said.

"I have to," he said.

"Why do you have to put him in chains?" she asked.

"He'll run," he said.

My father, shamed and helpless in the presence of his sister-in-law, hacked at the Johnson grass.

"Won't you, Rabbit?" Tipton said.

My father's eyes lifted from the ground and met Ross, but Ross stayed just out of reach. He had dealt with bad men all his life, and this whelp was nothing special.

"It's not right," my aunt Jo said.

But Ross got to say what right was.

My father dragged his chains past kin and friends and perfect strangers, stopping at dinnertime to eat a thin hamburger from Zuma's café. At dark, Ross unsnapped his holster and put a hand on his pistol butt, till my father handed his sling blade to the trusty and shuffled into his cage. In his cell, he murdered Ross Tipton a thousand times.

It went on for years like that. We rode our momma's hip, all of us, into city hall, as she made his bail a few dollars at a time.

If you are going to do right all the time, it matters very little who the police chief is in your town. You won't see him except at Kiwanis. But if you know that sooner or later you are going to do wrong, that doing wrong is a part of who you are, it matters a great deal. For twenty-five years, Ross ran our town, respected by many, feared by some, and hated by people with my last name, because Ross rubbed our noses in our sins.

Carlos Slaght, who has a kindness in him you can feel and almost see, is one of the people who believe my father was somehow better than the life he led. He believes that, with a little luck, my father's life would have been different, and, in a domino effect, other lives would have, too. It is a wonderful notion. But Carlos, Jack and others believe a series of events that began in the summer of '55 made this town all but unlivable for him, smeared his pride, and quickened his decline. It is a gothic story, the way they tell it, and you can see the bad luck tumbling, as if the devil himself had shaved the dice.

"It goes back to Everett, my brother, who whupped Ross when he was one-legged, and started the feud," Carlos said. "But I guess it goes back even farther than that. I guess it goes back to the killin' of Chief Whiteside by Robert Dentmon. Dentmon don't pull that trigger, there wouldn't have been no place here for Ross."

———

A S MUCH AS ANYONE, the people of the mill village and its close-in neighborhoods know violence. They accept industrial accidents and even a certain amount of murder, because some men just need killing. But there are things impossible to reconcile, and the killing of Chief D. E. Whiteside haunts the place and people even now. He was raised in the country, understood them and treated them like equals, and they lost him to a drunken meanness. D.E., whom everyone called Whitey, was an easygoing big man, bald as a boiled egg, and a respected member of the Mason's Lodge. D.E. and Mary had five children, Peggy, Charlotte, Sandy, Bill and Jack, so Whitey drove a truck on his off days, hauling corn. He could throw drunks around like feed sacks, but when his children were scraped or burned, he could be gentle as a grandmother. "It's him I remember looking after us," said his daughter Sandy, who was ten years old in the summer of '55.

"We never had trouble with Whitey," Carlos said. "When we was teenagers he'd see us hanging around someplace, and he'd say, 'Boys, I got to walk over here and check this building, and if you're still here when I get back I'll whip you all the way home.'" He tipped his hat to Velma, shook hands with Bob and the boys. He got along with my father, whom he treated with the respect due a returning serviceman, even if he had ended his hitch behind bars. "The thing about that cop was, he treated your daddy like a man," said Jack Andrews, "and he treated everybody alike. He didn't treat village boys any different than town or college boys." He remembers a Grand Ole Opry traveling road show with Grandpa Jones and String Bean, on the square. Two drunken village boys kept disrupting the show, till Whiteside snatched them up, banged their heads together like in a cartoon, and led them out. What was unique about that was the fact he did not sweep all the village boys out of the tent. He *distinguished,* and that meant the world.

His killing by a village storekeeper makes no more sense now to Whiteside's son Bill than when he was a seven-year-old boy on the front porch of their house on June 19 of '55. He heard the phone ring, then saw his mother tear screaming through the screen door. "It was foolish how it happened," he said. "That man killed Daddy on Monday, and they were going fishing Wednesday."

In the police report, it says Whiteside died because of a dispute over a water line, but if you believe in the tumbling nature of things, he died from changing times.

By the end of the Korean War, the parochial society of the mill village had come undone. The mill no longer generated the village's electricity, no longer gave workers a house. In '55, the mill cut off its water supply to the houses. City work crews dug up the village, tapping old lines and laying new ones as people grumbled, damned if they'd buy water God made for free.

The mood was black already, and many workers blamed the changes in their lives on the latest mill boss. Mill workers joked that, when the boss died, he raised up in his coffin as six poor men carried him to the grave. "You put wheels on this thing," he told the head pallbearer, "you can lay off five of these fellers." Backed by a new ownership group of New York investors, the bosses put in place slow-downs and stretch-outs. Bosses just laid people off when things were lean, then, when contracts were fat, worked people half to death in an attempt to see how fast the machines could run.

Then, the unthinkable happened.

The mill shut down.

It would only be idle a few months as another owner prepared a takeover, but for a few tense months there was a panic here. For store owners in the village, it was a death knell. One of them was Robert E. Lee Dentmon, a gaunt, sunburned, surly, besotted man who ran a little shack of a store, a Pepsi sign in the shape of a giant bottle cap tacked to the side. His friends knew he had a burning temper, carried a .22 in the bib pocket of his overalls, and drank whiskey like water when he was mad and sometimes when he wasn't. He told customers he would shoot anyone who tried to take his water line.

He and Whiteside had known each other for decades. It was an odd friendship—one was strident, quick-tempered, the other quiet, peaceful—but they both loved to fish, and when the weather was good on Wednesday mornings they would meet before dawn and fish the ponds and rivers they fished when they were boys.

In June, the taps in Dentmon's store went dry. J. T. Marible, a councilman and master mechanic at the mill, told the *Anniston Star* that Dentmon called him, incensed. "I told him he was talking to the wrong man. We [the mill] didn't have anything to do with the water in the village anymore. He said, 'I'll give you till six o'clock in the morning to get my water on.' " Dentmon seemed determined to turn back time.

Marible told Mayor J. B. Ryan about the call the next morning, on June 19. Ryan sent a crew of city workers to the village, to plug water lines in the vicinity of the store. Dentmon was drinking his breakfast when the city workers—Roy Wilkerson, William Barnwell and Roy "Tot" Turner—showed up. When the workers said they only wanted to locate the old line, Dentmon replied: "It don't make no difference. They ain't gonna move it." The three men went back to city hall, and told their supervisor Dentmon would not let them do their job.

Back at the store, Dentmon fumed about the water with Louis Snider, a produce salesman who sold the store owner watermelons and cantaloupes. As Dentmon griped, he reached under the counter and took out a box of shells, and began loading his .22, a poor man's gun. It cost a dime to fire a .38, but just a penny for a .22.

Mayor Ryan called Whiteside. Ryan told him to go speak to Dentmon, but Chief Whiteside said it would be smart to wait. "Daddy knew the man," said Sandy. "He knew his temper. He said, 'Let him cool off.' " But Ryan insisted and Whiteside drove to the store, followed by Wilkerson, Barnwell and Tot Turner in their city truck. Dentmon, wearing a pair of overalls faded almost white, his close-cropped hair shining with oil, stood outside. As Whiteside stepped from his car, followed by the three city workers, Dentmon greeted him:

"Whaddaya say, cop," he said, drunk.

Whiteside did not say a word. He just walked up to Dentmon, planning to pat him down for a weapon. As he came within arm's reach, Dentmon pulled his .22 pistol and fired point-blank into Whiteside's chest. The bullet, the size of an orange seed, went in below his badge, hit a bone and ricocheted into his heart.

"Kill him, Tot," Whiteside said, and died.

Turner and the other men did not move. A dog came up and started to lick at the blood, and one of the witnesses kicked at it. "Kick that dog again," Dentmon said, "an' I'll do the same to you."

Even as the bullet came to rest in Whiteside's big heart, its effect, its impact, was unchecked. "They gave Dentmon life in the penitentiary. But I didn't know life meant seven years," Bill Whiteside said. The bullet destroyed his family. Mary Whiteside, shattered, could not make enough money at the movie theater to feed, clothe and care for five children, and the county sent the children to live in a foster home. "That man," Bill Whiteside said, "took all I had."

City workers laid new water lines through the village, but for a long time, when people looked at scars of red dirt snaking through the streets, they thought of cemeteries. In '56, Union Underwear bought the mill and renamed it Union Yarn, and it was like the scare never happened, like a bad dream. The city hired Bill Harris to be chief. He, too, understood the village and had even worked in the mill, and in the village people said there would never be anyone as straight with them as Whitey, but that Bill Harris would do. But bad luck just kept tumbling, and Harris died of a heart attack that year. In October of '56 the job tumbled to Ross. He raised his right hand and swore to execute the duties of his office with professionalism, fairness and integrity. "So help me God," he said.

To look at him you would have thought the city had hired a knee-breaker and head-buster, just a redneck police chief with a turnip's IQ. But that wasn't Ross.

He was a conflicted man.

Born in Anniston in 1912, Ross was a respected welterweight boxer in his teens. He pumped iron and battered his sparring partners every day at Rubenstein's gym at Thirteenth and Moore. He was trim then, and his feet were light and his hands were quick. He went pro at eighteen in 1930, and outfought Jack Taylor for the Southern Middleweight title just a few years later. His toughest bout came when he turned heavyweight and fought the feared brawler Ching Johnson. Ross won the fight, but broke both his hands on Johnson's head.

When World War II erupted, he enlisted in the navy, as a healer. He entered the medical corps and served five years in the bloodiest theater of the Pacific, at Guadalcanal, Boganville, New Georgia, attached to the First Marine Division, Third Division, the Fourth Raiders and the Seabees. He slogged through the jungle muck and blood-soaked sand, carrying bleeding and shattered men across his big shoulders, watching them die, helping them live.

"There was always two sides to Ross," said Jack Andrews. "There was the evil side, and that other'un."

After the war he was a foreman in an Anniston foundry, then a deputy for county sheriff Socko Pate. He worked his way up to chief deputy by chasing down men who ran whiskey in the dry county, and was a logical choice for chief in Jacksonville. He took over a department with three officers and one car, unless you count the one they shared with Water and Sewer. He worked six days a week, twelve hours a day, for $150 a month. Ross took those humble seeds and grew an orchard.

He ran a loan business from his desk, lending ten dollars and asking back fifteen, and levied fines off the books. That was common knowledge among the working people, who paid the fines Ross levied with the money Ross loaned. The mayors and councilmen haggled over annexations and parade routes and judges ate lunch at the Ladiga Grill, but Ross ran the streets. He arbitrarily raised and lowered fines with his feet propped on his desk, settled cases based on his moods, and let you go early or kept you in his jail for as long as he felt necessary. He was just an old-time police chief, say older people in town, allowed to run his business any way he wanted as long as he kept the peace.

But Ross had beliefs. He believed in the dynamic of family, in the pureness of it. When his father, L.P., and mother, Elsie, died, he kept their house in Anniston just like they left it, and lived in a spare, concrete-block building off the square in Jacksonville. He had no family, no wife, no children, but preached his ideas on family values to civic clubs and schools. "Crime prevention can start the first day of a child's life, at home, at church, and school . . . [T]otal environment influences him, especially during these early years," Ross wrote in his speeches, which were covered by the *Anniston Star* and *Jacksonville News*. "The parent should be with the child long enough to make him understand right and wrong. This is best accomplished by an understanding between parent and child which is brought about only through close association."

In the village and poorer neighborhoods adjoining it, where mothers nursed babies on their ten-minute break and worked predawn to after dark, he saw his idyllic society come undone.

One family, in particular, seemed to live the way it damn well pleased.

They broke the law like it was written on the back of a beer bottle.

It was inevitable that they would collide. But he had barely gotten going good in Jacksonville when he lost, temporarily, the one thing a chief has to have in a small town, in a mill town, especially. He lost his invincibility, lost his swagger, and even lost his hat. Everett Slaght, my father's first cousin, took them from him. "Ross already thought we was trash," said Carlos, Everett's little brother. "But he hated us when Everett was done with him. Ain't no tellin' how bad Everett might have whupped him, if his leg hadn't come off."

R OSS SHOULD HAVE KNOWN there was too much magic in that boy's life, light magic, and dark, to mess with. Here you have a boy who gets blown into the Pacific yet doesn't get a scratch, then gets blown apart in his kitchen on the way to get a bowl of milk and cornbread. By the time Ross challenged Everett, he had already swam through a miracle, and danced on sticks. He was the most beautiful, most happy crippled man anyone had ever seen, and the only thing that could knock the smile off his face was a woman, and should that really come as much of a surprise?

Everett never told people his miracle. He never explained what happened to him after the shell exploded in his gun turret on the

Iowa, sending him cartwheeling into the deep. His mother, Eldora, got a letter from the War Department after it happened, giving sympathies. But a few months later he came walking up Pelham Road, and she saw him there, at the corner of Mountain Avenue. "Hey, Momma," he said, "it's just me."

He didn't have a mark on him, not a burn or a cut, as if angels had snatched him in midair and carried him home, and that was what a good many people came to believe.

He was Michelangelo's *David,* with freckles. He was six feet one and 235, with slabs of muscle rippling across his body, hard as the marble he seemed to be. He had blondish-red hair and laughed all the time, like he knew he was living on bonus time.

He married when he came home but there was no happiness in it. One night, after another argument with his wife, he came home late and asked her to fix him a bowl of milk and bread. He pushed open the door to the hall and there sat his father-in-law with a single-barrel 16-gauge shotgun. The old man pulled the trigger but he shook a bit as he did, and blew Everett's left leg off at the knee.

"But they stayed together, him and her, a few more years," Carlos said. "It didn't get no happier."

Tennessee Williams wrote that a one-armed, beautiful boy was even more like a statue, with that missing part, and I think it was that way with Everett. He was still fit and trim and raced two-legged men on his crutches, until the VA fitted him with a wooden leg. Not long after that, Everett and his wife got into another fight just off Alexandria Road. Carlos and his brother Red happened to be there when Ross's cruiser pulled into the yard. Ross liked being the champion when women were involved.

Carlos and Red tried to calm Everett down.

"I got it, boys," Ross said.

He walked carefully up to Everett.

"Let's go, son," he said.

"I ain't done nothing, Ross," Everett said.

"Just till you cool off, boy," Ross said.

"I ain't going with you," he said.

Ross grabbed his shoulder, and Everett hit the big man so hard on the side of the head it staggered him. "But as he swung he broke the straps on his wooden leg, and his leg come off, inside his pants leg," Carlos said.

Everett had been a boxer, too, on the *Iowa,* but he couldn't fight Ross in a stand-up fight teetering around on just one leg. So he lunged forward, wrapped his arms around Ross and dragged him down.

It was a fair fight in the dirt. With Ross on top of him, Everett locked one ironlike arm around the chief's neck and started jabbing him in the face with his free hand. Ross fought back, punching, and you could hear the fists landing like drumbeats on rib cages and heads, but Everett was choking Ross blue as he pounded his face.

Carlos and Red watched.

"As a family," Carlos said, "we don't respond well to being run over."

But fearing that Everett would kill the chief, or that Ross would blow a hole in their brother, Carlos and Red wrenched the men apart and the chief wheeled away, holding his throat. Carlos and Red stuffed Everett and his dangling leg into the back of Ross's car. Not even Ross could shoot a man in back of his own cruiser and claim self-defense. Ross had no choice but to drive Everett to jail. Carlos and Red followed in their car, just in case.

Ross was too embarrassed to bring serious charges against a one-legged man who whipped him in the dirt. Word got out anyway, as it always does, and people snickered.

Everett's house burned down not long after that, under suspicious circumstances. He and his wife split up, and he just wandered, rootless, on that wooden leg. His magic, good and bad, leaked out of him, and he died of a massive heart attack as a young man.

It would be easy to say that, after his whipping, Ross picked on my family for no reason, but that would be untrue. My people always gave him reason. Police turned their cars around in the yard, on the chance they might catch them doing something illegal. "He took Roy to jail for a gallon of cold water, 'cause it looked like moonshine," Carlos said, but conceded that any other time, it probably would have been. If Bob tried to be Bob, if he tried to hitch up his wagon and take a spin around the village drunk, Ross sent his men with guns. You can shoot a man for a lot of things, but should never even think about shooting a man for driving horses under the influence.

"When someone is arrested," Ross told the Exchange Club, "you usually make at least five enemies: the individual himself, his relatives, and his close personal friends." But an officer of the law, he said, must treat everyone the same. "You can't treat your fellow man like you're a bulldozer. Give him a fair shake, and then you've got nothing to be afraid of, and nothing to be ashamed of."

All you had to do to earn his benevolence was to say "sir." But it is funny, how that little word sticks like a fishhook in some men's throats. Bobby and his sons did not say "sir."

Long before my mother made her first walk to retrieve my father, Velma walked to fetch her men.

It is hard to truly capture the dignity of that little woman, her home-made dresses half covered by an apron, her face and shame shielded by her bonnet, change purse in her hands with just enough money to get Bob out. She stood in front of Ross's desk because she was never asked to sit. He lounged in his chair, treelike legs across his desk, to show Velma the bottoms of his shoes. He stood up when ladies from the East Side approached, but he never stood for Velma.

He harangued her as if it was she, and not Bob, who had gotten drunk and acted a fool. One day he went too far, got too mean, and she told him, her voice a squeak, to go to hell.

"DO YOU KNOW WHO I AM?" he roared.

Nobody talked back to Ross.

"I'M ROSS TIPTON."

He came to his feet then, so he could look down on her.

"Do you know who I am?" she said, her little voice trembling.

"WHO?" he said, in contempt.

"I am Velma Bragg."

She stood there shaking till he dismissed her.

He despised the drunkenness most of all, though he went home after locking them up and drank from gallons of whiskey left as tribute by whiskey runners outside his door. Even though they worked in the mill, the Bragg clan had everything he did not. Their women were beautiful and their lives, while certainly not rich, dripped with excesses. Their cars smoked but gleamed, and they lived in mill houses but wore neckties. Worse, they denied him things that were rightfully his. He could not make them afraid of him.

My father saw it as a game, a chance to dance with the devil in his own backyard. In the mid- to late 1950s, he engaged in a period of self-destructiveness that could have, at any drunken moment, left him cold on a slab. The infractions blurred together, but my mother remembers how he banged through the house, lunging for the back door, gleeful, as Ross rolled up in the yard. It was like hide-and-seek to him. He would see Ross pull in behind him at night, and he would slam his foot on the gas and speed away, then turn off his lights and race blind down the streets. As soon as he was beyond the glow of Ross's headlights he would zigzag through side streets, pound down a dirt alley or back his car into a stranger's driveway, kill his engine and sit, heart pounding, the orange glow of a cigarette bobbing in time.

It was foolish for any man, especially a married man with sons, but it was who he was. I guess it made him feel alive. I guess Ross was his wire.

"He'd always say, 'I outsmarted Ross,' as he come in the door," my mother said.

It wasn't like it is now, when the cars could hem you in. There was no other car in Jacksonville, especially on days there was a sewer emergency, so police had to run a man to ground to take him in. Ross would always find him, sooner or later, as he did that day he rolled up to the house where my father, mother and grandfather were working on the roof. He fired his invisible bullet, then walked to the ladder, and waited.

"He was always telling everybody how sorry Charles was, how

somebody ought to take him out in the woods and beat him to death," said Jack Andrews. Sometimes, when my father was drunk or fighting or sometimes doing nothing at all, Ross would walk up, moving light and quiet for a big man, and crook his finger. My father would run if he could and fight if he was hemmed in, but Ross would just snatch him off the ground, bang him against the side of a car, then carry him like a child to jail.

"Ross had a big belly, but was fast and he knew how to use his fists, and Charles just didn't have no chance," Jack said. "He'd have made two of your daddy."

He never beat or whipped him when he was in custody.

He never starved him.

He just put him in chains, in plain view.

"Ross wanted to own him," Jack said. "What it was, he had to break you. He hated disobedience. If you didn't cower down, didn't bow, he wasn't satisfied. Charles wouldn't. It wasn't enough that he put you in jail, or on the work crew. He had to break your spirit, and he couldn't break Charles."

One day, when my father was free, Ross saw my mother in town.

"How's your man?" he asked.

"He's working, doing good," she said.

"Well, I know he don't treat y'all right," he said.

He tipped his hat.

"You call me if there's anything I can do."

It stopped being fun after a while.

He and Jack liked to string trotlines then in the Coosa, up near the little town of Ohatchee. They would take Purex jugs and nylon cord, and bait the lines with whatever foul-smelling meat they had. The next day they would pull them in, and there might be crappie or catfish, always something. One day the lines were gone. Close by, they noticed varmint traps. A man named Johnson, a good friend of Ross's, was the only trapper they knew.

Johnson sold fur to department store buyers, and supplied fish to Ross in return for occasional favors. "No matter what he ever got into,

Ross took care of it," Jack said. Johnson was gray-haired, crew-cut and stocky, and had a reputation for smiling in a man's face, "and popping a knife in you," Jack said.

"Well, we went to his house, me and Charles, and we'd both been drinking," Jack said, "a little bit."

They found Johnson on the couch.

"What you want?" he said.

"You know anything about that trotline?" my father asked.

"I know about lots of trotlines," he said, and laughed.

"Well this'un was ours," my father said.

The man's smile faded, but he didn't move, just lay there.

"We saw your traps, right close by," my father said.

Johnson ignored him, like he wasn't there.

He was so unconcerned, he looked like he might take a nap.

"You gonna just lay there," my father said, "or do I have to pick you up to knock you down?"

Johnson jumped to his feet as my father clubbed down with his fist. There was a crack, and the man crumpled to the floor, holding his face. My father had on a pair of pointy-toed cowboy boots, and drew back his leg, to kick the man in the head.

"Whoa," Jack said, and grabbed him, and half carried him out the door.

"What you gonna do, stomp him to death?" Jack said.

"Yeah," my father said.

His face was bright red, twisted and ugly, but he let Jack push him into the car. In his mind, Jack said, my father could see those fish sizzling in Ross Tipton's kitchen.

My father knew Ross was untouchable. The best he could do was knock the hell out of his friends.

Ross got serious, then. There are two definitions of wrongdoing in my hometown, and they have nothing to do with felony or misdemeanor. All that really matters is whether your crime required you to be sent off, or do your time at home. You could be sent off for stealing a car radio, and not sent off for opening up a man's belly in the parking lot with a hawkbill roofing knife. If you were not sent off, you did your time in the city jail, so your momma could come see you. But if you were sent off, you went to county, or to an institution. Back then, it was at the police chief's discretion where you did your time, and it was then, around '59, Ross sent my father off.

It was just a few months, for driving drunk, but it was a different jail. In county, the junkies screamed all night, peed on the floor and toted shivs made from melted pocket combs rubbed against the floor until they were needle-sharp and hard as bone. He would lay in his bunk and hear men's teeth clack from the violent DTs, see them rock back and forth when the truth was he could have used a drink himself. Whiskey runners in overalls and dope peddlers in pointy shoes stared at each other, white and black, through the cells. But my father was a model prisoner, and worked his way up to trusty. He moved through the jail without chains, pushing a mop, emptying trash. He only had a few weeks left to serve when he escaped, and no one knew why he took the keys when he did, except to stick his thumb in the eye of the men who put him in a cage.

Later, free again, he and Jack sat in his car at Germania Springs, listening to the radio and smoking cigarettes, as my father planned the destruction of the chief of police.

He laid out a simple plan. He and Jack would put in a call to the dispatcher, late at night, and say that two delinquents were throwing trash, breaking beer bottles and raising cain at Germania Springs. Ross used prisoners to keep the park clean—it was his pet project— and would be livid. He would rush over alone, because Ross wouldn't need help with delinquents. "We'll lay for him with baseball bats," my father said. As Ross stepped out of the car they would smack his head and break his legs, to bring him down, break his gun arm, and beat him to death.

Jack just looked at my father's dark silhouette.

"We can't," Jack said.

"Why not?" my father said.

" 'Cause they'll put us in the electric chair," Jack said.

"I don't care," my father said. "I intend to kill the son of a bitch."

It is not unusual here, for men to get drunk and talk about killing. If you're not talking about women, you must be talking about killing somebody. Jack spent a big part of the night talking my father out of his revenge, reminding him what he had to live for. He was pretty sure Ross would be hard to kill, would have shot my father or beat him to death or put him in prison forever. It was crazy. My father should have been home with his wife and babies, not out with Jack plotting the death of a chief of police, on a school night.

Jack talked all night.

The electric chair didn't scare my father, but life in prison did.

Jack talked on that, on the eternity of it.

He told him it was a long way to the prison at Atmore, down on the Florida line. Poor people, sometimes, didn't have a way, couldn't afford the gas.

"You won't never see Margaret again," he told my father.

Men are forgotten, he said, so far south.

"Oh hell yeah, he'd of done it," Jack said, thinking back. "Your daddy wasn't afraid to die."

But he did not want to disappear.

M Y FATHER WAS ALREADY WAKING with the shakes when I was born. He never stopped hating Ross, but as his life dwindled it wasn't much of a contest. People who knew my father still blame Ross for quickening his end, and I guess I do, too. But the truth is he never broke my father down. The whiskey and TB did that. It is a hell of a way to win.

As his career as chief neared its end, District Attorney Bob Field was finishing an investigation into Ross's dealings, prompted by complaints from private citizens who served on grand juries, and by police officers and ex-officers who felt "the system may be breaking down."

Field said the major shortcoming in Jacksonville seemed to be the disposition of cases made by police officials outside the authority of the court, and, while it was found that Tipton had signed judges' names to docket sheets and warrants and established the amount of fines on his own authority, he felt there was no criminal intent. He said, though, Jacksonville was the only police department he knew of that had no systematic way to keep up with evidence. People in the village laughed. Evidence was what Ross said it was.

Ross Tipton was chief until he was sixty-eight years old. When he retired, on June 17, 1981, the State of Alabama had Ross Tipton Day. People wrote to the *Jacksonville News* to applaud him, to thank him for the money he gave to hardship cases, food to hungry dogs, and the justice he meted out to men who thanked him for sending them to prison. Faye Pritchett-Renfroe, of Tenth Avenue, wrote: "Thank you for the many fines you paid out of your own pocket on Monday morning so a father or husband could go to his job after squandering his family's grocery money on booze, for the clothes and food you purchased for less fortunate, for the care given to the habitual drunks of our town, and for looking the other way when young people were arrested for minor things, for taking children fishing, and thank you for having been our friend. It is my family's wish that your retirement will bring you joy and contentment, and may you know the peace of the Lord."

In the years my father dwindled, Jack still had occasional run-ins with Ross. He was married then, working third shift at the mill. He tried to stretch a dollar where he could, and was using old tags on his car, hoping no one would notice. Ross did. He told Jack not to move the car out of his yard till he bought tags. Jack told Ross if he couldn't drive he couldn't work. "I got two babies got to be fed," he said. Ross told him he would have to walk. But later, he sent word to Jack that he guessed it would be all right to drive the car to work. "That's what I mean, about the two sides of Ross," Jack said. "There was evil, and something else. Once he had power over you, he was happy."

I HAD JUST ONE criminal encounter with Ross Tipton, if you
don't count the ones I committed behind the wheel. It was a weekday in summer and I was about eight years old. I walked to Germania
Springs, where my father once plotted to kill Ross Tipton, and
amused myself. I swung on a swing set and bounced rocks against a
tree till I was hot enough to wade in the cold stream. I was still might-
ily bored, so I found some chert rocks the size of cantaloupes, and
started a new dam.

"What you doin', boy?" a big voice said.

I looked up to see the biggest man I had ever seen above me on the
bank. He had on a white shirt and black pants with a yellow stripe running down each leg, and a big black gun belt. I had seen him a hundred times, but he had never spoken to me.

"You can't dam that water up," he said.

"I didn't know," I said.

"Well, now you do," he said.

There were no cars in the parking lot, so he must have wondered
how I got there.

"Where you live, boy?" he asked.

I pointed across Roy Webb Road to Ava's little house.

Everyone knew we lived there when we ran from my father.

"You're Charles Bragg's boy?" he asked.

"Yes sir," I said.

He did not say anything mean, did not say anything about him at
all.

"You tear that dam up, and fish them rocks out," he ordered.

"Yes sir," I said.

He turned and walked to his cruiser, an old man in thick glasses
walking soft on tender diabetic feet, but I was still scared to death. I
fished out a rock or two, but as soon as he was gone I was running
wide-open, stopping just long enough to check both ways on the

blacktop before springing across, tearing through the yard, jerking open the screen door and stumbling into the hot little house.

"Ross Tipton's gonna put me in jail," I shouted.

My mother told me to stop playing folly, to go outside and play. But she told me not to go to the spring again, for a while. I hid in the bushes and watched the police cars circle in the gravel lot. After a few days, I figured I was safe, that they had forgotten my crimes. But now that I know my father better, now that I know Ross, I know I finally let him win, after all this time.

He got one of us to call him "sir."

The Boy

THE BOY STOOD at my side in a black tuxedo, holding the ring. He was grinning, grinning. I thought his head would pop off, from grinning like that.

I had been single twenty years, when the woman's middle boy walked his lovely mother down the aisle. It took guts, for that boy to do that. I guess it took guts for both of them.

Later, a rhythm and blues band played into the night on the roof of the Peabody Hotel, the big river pushing by, immense and silent in the dark. The boy danced until the last bass note fell on the floor, his shirt-tail out, his face covered in sweat. He did the electric slide and the funky chicken and probably the boogaloo, and of all the things that happened that night nothing impressed the old people more than that boy, dancing like he did. I don't know what animated him that night, but if he was worried about me, about how he fit into all this, it didn't show a lick. He just tore it up on that shaky ground, and figured it would all be all right in time.

The script for the nuptial had me coming down at the last minute, just before the bride.

The man holding the stopwatch was a competent, pushy if not imperious friend named Dana Rosengard.

I came down from my room a few minutes early.

"It's not time for you," he said. "Go away."

I turned and walked back into the elevator.

I could run for it now.

No one could say I had not given a good-faith effort.

One of my best friends, Chris Smith, watched it happen.

"You sent him away?" he said, incredulous. "You had him here, and you sent him away?"

But I came back.

And now I stood there, watching that boy throw down to "Mustang Sally."

In the din, in that whirl of friends and relatives, I remembered my last year in the wild. I washed my hair and my laundry in dishwashing detergent, and both got squeaky, lemony clean. I never wore an ironed shirt or even wished I had one. I still lived in hotels, mostly. I spent some nights in my mother's cabin in the foothills, some nights in a house near Mobile Bay, some nights with friends in Tuscaloosa who had a magic refrigerator filled with limitless pie. I left clothes scattered 'round so I could travel light, and my mail piled waist-high. There was nothing in it that could not wait, even bills. I shot water moccasins with a .22 pistol for relaxation, wrote some words, waded a sparkling river in Montana, made some good money in Miami and still spent a good bit of time walking in New Orleans, till the water washed so much of it away. Then I was caught, and the wild was in my mind.

This year, we added a new laundry room. I got a flu shot. I put the silver car, the one like James Dean had, up for sale.

They took a million photographs the night of the wedding.

Me, I have never taken pictures. I just figured I would remember for as long as I can, and then when I am old and lost, I will not have to sit at the county home, a photo album on my trembling knees, and wonder who all those people are.

But I would like a picture of that boy dancing. Even if I forget his name, I think it would make me happy to look at it.

"Whose boy is that?" some codger will ask me.

"I ain't sure," I will answer, "but look at him go."

CHAPTER THIRTEEN

Dallas

———

MY FATHER'S LUCK was running out in '62, '63.
He might have been snuffed out in the day-to-day violence of his time, but Jack believes God protected my
father, for one last chance to be with my mother, to be with us.

"I knew a man in Atlanta who sold pistols cheap, Saturday night
specials, and I would go over to Atlanta and get some and sell 'em
from the trunk of my car at the Spur service station I was running in
Anniston," he said. "Well, one day me and your daddy was comin'
back from Atlanta with some pistols. I had that '56 Chevrolet, brown
and bronze—your daddy loved that car. Well, it started snowing, and
there wasn't but one way to get to Atlanta then, one good way, and that
was on ol' 78. And it was a dangerous road, and the more we drove the
harder it snowed, and there wasn't nobody on the road but us. I guess
the rest of the people had more sense. Well, you couldn't see nothin',
and I told Charles, 'I hope this road don't freeze over,' but it did. We
topped this hill, blind, and here come a eighteen-wheeler off the top
of that mountain. I cut the wheel to miss him, and it was like we was
in slow motion, as that car began to skid to the edge of the road, to
the drop-off down the side of that mountain. 'Hang on,' I said. 'Here
we go.'

"I come to, and saw we'd rolled. The first thing I said was, 'Charles, you all right?' And he told me he was. 'Don't kick that door open, Jack, 'cause I got a door open over here,' and we crawled out, it just snowin' like hell. I looked at your daddy and said, 'We're gonna freeze to death,' but he just smiled. Well, we climbed back up to the road, and that's when I heard a car comin'. It was a Chevrolet, black, and there was this old man in there with a hat pulled low over his face, this wide-brimmed hat like they used to wear, and I guess he might have been ninety years old. He said, 'Where you need to go?' and I told him we needed to get to Oxford, and he said, 'I'll take you there.' He had on dark clothes, and that black hat, and I wondered all the way home what that old man was doing out there by himself on that dangerous road. But he drove us home on them slick roads, and let us out, and I never did even get his name.

"When he pulled away I told Charles, 'Charles, I believe that was an angel.' He just smiled again. 'You do?' he said. 'I do,' I said. But your daddy didn't believe in angels, I don't believe. But you know, the Bible says you don't have to pray to God to send angels, 'for you will entertain angels unaware.' "

It was about that time he took us to Texas.

It was '63. My father came home one night, sober, and said, "Margaret, how would you like to go to Dallas?" The brothers had found long-term work in Dallas at a big auto body shop. It was life-changing money, and it seemed like the whole Bragg family was planning to move out there overnight. My mother stared at the floor. He was asking her to leave home, leave her sisters and lovelorn mother, to follow a man who could self-destruct anytime, who might choose not to go to work any day, or pop the top on a single, sociable beer, and stay drunk a year. But he leaned across the table and took her hand, and told her this was their fresh start, their second chance in a place free and clear of accusing kinfolks and the persecutions of the law, in a big city where no one knew your history or cared. He said he had just used up this place, just wore out this little town, where he couldn't drive to the store for a pack of cigarettes without Ross asking him to walk a straight line, and couldn't go a mile without his junk car breaking down at an intersection, shaming him. He promised her a lot that night, promised to work steady and make a living they could be proud of, promised not to drink in the house in front of her and the children, or drink so much or so often. But he had promised her a lot before. He stayed sober for several days after that, to show her he was serious, to prove to her she could trust him this time, and every night he begged her to go with him, and start over. She finally gave in, but the day they left she got so nervous she dressed the baby, Mark, in new clothes, picked up her suitcase, walked out and left him on the bed.

"They was hurryin' me," she said, the kinfolks swirling around, fussing, crying, saying goodbyes. Bot Wall was giving her and her boys a ride to the bus station in Anniston, but he was bad to let his car run out of gas on the way to anywhere, so they had to build time into the trip for that. "Well, I got Sam in the car, and you, and then I got in and said, 'Let's go.' And Granny Bragg stuck her head in the window and said, 'Margaret, honey, are you not gonna take the baby?' "

We rode a bus halfway across the country, on faith. Sam was seven, I was four, and Mark was one, and I would stare for hours out the window at the swamps and rice fields and piney woods, at the vast, tea-colored ocean I now know was Lake Pontchartrain, at cattle without end and the oil wells that looked like iron dinosaurs. I would watch until I couldn't keep my eyes open, then crawl to the floor and sleep under my mother's feet. It was just a two-day trip on that lumbering bus, but it seemed like a great journey, some vast expedition, before I heard the bus driver announce "Dallas, Texas," and we stepped out onto the hot asphalt. My mother wondered, every mile, if he would come apart before she even got there, if he would have forgotten us. He did things like that. But there he was in that vast parking lot, waving.

Then, the most amazing thing happened.

He kept his promises.

We lived in a house of our own, a little white wood bungalow with big porches and porch swings, and at three-thirty in the afternoon, every day, we would hear the tinkling music of an ice cream truck coming closer, closer. We had never seen an ice cream truck. My mother had a bottomless change purse, full of silver, and she handed out dimes to my brother and my cousins, and led me by the hand to the cut-out door at the side of the truck and said, just like we were somebody, "Two ice cream sandwiches, please." I would eat all of mine as fast as was possible, and she would give me the bottom half of hers.

I thought I had stepped through some magic window. One day she was dragging me on a cotton sack, pulling all day for a dollar and change, and the next day we were sitting on a porch step eating ice cream.

"You remember the ice cream truck?" she asked me, forty-two years later.

I nodded.

"The other kids sat and ate their ice cream there, from all up and down the street, because we had the best steps, big, wide steps," she said. They left their wrappers on the steps as they ran off with Sam to play. I would help her pick them up when they left, and if there was chocolate left on them, and she wasn't looking, I licked it off. She caught me once and told me never to do it again, because it was plain nasty, but I was four, and it was chocolate, and you know how that is.

It seemed like all the yards were dressed up for a party, but now I know it was just an election summer in Texas. Campaign posters in red, white and blue seemed to blanket every lawn, most of them for Governor John Connally, who would take a convertible ride here with President John F. Kennedy in the coming fall.

I remember our time there in specks. I remember walking between them at the Dallas Zoo, her toting my little brother, and Sam running around and around in circles, forgetting for once in his life to be a serious boy, because he just glimpsed a live elephant through a fence. I remember seeing the monkeys, what kind of monkey I will never know, only that they smelled like something I won't even say and really did fling their poo. I remember the baboons, or maybe monkeys, that for some reason did not have any hair whatsoever on their incandescent behinds, and how that made my mother go, "Oh. Lord," and avert her eyes. For some reason I can still see my father's clothes in my mind, his short-sleeved shirt with little palm trees on it, and dark pants, cinched high at the waist. He had always gone spiffy. But we were all spiffy now. I remember staring at some big cat through a forest of legs, and reaching a hand up to my father. He did not gently scoop me up but just reached down and grabbed my arm between the wrist and elbow and, because he was so strong, dead-lifted me, dangling, up to his shoulders. He knew I wouldn't break, or squeal. I was his.

He went to work every morning, early. He walked, because the shop was just a few blocks away, and if I had been older I would have marveled at that. In a car culture, you didn't walk much further than the mailbox. It humbles a man, to walk to work.

On Friday, every Friday for two solid months, he cashed his check and gave my mother money, enough money to live on, to buy clothes, groceries and ice cream.

"We was fine," my mother said. "We was all just fine."

For her, it was all as mysterious as it was to me. She had never seen a city like that, had never even been to Birmingham. The grocery store, a supermarket, really, was almost across the street, and it was just all so easy, somehow, compared to what she was used to.

Mostly she remembers the beef, the slabs and slabs of red beef, and we ate it all the time, whenever we wanted. We had steak and biscuits and gravy for breakfast. Velma came for a long visit, and for supper there was Velma's giant meat loaves, and short ribs with potatoes and onions, and homemade hamburgers with hot Spanish onions and slabs of yellow commodity cheese. "I mean, it was some of the prettiest meat you ever seen," my mother said. "Me and Charles would go to the store together. We'd never done that before."

After supper, he and his brothers would go out in the backyard, or sit on the back steps and sip a beer. The rhythm of the bootleggers finally seemed to be broken here, and they drank a beer or two in the afternoons and quit, unless it was the weekend, when it might be a beer or six. But it was never the spectacle it was before, never the painful, grinding drunks that made her want to go find a hole and slip down in it.

"He did good then," she said. "He did real good."

I wish I could remember more.

Sam explored the neighborhood, playing ball and hide-and-seek with the like-aged children until he discovered the home for old men down the street. They would sit in their chairs in the sun, and yarn. Once Sam discovered them, he spent all his time at the home, listening to stories, nodding his head, learning how to whittle or roll a cigarette or fill a pipe, "and at first I was worried about him, because I was afraid some of the old men was mental cases, but they wasn't, they was just old," and they loved the boy. He was in his true element, my brother, who has always been an old man trapped in new skin, and they would bring a chair for him, and a Coca-Cola, and from a distance he looked just like one of them, my mother said, but with shorter legs.

There was a Laundromat on the corner, but she still lugged the wet clothes home, to dry on the line. She never liked machine-dried clothes, because they smelled just like that, not like the breeze and the sun. He went with her to do the laundry, too, as if he had remembered why he wanted to be with her, with all of us, and wanted to be with us again. He had never lived in a big city either, but he laughed at her when she saw things she didn't understand, like pigeons. She had never seen uppity city birds before, birds safe from shotgun reprisals, and the first time she heard them squabbling she panicked. "I was afraid it was somebody beatin' on them old people, it sounded so awful," she said. "But your daddy took me by the hand and led me over to the window, and showed me all the pigeons, making racket on the roof—and he didn't laugh at me. Why, I'd never seen pigeons. I didn't know they made the awfulest, unnatural sounds." She never did think much of pigeons after that.

When it ended, after two months, it ended over a $54 welfare check.

"Maybe I should have had more faith," she said.

This was a wonderful dream, this life, but it couldn't last, it couldn't be that real. She waited for the inevitable, for the night he didn't come home, for the morning he just rolled over and told her to call his boss and tell him he was sick. She waited for two months, and there is a chance she might have waited forever, or maybe quit waiting, and believed in him. But there was a crisis at home that made her have to choose too soon.

All she had to live on in much of her life with him was money she made picking cotton, taking in ironing, and cleaning people's houses, never enough to feed and clothe three boys. But she got $18 apiece for us in welfare, $54 for the three of us, and that was enough. But the welfare was writing letters to her at her mother's house, asking about her status.

If she was with her husband in Texas, and he was working, then they would stop the check. You cannot explain to a bureaucracy the realities of living, that, yes, she was in Texas now, and yes, he was working now, but that it could all come apart with one popping top or breaking seal. In late July, the welfare woman came to Ava's house.

"Where is she?" she asked Ava.

"She's out," Ava said.

"Out where?"

"In Texas," Ava said.

"I walked the floors then, hon," my mother told me. "I walked them over and over again, day after day." On top of it, there was simple guilt. Ava had never lost a daughter to such distance before, and wrote her every day, begging her to come home. Other kin did, too, not believing the fairy tales she fed them about supermarkets full of cheap beef, and door-to-door ice cream sandwiches. They pleaded with her to come home, these kindhearted people who always took her back when things went bad with her man. They did not trust him to do right for long, and in the end, she decided she did not trust him to, either.

She told him she was going home, and she thinks, although she hates to, that she saw something break in him a little then. "I didn't know what to do," she said, so she tried to do what she believed was the safest thing for her boys.

At first he was mad, but he didn't hurt her, or even yell.

He begged.

"Please, give it a while longer," he said, but she wasn't leaving because he had disappointed her this time. She was leaving because of all the times before, and he just couldn't get his mind around that.

"We was happy," she told him, "and you done good. But I got to go home."

"I won't send you home," he said. "I won't get you no ticket."

So she wrote her mother and had her send the check, and she cashed it at the convenient grocery and bought three tickets on a bus for home.

The night before we left he begged her again to stay, and bought her a giant bouquet of flowers. He bought them, for the first time.

The next morning she lay in the bed and weighed two months of happiness against eight years of everything else, and walked to the phone and called a taxi.

Fifty-four dollars, guaranteed.

But first, she put her flowers in the refrigerator, because she thought they might live a little bit longer there. "I hated to think of 'em dying.

"He was sittin' on the banister on the porch when we left," she said. "He looked whipped."

He found a girlfriend in Texas, not long after we left. My mother knew because years later, as Velma showed her some family pictures, she came upon the woman's picture and hid it, quick, under her apron—just not quick enough. He told people he planned to start over, maybe even start a new family out there, and he should have.

He should have stayed in Texas. He should have built a good, clean life with that new woman and had a whole new round of boys, and lived happy in the Lone Star State.

But after a while he just followed my mother home.

The Boy

———·+·———

IT WAS LIKE she drove a ten-penny nail through the last feeble, halting heartbeat of the man I was.

"Can you pick the boy up from school?" the woman asked.

At forty-six, I drove car pool.

At first I was terrified I would run over half a dozen nut-job children on the way to get him, because when the bell rang they exploded from doors as if propelled by a cannon. They all wore the same damn clothes and all looked alike to me, at least at first, and what if I got the wrong one? I was always afraid I would be late, or he would perish from the elements, or get in a car with a stranger, even stranger than me.

But I always snagged him clean, and we headed for the Sonic, for his tribute. The boy, the woman instructed me, was to have only a small drink, maybe a slush of some kind, so he would not "ruin his dinner."

It was a surreal thing, to hear that, like she was emanating from the speaker of a black-and-white television from 1963.

But the best thing to do, I had learned the hard way, was make like some bobble-head doll.

Few men get in trouble when they nod.

I know the boy liked it, when I showed up. I watched for him in the rearview mirror, and when he saw it was me he started to grin.

"Hi, Ricky," he always said.

Nobody but him and my momma get to call me that.

"Let's get us a treat," I always said.

The Sonic was just around the corner.

"What do you want?" I always asked the boy, as I punched the magic sugar button and the voice on the other end said hello, and he dutifully gave his modest order, like the good boy he was.

One day, about nine months into our time together, I punched, waited.

Three seconds is a lifetime, at the red button.

"May I help you?" the voice said.

"I would like a forty-four-ounce root beer float with vanilla ice cream, and a corn dog," the boy said.

I just looked at him.

"Please?" he said.

"Your momma won't let you," I said.

"Well," he said, looking around the truck, "is she here?"

I thought a minute about that.

"Well okay," I said.

Over time we were found out—I would learn that the boy had a perverse need to confess all his sins to his mother—and she said I had to be responsible, said her son had not inherited a stepfather, but a coconspirator.

I told her I would do better.

Not long after that, another driver almost hit us as we drove through town. People in Memphis all drive like God is on their side.

"I know what Rick would say," he said, from the backseat.

"What?" she asked.

"He would say, 'What the hell does that damn fool think he's doing?' "

Then he just grinned, all proud of himself.

She stared into me.

"What?" I said.

"Don't 'What' me," she said.

I knew I needed some vitriol here, some passion, to get out of this.

"Shame on you," I said to the boy. "Just because you hear me say things, that doesn't mean you can say them. If I was a smoker, you couldn't smoke. If I was a drinker, you couldn't drink. You're a little boy. You are not me. You are not me."

He beamed.

He had root beer residue on his cheeks.

He had stains on his school clothes I did not want to think about.

His halo hung lopsided on his head.

And in mid-rant I started to laugh, not at the boy in front of me, but at the boy I was such a long time ago.

I was five, maybe, playing on the porch with a few plastic army men. Suddenly, the yard was full of cows. A neighbor's Herefords had found a gap in the barbed wire and wandered into our garden.

"I ought to shoot them damn cows," my father said.

"Shoot them damn cows, Daddy," I said.

He laughed and my mother pretended to whip me. I ran and hid behind him, grinning at her from around one leg of his big-legged pants, the kind Ricky Ricardo wore. I never wondered then why that blue-collar man dressed so nice, like the invitation from his rich friends was lost in the mail. Anyway, it was the last time I ran to him in my life.

Instead of shooting the invading cows, he jumped to the dirt, found some rocks and let rip. He never missed, not once, till he caused a stampede.

In real time, I rolled my window down to feel the air on my face.

I found I could remember better, that way.

The woman and boy must have wondered where I went.

CHAPTER FOURTEEN

Ride

————•‡•————

MY MOTHER TOOK HIM BACK when he came home in
summer of '65, but whatever magic there was in the air in
Texas did not blow this far east. It would be our last year, a
nightmare year. But at least, if we all perished, we would be buried like
sultans.

My mother took out a burial policy on me, Sam, and the baby boy
Mark. It cost a dollar a month, and would have paid three hundred
dollars if one of us had died. At the first of the month, a man named
Dee Roper knocked on the door, took an envelope from my mother's
hand, wrote out a receipt, and chatted long enough to be civil. Sometimes my father was there, sitting at the table in the middle of the day,
a thin line of puckered scars showing through his undershirt at the
bridge of his shoulders, a glass of whiskey in his hand. My mother
called it "shell-shot," and I think she meant shrapnel. "You got to be
patient with that boy, because he's been through something you and
me can't even imagine," Dee Roper told her, and she told him, politely,
yes, sir, she would be. I was five years old, sick and puny and almost
translucent. I remember being ill, but did not remember it as so bad,
or often. The croup and flu settled in for weeks and months. The
worst was whooping cough, pertussis. My grandmothers treated me
with white whiskey mixed with crushed peppermint, rubbed my chest

with salve, and I still couldn't breathe. There was only one place I could catch my breath, in the wind rushing through the window of my father's doomed, raggedy cars.

"You won't drink with the boy in the car?" my mother admonished him, every time.

Even that much could have set him off.

"I won't," he lied.

My mother remembers only letting me go once or twice. As I remember, we rode around the world. My father would set me in the front seat, against the passenger-side window, and we would motor. We would cross over into west Georgia on the mountain roads, the car radio blaring bluegrass and Texas Swing. It seemed like there were always five beer bottles—always five—rolling and clinking in the back floorboard, and one last, brown bottle dangling from the fingers of his right hand. He drove, always, with the wrist of his left hand draped across the steering wheel of the heaps he would ride to death, and jump from the saddle as they collapsed underneath, like an Indian off a dying horse. I would roll down the window—all the way if it was summer, halfway when it was cool—and the wind would rush in and fill my nose and throat, till I was pacified. If he was four or five beers gone, he would let me thrust my head and shoulders out of the car and I would ride that way for miles, until my teeth began to click. Sometimes he held to the back of my pants, to keep me from falling to my death, but most of the time he would not.

I wasn't afraid of him yet, not all the time.

I didn't understand it all that much.

"You will feed the boy?" my mother always asked.

"Hell, yes," he would answer, mean, as if she thought he didn't have sense to do such a simple task. Then he would run into a gas station and hand me a pack of Golden Flake Cheese Curls and a big RC.

It was the only place I remember him talking to me. I guess he talked baby-talk to me when I was littler, but here he talked to me like I had some sense.

"What you read in school?" he asked.

"Dick and Jane and Spot an' 'em," I said.

He asked me if Spot was a girl dog or a boy dog.

I told him I didn't know. I remember it because he thought that was just funny as all get out. I think it was the first time I realized that drinking, before it killed you or at least sent you to hell, could make you happy.

He conducted slurred spelling bees, mile after dark mile. The head-lights would settle, just a second or two, on a road sign, and he would ask me to spell it as it vanished in the dark.

The towns and wide places in the road were easy.

"Spell 'Broomtown.'

"Spell 'Ringgold.'

"Spell 'New Moon.' "

The rivers were hard.

"Spell 'Tallapoosa.' "

The creeks were impossible.

"Spell 'Choccolocco.' "

He rattled across Ketchepedrakee, Enitachopco and Tallassee-hatchee.

We didn't even try.

I guess I should just be glad we didn't kill anybody we met on those narrow, one-lane and two-lane bridges, his headlights weaving from one guardrail to the next. I was good at spelling, in a car, anywhere. I hated math, because it was dull, and once you were behind, you were behind for life. I was behind on the second day of first grade, and have been behind ever since. But I could spell at fifty-five, sixty miles per hour, spell even on the wrong side of the road.

The police stopped us one night in Piedmont. I remember because the only part of the officer I could see was his flashlight beam, his belt and gun, and how he kept his hand on it, as he stood there. My father might have had a license but he didn't have it then, but it was a different time, when such laws were more like suggestions. He asked my father if he had been drinking, stabbing his flashlight beam at the bottles. All my life I have wondered why he didn't throw his empties out, instead of holding on to the evidence. "No," Daddy lied. "Them's old."

"Your daddy been drinking, boy?" he asked me.

"Un-uh," I said.

I wondered if they had little jails, for boys and midgets, or if we all went to the big jails. I had seen a television show where little children just slipped through the bars, and I told myself I was brave enough to try.

But he just let us go. They often did things like that. They would even help a drunk in his car, and tell him to drive straight home.

Sometimes we went just to get beer or bootleg whiskey, sometimes to pick up his paycheck at a body shop or garage, and sometimes to pick up his father, Bobby, and take him for a ride. They would listen to the radio—the old man liked Ernest Tubb—and either pass a pint bottle of homemade whiskey back and forth or sip from beers wrapped up to the neck in brown paper bags. One of my most enduring memories of my father is tied to that old man. We were driving through Piedmont, past the hillside cemetery that is so steep you wonder if they have to bury people standing up, and my grandfather Bobby was holding to a bottle half hidden by a popcorn bag.

"Don't turn that beer up, Daddy," my father said. "We're in town."

"I know how to drink a damn beer," Bobby said.

I lived a long time after that believing you could hide any sin in the Bible if you had a big enough brown paper bag. I wish they made them people-sized. I would carry one in my trunk, or sleep in one, just to be sure.

I was always glad when he dropped the old man off. This was our time, mine and my father's. In cold weather he would crack the glass, just a little, turn the heater on wide-open, and I would ride with my feet and legs warm and a drill-like sliver of frigid, beautiful air boring into my lungs.

"You got a girlfriend?" he asked.

"Yeah," I said.

"What's her name?" he asked.

"It's a secret," I said.

"Why?" he asked.

"She don't know she is."

He laughed and drank and drove.

He never took Sam or my baby brother Mark—he would have been more likely to be alone with a viper than a needy infant child. My two grandmothers, Ava and Velma, would keep them, or our aunts and uncles would. It may not make much sense, but I believe he left Sam at home because he believed my older brother could see into him, and disapproved. I think he didn't like to ride the roads with that disapproving gaze against the side of his face. Me, I betrayed them both, my mother and brother, for an RC cola.

He took me to the chicken fights, at least twice. I had seen chickens fight to the death in the backyard, so there was no horror or mystery in the cockfights. Like a lot of country boys, I had already begun to rate life on the kind of covering things had on them. Scales, on fish or snakes, didn't count for much, and feathers didn't count for much more. When told by my grandmother to "go get us a chicken," I would take the broom handle from behind the door and leap from the porch into the backyard. I would play God and choose the one I believed to be the tastiest, then run it down and whack it hard about the head or neck. Then, I would go play until the plucked and fried pieces reappeared with biscuits and gravy. To demur at death at a cockfight would have been hypocritical. I guess the supper birds didn't suffer, but if I had a choice of how I would go out, I would rather be a gamecock than a Sunday dinner.

He might not have wanted us at all, his boys, but he sure didn't want weak boys, boys with no guts. He took me, I believe, to see what kind of boy I would be. I never cried over a damn chicken in my life. He even let me ride his shoulders once, so I could see better. It is no wonder, surrounded by such spectacle, I didn't really notice the dollars that slipped through his hands, and what it all meant. He bet a piece of the rent on a speckled Dominicker, and let the rest of it ride on an orange and black game rooster. He spent milk and bread for a pint jar of clear whiskey, and the electric bill on a gallon can.

We would get home after the other boys had gone to bed. My mother sometimes worked the night shift at a truck stop, but if she was home she would be sitting up, or on the porch. I would crawl into the bed I shared with Sam and try to tell him what I had seen or heard, but he would tell me to be quiet and go to sleep, and I would lie awake for hours and listen for the train. The tracks ran right close by, and the train put me to sleep like a drug.

I didn't know, of course, how bad it was going to get. My brother Sam did understand, understood the levels of drunkenness, and could see ruination day coming closer.

My father lost all of us that year.

But he lost his oldest son first.

———·———

I T TAKES A SPECIAL KIND of man to stomach a dogfight. I grew up with hard men, but only my father was able to choke back enough of his finer nature to handle a dog in the pit, and I believe he could only do that drunk. It was a ferocious battle till one dog turned cur, and began to yelp for its life, as if it was begging the all-powerful circle of men to spare it, and pry the jaws off its torn throat or mangled leg. It was not supposed to be a fight to the death. Two dogs, pit bulls, mutts, others, would be loosed in a shallow pit or barn or squared-off place in the underbrush, and fight until one of the dogs tried to quit. The problem was, some dogs would not turn cur, and others would not stop savaging the dogs that did, so some would be so badly mangled by the time a fight was called that they died right there, or in the truck beds on the way home, or were put out of their misery with a pistol shot just outside the circle of lantern light or headlights that lit up the pit.

There was always a fight on the state line, because there was something about that invisible border that seemed to accept a stronger dose of meanness than other places. He always owned dogs, scarred, one-eared brutes that spent their wretched lives desperately jerking against a logging chain, till a night would come when he would hook a two-foot length of lead chain to their collars, and drag them off. They snapped at us but never bit at him that I could see, as if they recognized one of their kind. We never saw them again, so I guess he never won.

In the fall of '65, he opened the passenger door of his car and something wonderful sprang out.

He was a boxer, and he was the prettiest dog I had ever seen. He was mostly brown but with a touch of white on his chest and black around his face, and he had brown, intelligent eyes and a two-inch stump of a tail that was always in motion, not just wagging, but damn near vibrating. Even with that ridiculous tail, he looked dignified. His eyes had a natural squint, and that made him look like he was always thinking hard about something, though he was probably just thinking about what all dogs think about: biscuits. He was as tall as my baby brother was high, and when he was told to "stay" he did not so much stand as pose, his head high, like a show dog. He never growled, even when I tried to ride him around the yard, and he would chase us for fun. His muscles rippled under his coat and he was hard to the touch, and when he ran he bounced from the ground, like a hard rubber Super Ball.

From the second he leapt from the car, he was Sam's dog. There are no magical stories to tell of it. The dog did not drag my brother from quicksand with his teeth, or crawl home after being mauled by a bear to lead a rescue party to starving children. He was just a good dog, and my mother and I would sit on the front porch of the falling-down house we rented, and watch the boy and dog run through the cornfield across the road. When they were tired they lay together on that porch, the big dog on his back, paws in the air, as if dead.

"Crazy dog," Sam said.

Always that.

"Crazy ol' dog."

We never found out where my father got him. But people who know drinking, gambling men know that they bring home all kinds of trophies—worn gold wedding bands, cheap wristwatches, porch furniture, rusted bicycles, wrench and socket sets, suit coats, cowboy boots, used tires, car batteries, stereo speakers, car radios with the wires still hanging from the back, Saturday night specials with the three of the six chambers still loaded, leather jackets, dogs, but never cats. We figured he won him. It wouldn't have mattered to us if he stole him. He gave my serious brother a gift that made him laugh out loud.

"You can't fight that dog," my mother told my father.

"I ain't," he promised.

Like I said, he wasn't a magic dog. He didn't make everything all right. My father was mean to my mother, more and more, but for a while, maybe, we didn't notice it as much. My father's self-respect continued to peel, and finally he gave up on work altogether, living off the welfare check that my mother drew. He was living drunk, now. One night he staggered into the house and greeted my mother with a big smile. He was missing his front teeth. The thing she had loved about him most was his white, perfect teeth, and he had gotten them pulled, for meanness. He said it was because the teeth knocked loose in a long-ago wreck were bothering him, but the dentists had said there was no reason to pull them, that they could be saved. He had gotten drunk and had them pulled, and then followed her around that bleak house, smiling and smiling.

I was sick then, and had to stay inside with all that meanness. Sam and the dog ran free of it outside.

"What was that dog's name?" I asked my mother, four decades later.

"I don't know if it had a name," she said.

"How long did we have it?" I asked.

"Three days," she said.

At a gathering of other drinking men, an older man told my father he had seen the dog in our yard, and would give him two-to-one that his brindle pit bull could eat him alive. My daddy told him no, the dog was a pet. The man told him they would call it, quick, as soon as one dog turned cur. My daddy said no, the boxer was a lapdog. But the more he drank, the more reasonable it became. One afternoon, he loaded the dog into the car. My mother begged him, and Sam just sat outside on the steps, arms around his knees. He was not a crier, not then, not ever. He just sat there, till way after dark, waiting for his daddy to bring his dog back.

The next day, my father's car rumbled up in the driveway. He opened one of the rear doors and lifted the boxer from the backseat. The dog did not yelp or whimper, and must have been in shock. His guts had been opened up, and the skin around his neck and intelligent face was not just ripped, but ripped away. His dark eyes looked as hard as marbles, and his chest rose and fell in a jerking, ugly way. I wanted to pet him, but there was just so much blood, and no place to put my hands.

Sam had come running, and just froze there, and went white as bone. My mother tried to get in his way, to shield him, but he was a big boy then, and too old to be protected with an apron. She told me, later, how he looked, like he had been stabbed, and just didn't fall down.

"Just stood there, a'starin' and a'starin'," my mother said.

My father, hungover, listing a little, had not spoken.

"Why did you bring it home?" my mother asked, quietly.

He was not the kind of man you screamed at, even in times like these.

"I didn't know what to do with him," he confessed. If he had been sober, maybe he would have known not to bring it home.

Then something happened that never, ever had. My meek, gentle mother told my father to leave. She walked up to him, within range of his fists, and with her hands down at her sides, accepting of what might come, she looked him in his bloodshot eyes and ordered him away from her, from us. "Take the dog," she said, and instead of turning on her, in fury, he scooped it up in his arms, and left.

"I run him off," she said, and forty-one years after the fact, she still sounds a little surprised.

Sam went missing for a while after that, for a day or more. He hid in a tree.

"He was nine then. He remembers it better than you," my mother said.

I remember it. Boys remember dogs.

It never haunted me, not like it did him.

"Sam feels things more than you do," she said.

She was not being mean. She just knows her boys.

I don't know what happened to the dog. If my father's head had been clear, he would have just put him down, quick, with a hammer. He had done it before. Ours is a culture of cruelty, as to dogs. Runts are bashed against a tree. Strays are tied up in a sack and dropped off a bridge. I wouldn't do it, couldn't do it, but it was done. As it was, my father probably just rode around from bootlegger to bootlegger, seeking credit, and somewhere along the way the dog suffered and died, and was thrown off in the weeds.

She relented eventually and he came home, but she never forgave him for what he had done to her son. There is no patch for that.

His life had spiraled to nothing, taking us down with him. He was at a place where he was even willing to gamble his son's heart in that pit, and maybe he could come home with cash money in his pockets, and show those men and his own family that he was more than what he had become. Wasn't that worth the life of a dog? "He just needed something good to happen to him," she said, and the dog was the only currency he had left.

I had not realized, after all the hatefulness we endured in that time, how long that particular hurt lasted in my brother. We have buried, between us, fifty dogs since then. "But it stuck in him," my mother said. "If he thinks about it, even as old as he is now, he gets so mad he can't stand it. That's why he will not talk hardly at all about your daddy, because it makes him think of that dog, and what your daddy did to him."

One night, a lifetime later, she picked up the phone, and dialed seven numbers. It always starts with 435. If it wasn't for me, running off to join the circus all the time, she would never dial more than seven digits, and every one of them would start with 435.

"Sam?"

Seconds later, she hung up the phone, and called me.

"His name was Loco," she said.

———

THAT IS WHY I COULDN'T whitewash my father, because of that dog, and what it had done to the brother who spent so much of his life coming to rescue me from the side of the road. I stood a hundred times in a hated necktie, ineffectually holding the flashlight as his wrenches slipped and he gashed his knuckles on the fan blades of my junk cars, working for hours stooped over in black grease just to get me rolling again, to get me chasing something cleaner, easier. "Don't get dirty," he would hiss as I reached in under the hood to try to help. I have sometimes said that my older brother is who I want to be when I grow up, but that's a lie. He works too hard and lives too straight, for me. There have been times in my life when all I truly cared about could dance on the point of my pen, but not Sam. He feels what he feels all the time, and would rather stand in the dark and listen to his dogs trail a coon than carry on a conversation. He discarded our father more than three decades ago, just took him out with the trash, because of a dog whose name I could not recall.

There was more to it than that, of course, but the dog gave his anger a place to rest that was easier to remember than some of what happened to us then. It was the year of the great disappearing tricycle. Every word I wrote only brought me closer and closer to this point, and with every finished page I knew I was building him up only to have to tear him down again.

The night he left with the dog, she started saving dimes, nickels and pennies, for our escape.

"I loved him," she told me, and in all my life I had never heard her say those words.

It is why she ran away, and ran back.

"I might could have run forever, by myself," she said.

"But I couldn't run and carry y'all."

· I told her I guessed some people were not meant to be daddies, and she told me she guessed that might be right. He never sang a lullaby in his life. But one night, before we were free of him, he was precisely the kind of man we needed him to be, in precisely the right moment, and if I had more faith, or put more value on my own life, I would believe that everything he had done or been in his life had led him to that moment. I don't believe that. I just believe that, sometimes, you need dark men to do dark things.

———

WINTER IS A BLEAK TIME in the Mountain South, a gray, wet, messy time, without the dry snows of the north or clear sunshine of the Gulf Coast. It can be humid and warm on Tuesday and 16 degrees on Thursday morning, with ice forecast for Friday night. I have always hated winters here, not for the cold or the ice but the gray, the unrelenting drizzle and rain that can settle in for a week at a time, turn the ground to soup and plaster the leaves to the car windshields like wet toilet paper. It was in weather like that, that mess, that I got sick for the last time in the big, cold house in Spring Garden, where we lived after coming home from Texas.

The rides had stopped altogether. He rarely had money for gas anymore. Almost as if there really had been something medicinal in that open car window, my breathing got worse, and worse. My little brother Mark played on the floor as my mother perched day and night on the edge of the bed I shared with Sam, rubbing my chest, singing. She sat up all night, sometimes, just watching me, fingers on my chest, feeling it rise and fall. I believe that even if she had fallen asleep there in her straight-backed chair, she would have known if I had ceased to breathe, from the touch. One late night, the night before she was going to take me to the doctor in Piedmont, I took in a weak, ragged breath, and began to choke. Thick fluid, like left-out rubber cement, clogged my throat and nose and stopped my air, completely. My mother screamed, and lifted me from the bed like I was a baby. My father, who had already gone to bed, walked barefoot into the room and asked her what was wrong.

"We got to get him to the hospital," she said.

The car wasn't running. There was no phone in the old, creepy house, and never had been.

"You got to do something," she begged him.

I had begun to turn blue when he took me from her, ran with me to the kitchen, and laid me on the table. He grabbed a box of salt, and dumped a fistful of it into one hand. In my panic I had clenched my teeth, and I ground them together as he clawed at my mouth with his free hand, trying to pry them open. Finally, he balled up his fist, to knock them out, and I opened my mouth to scream, with no sound. He poured the salt down my throat, then clamped his hand hard over my mouth as I convulsed, jerking in his arms.

"You're killin' him," my mother told him, but he just pressed down harder. When he finally lifted his hand I vomited with such force that the mess clogging my throat exploded outward, and I could breathe.

He handed me, limp, to my mother.

"Here," was all he said.

He went back to bed.

She sat up with me all night, trying to rock me, big as I was, in a straight-backed chair.

We left him not long after that. If I had lived, or died, it was done. She was pregnant then, and lost the fourth son not long after that. I blamed him because he made her life so hard.

"But he saved your life," my mother told me.

I should have remembered it better.

"But he did," she said.

"He didn't seem real damn happy about it, did he?" I said.

In my mind, all those years, I thought he was trying to hurt me. Now, just as my brother never forgave him for his nature and what it cost, I know that if he had been any other kind of man, a gentler man, I would most certainly be dead. They would have huddled together over me, man and wife, watching me die in as ugly a way as you can, as my older brother ran a mile to a phone, to call an ambulance that would come too late.

The Boy

———

S O LET ME TELL YOU about my boy.

It tickles him when I say things that make his mother's head hurt, like the other day, when I noticed how tall he was. "Next thing you know," I told him, "you'll be running around with loose women and dancing the boogaloo."

"For Pete's sake," the woman said.

"He doesn't know what loose women are," I said.

"Yes I do," he said.

"No you don't," I said.

I looked at him.

"Do you?"

His mother wished herself someplace else.

That made us both happy.

He hates it when I hurt. I have arthritis in my busted-up knees and feet and I limp a lot, and one day a pain like broken glass in my joints gouged me and I sagged against the car. I felt his hand at my shoulder. "Are you all right?" he asked, and there was a fear in his face.

"I am fine," I lied.

I straightened up, and walked inside.

I don't want that boy to ever see me weak and broken-down. He thought I was ten feet tall and bulletproof when he first saw me, and I want it to always be that way. But it may be he already sees me as used-up, and is too gentle to say.

It is the first price you pay, for getting your boy so late in your life, but it is not the last.

The fact is that he was improving, as our first year slipped by and he turned eleven, becoming the boy I needed him to be. He would never cry from a carpet burn again, or because he needed a nap.

Or maybe the woman was right. He was just a little boy becoming a big boy.

I bought him a bow and arrow and taught him to shoot, and told him to never, never shoot me. My brother Sam shot me in the hand, and being shot with an arrow once in a lifetime ought to be about right. My niece bought him a BB gun, because boys need one, and it was worth any potential danger just to see the look on his mother's face.

I even let him shoot a .22 rifle at a tin can on my mother's farm. His arms would not quite reach the trigger and the front sight wobbled drunkenly, but when he pulled the trigger the can jumped in the air. I have only seen pure joy a few times in my life, and I saw it then. (I am pretty sure he closed his eyes when he fired, but I slapped him on the back anyway, and pronounced his new name to be Dead Eye Dick.)

At the pond, I taught him to cast with a Zebco 202, how to gently twitch the rod tip to make the rubber worm dance across the bottom, and he didn't know I was the worst fisherman who ever lived and I didn't tell him. But I got Sam to show him the fine points so the boy could actually catch fish.

Mark taught him card tricks when he was home. I showed him how to cheat at poker, how to hide jacks in the waistband of his jeans.

"You didn't really teach me," he said. "I just caught you."

I like to watch him live.

He walks funny, like his feet don't fit yet. But when we walk across a parking lot he never runs ahead or lags behind. He still walks with me.

He has long, artist's fingers, not little hands like mine. He has brown hair. I cut it once and did a good job, and cut a second time and made him look like Moe, from the Stooges. He is still a little upset about that.

He has his mother's eyes. His eyes are perfect. He can see a mile, more.

His teeth will be perfect, a million dollars from now.

We can't keep his fingernails cut, let alone clean. I tell him he looks like a can-can dancer with those long nails, but he doesn't know what that is either, so it's all right to say.

He couldn't whistle a lick at ten. But he learned and now he whistles all the time. Maybe by twelve, he will whistle in tune, and my headache will ease.

He still has trouble breathing, sometimes, from his allergies. In winter he has a chronic cough, deep in his lungs. I tell him he is the snottiest boy alive, to cover up what I really feel. I never believed I would hear a child cough, and hate it so much.

He forgets things. He forgets to close the bathroom door. I walked by once and saw him on the toilet, perfectly at ease.

"For God's sake," I said.

"What?" he said.

He forgets homework. He forgets to change his underwear.

The woman made him learn the piano, but his heart wasn't in it. He banged at it anyway, beat it like he was mad at it. I know it is wrong to hate a child while he is playing church music. God help me I did.

I waited for him, as he got older, to torture me with rap, or heavy metal, or plastic Top 40. But one day he heard Johnny Cash, and his life changed. I heard him in his room, singing "Get Rhythm" and "Folsom Prison Blues."

He sings well. His voice is deep, strong. He sings from the backseat. He sings to the dog. I stood in the kitchen recently and watched him sing as he walked around in the yard. It was one of the finer moments in my life.

We got him a guitar for Christmas, and a genuine Johnny Cash songbook. Someday we might see him in the Opry, but I don't know if even Johnny could play Nashville now. Those new guys, I told the boy, all look like they would run from a fistfight.

"All hat and no cow," I told the boy.

He nodded, like he knew what I meant.

He likes barbecue sandwiches, any gum that smells bad, and pie.

We play the pie game in the car. He asked me if I would rather have a million dollars, or pie. I tell him a million dollars. But it has to be something real good, to beat pie.

He does not like girls, yet.

"Why do they talk so fast?" he asked me. "I can't understand what they say."

"That's all right, boy," I said. "You won't be able to understand them when they talk slow, either."

He still loves his go-cart, but wants me to leave the silver car to him in my will.

He believed in Santa Claus until he was eleven. He says he stopped believing at ten, but we know better.

He loves my mother. I was afraid he would see her as something from the dark side of the moon, too, but he didn't. He says "yes ma'am," and she drops another biscuit in his mouth. I think of Sea World, when she does that.

He loves his mother more than anything, more than air.

He calls her "evil," and I call her "spiteful," and we snicker. But the planet ceases to move, when she really gets mean, the way mothers have to when a boy does wrong, like ignoring his homework for a big part of the sixth grade. She can still make him cry, but not much else does.

Sometimes I am obliged to side with her.

Sometimes I pretend to, till she has stomped away.

Then I shake my head.

"Women," I say.

"Yeah," he says.

CHAPTER FIFTEEN

One Friend

———

H E SHOULD HAVE BEEN in the tuberculosis sanitarium with a warm blanket on his legs, watched over by a mean big woman with a beehive hairdo and Scripture pamphlets in her smock. Instead, he lurched around town in an old white Pontiac, the engine missing time. The steering wheel bumped through fingers as thin as No. 2 pencils, and his breath rattled round his cigarette when he took a pull, with a sound like feathers rustling in a paper bag. "He'd come to the house in that ol' car, it hitting on about two cylinders, and have a pint of vodka or some Seagram's with him. He'd say, 'Jack, that seal ain't been broke. Pour as much of this as you want to drink.' Charles didn't want me drinking after him. He was always careful not to give me the TB. I'd pour a little in a glass, and he'd take the bottle and go sit in the door, 'cause it was easier for him to breathe. I'd say, 'Charles, let me make you something to eat, some soup or something,' 'cause I knew he liked that Campbell's tomato soup. But he wouldn't eat nothin' then. He didn't want to deaden that liquor. He just sat in that open door and talked, and drank till it was gone." The Pontiac, ragged, dented and rust-flecked, means it was '74, since cars are the way the working-class people of the Deep South truly mark their time. Listen to them, sometime, when they are groping for a memory, and they will find it beside a yellow Oldsmobile, or a baby blue Malibu. Life flutters past us here in pink slips, not diplomas, birth certificates or Christmas cards, and for the rest of Jack Andrews' life he will think of my father's suicide when he hears a Pontiac skipping time.

"He killed himself, and he knew what he was doing," Jack said. It would have been awful to witness, but as the liquor poisoned my father it numbed Jack and made it so he could stand it. It takes a long time, sip by sip, to stop a human heart, and it seemed like Jack and my father replayed their whole lives before his was through. It should have been a joy. Jack would get out a guitar and pick the lovesick blues, and they would laugh about being boys, fishing in the air. But after a while every breaking seal began to sound like a cocking gun, so Jack took a few sips for warmth, and followed his friend across the times they had. They were not old men. Both of them were in their late thirties. But there was no future together anymore, so they remembered like two old men in a nursing home, knowing that was all there would ever be. His death was so certain it was like it already happened. "You hear people talking about a wake?" Jack said. "Well, I guess that's what we had."

In the last year or so of my father's life, the alcohol was the only sustenance he cared to receive. He burned the sugar in it to power his feet and animate his mind, as everything else inside withered from disease. The TB squeezed his lungs and the cirrhosis ate at his liver, and it was a cruelty, what he did, forcing Jack to watch him die. But Jack doesn't see it that way. There was no way to save him that he could see, and just running him off, making him do it someplace else, would have broken the promises they made to each other when they were still boys clicking down the sidewalk in Jacksonville with steel taps on their two-dollar Steinberg shoes.

"We talked a lot about souls, there at the end," Jack said. "We figured it was like the blade on an electric fan, running. You can't see it, but you believe it's there."

Jack was sure he had a soul, but not sure of its destination.

I think it is better to think you don't have one, than to think it will burn.

Jack wiped at his eyes a lot as he talked of the last days. It is an acceptable way for a Southern man to cry. You can leak, when your heart busts in two, but you by God better not make any noise. I didn't cry with Jack. I laughed with him, at the fun they had, but I still weighed everything I heard against the time I lived with him, and wondered what happened to that boy, that man, to the still-beautiful, indestructible boy my mother loved. He put us, his children, on this rock even as he was coming apart, ignored us as we did without, and never believed he did anything wrong.

I told Jack that much.

"That," Jack said, "is not true."

"I guess we talked about everything, right before your dad died," Jack said, "but mostly he talked about your mother. He talked about Margaret, and he talked about you boys."

I believed all my life we somehow just reoccurred to him before his death, as we had reoccurred to him every few years, when we were children. I had not seen him for nine years until I saw him for a fraction of one day in '75, and then he was dead. But Jack told me he talked about us night after night, over years and years, and when he did he cried so fiercely he could barely tip the bottle to his lips.

"Why?" I asked Jack.

" 'Cause he hated what happened in his life," Jack said.

"He felt sorry for himself?" I said.

"No," Jack said.

He closed his eyes, to see his friend better.

"He was sorry for what he done."

Jack has seen a lot of regret in his life, a lot of mistakes.

"But I never seen a man more sorry for what he'd done."

I wrote, when I was younger, that hearing my father say he was sorry would do me no good at all.

I am older than that now.

I still didn't believe it, not completely.

A few years after they split up, my mother went to him, asking for money to help raise his sons. He ignored her. Then, on the urging of her sisters, she got a lawyer, and my father came to meet with her and her sisters, Edna and Juanita. They were all beautiful women, and he walked in and cursed them all. "Y'all look like three ol' Dominicker chickens," he said, and laid a ten-dollar bill on the table. He mailed her one more ten-dollar bill, and that was it forever: twenty dollars' cash, for three lives.

Saying you are sorry for what you did when it is too late to change is like saying from the wheelchair that you used to do a mean soft shoe. You can say anything, from the chair.

"You can believe it," Carlos Slaght told me later, when I shared what Jack had shared with me.

"Why?" I asked.

" 'Cause Jack ain't got no reason to lie."

Jack didn't need to improve my father to love him.

He loved him just fine.

It is as close as I will get to knowing that he had regret, till he climbs from the grave, pays the light bill, steals my mother a fresh bouquet, pounds out the dents in that phantom tricycle, and buys my brother another goddamn dog.

"He would sit and talk about y'all and he would cry and cry. I seen him, God, so many times. He stayed all tormented, all tore up," Jack said. "Lord, how he did love your momma."

I had heard he had a new woman, and that he was living with a woman named Noby at or near the time of his death. "Noby was good to him," Jack said. "She made sure he had things to eat, if he would eat, and made sure he had plenty to drink. But there was never nobody in his heart but your mom. He wanted a home, to be happy. But he knew he threw it away, and I never heard him blame anybody but his self. But he knew all about y'all, everything you did."

I learned that my father talked to friends of friends and kin of kin, and followed our lives twice and three times removed, from a safe distance. Once, when a man wanted to court my mother, he went first to my father, to ask permission. "I got no say about it," my father said, "but if you ever lay a hand on my children, I will kill you."

"He talked about you, most of all," Jack said.

I thumbed my own chest.

"Yeah, you. He knew all of what you did."

I didn't do much. I lost a spelling bee, won a speech contest, wrecked a good motorcycle and burned my leg, broke the same leg playing basketball, twice, then broke my collarbone on the same damn motorcycle, but a different street. I hit two in-the-park home runs in a softball game against a team called the Jacksonville Merchants, but that was only because they had a bunch of rag arms in the outfield. But my father knew about the emergency rooms, saw my picture in the newspaper, and did not give me a call or write me a letter or reach out to me in any way, not until the end, till it was too late to say very much of anything except goodbye.

"But he knew about it," Jack said.

He believed he was too far gone to try and be part of it, Jack said.

He was just the drunk, the raggedy man.

"He didn't know how," Jack said.

Jack said he told him to call us.

"They wouldn't believe what I have to say," my father told him. "When it's all over and done, they'll make me out to be one low-down son of a bitch. They won't have one good memory of me."

Jack went to see him after we left him for good. My father was planting cedar trees. There are a lot of ways, down here, you can spit in the eye of God. You can sweep your house on New Year's, and sweep your future right out the door, or let a bird in your house, which means someone you love will die. But the worst curse is cedar trees. No one plants a cedar tree, until they are ready to die.

"When those things get big enough to shade your grave, you'll die," Jack told him.

"Where'd you hear that," he said.

"I heard it all my life," Jack said.

My father laughed.

"It was like he knew the only thing that could kill Charles, was Charles," said Jack. "And when he made up his mind to go, he did."

We talked a long time that night, Jack and me.

Finally, he walked me to the door.

"Thank you," I said.

He told me to come anytime, and not just when I needed something. He seemed to have something else to say, something he had a hard time getting out of his memory. It was a confession, I suppose, although he didn't do anything wrong.

Near the end of my father's life, the phone rang in Jack's place. It was well past midnight.

"Jack," he said, "will you come get me?"

"Sure," Jack said. "Where you at?"

"I'm in the hospital," my father said.

Jack didn't know what to say.

"They got me in the TB sanitarium."

"You want me to break you out?" Jack said.

"Yeah," my father said.

"Charles, they'll put me in jail," Jack said.

"I want to go home," he said.

Jack can still conjure him in his hospital dormitory in the middle of the night, the phone pressed to his ear. Three decades later, it still stabs his conscience, and breaks his heart.

"They won't let me take you out, Charles," Jack told him.

"I just want to go home," my father said.

They talked awhile, my father coughing. He was always coughing then.

"I didn't go up there," Jack told me.

I told him not to worry, that there was nothing he could do.

Near the end of my father's life, Jack drove past the cedar trees he told my father not to plant. "They were head-high," Jack said. They cast a shadow six feet long, but my father didn't believe in that and neither do I. You live until you drown in your scarred lungs, till your liver goes green. Then you die, begging and praying for one more breath, or in peace, or desolation, or in awful pain. You die asleep or you die surprised, die with angels in your arms or your feet on fire, or just die into a never-ending nothin'. Or, you just get tired of living without the things you threw away and you die remembering, and, if you are lucky, with at least one good friend.

The Boy

—·—

THE WOMAN WAS RIGHT.

The little boy just started to fade, like we left him in the sun too long.

He had been a ragamuffin, hurled into space by the seat of his pants. Suddenly, he shopped for shirts, and worried about his hair. He got too heavy to throw.

Girls giggled and passed him notes.

He began to care if he had pancake in his hair.

He turned twelve, then thirteen, and then the little boy just disappeared.

Me? I was no longer the coolest thing around.

"No offense, Rick, but I'm going to watch TV in my room," he told me one day.

He made his junior high basketball team. The first game I saw, he walked onto the court with the starting five, and even though that only left three boys on the bench, I was so, so proud. When he was still little and played on his church team, he would glimpse me in the bleachers, wave and grin. But now he was all business.

"Don't yell anything to embarrass me," he admonished, before one game.

The first game I saw, he put one boy on the floor, hard, on a rebound, not playing dirty, just aggressive, and he fouled out in the third quarter.

233

He still goes to Baptist Camp. He came home with a new trophy, the summer of his twelfth year. He was voted best cardsharp, to his mother's shame.

He is not helpless, not needy.

He is everything I rushed him to be.

I had missed this transformation in the middle son, or all but missed it. I never really knew the oldest boy, who was in college when I arrived, but in the middle boy I saw enough to scare me, as he was preparing to date, preparing to drive. His whole senior year of high school he wore only orange—skull-popping, eye-hurting orange—because he is a Tennessee fan, or because it is the only color they have on his home planet. He believed homework was an elective, too, but could tell you how many points UT scored in the fourth quarter in 1973. He was good-looking, blond, engaging and could talk paint off a wall, but went days without eating or sleeping, practiced the drums at two in the morning, and asked me questions like: "How deep is the Gulf of Mexico?"

"Well, it varies," I said.

"Oh," he said.

The woman told me once—she must have been in a fever—that I might have a talk about human reproduction with the middle son, and I told her no way in hell. But he cornered me one night, asked me a bees question—or birds, hell, I don't know—and I listened till I had the gist of it, then told him to go to bed.

He drove like everyone else in Memphis, like he woke up drunk. But just months after the wedding he went off to join other orange people in Knoxville, and I was spared. I meant to check his head for antennae, before he left for school.

But what if my boy, my littlest boy, took to wearing orange, too, or asked me hard questions about the biology of love?

What if he got cleaner, tougher, but stranger?

I did what the woman did, with all her sons.

I pretended it wasn't happening.

It did not stop the process. But now and then, the little boy peeked through from that hulk. I recognized him, on those big feet, behind that fine face.

On the long rides to the coast, we still played his favorite game. The boy wants to be a marine biologist, wants to study sharks, and as we ride he makes me ask and answer questions about the sea.

"What's the fastest shark?" he asked.

"Mako," I said. "Gimme a hard one."

"Do you know what a narwhale uses its horn for?" he said.

"Nope," I said.

He got a little smug over that.

I fought back.

"Is a sea cucumber a vegetable or—" I asked.

"It's a worm," he said.

"Well, hell," I said.

And so it went, mile after mile.

"My daddy and me, we used to do something like this," I told him.

He liked that.

He asked me if I knew what plankton was.

"Little-bitty shrimp," I said.

You know stuff like that, somehow. You know it because the television remote got lost in the cushions with three boys' worth of abandoned toys, and you sat with a boy, a little one, through a thousand hours of Nature Planet. You learn to stand the smell of sour-apple bubblegum and the company of a boy who jabs you in your belly before he makes himself comfortable, and tells you that you are "comfy," not to be mean, just stating fact. Then, just when you get used to it, to not minding it so much, it all vanishes, and the little boy you launched into the air stands at your shoulder like a man, and when you turn to say something you find yourself looking right into his eyes.

CHAPTER SIXTEEN

Amen

———·———

WHAT PEOPLE DON'T TELL YOU shapes a man, too, shapes the way he rides through your mind over a lifetime. I told my mother what Jack said, how my father loved her till the day he died, and all she did was nod. It was not news to her. He called her every day in the last year of his life, and told her that. But she never told me because it didn't matter anymore. He pleaded with her to take him back, to let him try again. "He wanted to get married again, but I couldn't," she said. "I did think about it. I surely did." But time ran out. "The doctor said he would have three or four years, but he didn't. He didn't even have a year." I saw him once toward the end. It was like looking at a burned-up house.

———·———

PEOPLE SAID HE WEIGHED less than a hundred pounds, and I know he hated that, to have people see him that way. My mother went to the visitation in the winter of '75, and my father's people were kind to her. They always were. The next morning she asked her boys if we wanted to see him buried. I was in tenth grade, Sam had quit school and Mark was a little boy. Sam, who went to work at thirteen, who dug coal out of the mud so she could heat the house, looked at the clothes laid on the bed. "Momma, I didn't know him," he said, but

I think that was a lie. We walked out of the room together. Mark, who truly didn't know him, who cannot even remember his face, went to play.

My father told my mother he did not want a crowd at his funeral, just us, Velma, and Bob, but there was a nice crowd. He had also said he did not want to be buried in a tie. I understand that now. He would have considered it foolish to lose his looks and hang a tie on the wreck. They put one on him anyway, and there he lay, in a clip-on. Prince or not, the dead just don't have much pull. But before they took him away his momma tugged the tie off his breast. What her boy wants, he gets, if it was in her power to give.

I have it now. It was in the box Ruby gave us after Velma died, with the wallet and dice. I still don't believe in ghosts, but it seems funny in a way, like he was trying to send a message somehow: Rig the game if you can, 'cause luck is a bitch for a poor man; and don't worry what people think, because once it's all over the people who love you will make you what they want you to be, and the people who don't love you will, too.

I WISH IT HAD BEEN DIFFERENT, but I cannot see it. I cannot see him living off his pension, or singing a hymn, or lining up to vote. I cannot see him in shuffling old age with a little potbelly and bifocals, fretting over prescriptions, waiting in line at Wal-Mart. I cannot see him in a sensible car, driving the speed limit, police waving, saying: "You know, there goes a good ol' boy." I cannot see him going home to a paid-for house, with pictures of his boys on the wall. And I cannot see her there with him, to make it complete. But now I know he did see it, and that has to be worth something.

The Boy

---·---

W̲E̲ W̲A̲L̲K̲E̲D̲ O̲N̲T̲O̲ T̲H̲E̲ C̲O̲U̲R̲T̲, my boy and me, on a Saturday morning. My feet hurt and my knees throbbed, and all I had done so far was walk in from the parking lot.

The boy had never beaten me. I was too big, too tall. But every day he got bigger, stronger, and I just got old.

"You want to warm up?" the boy asked.

I shook my head. Warming up was playing for nothing. You don't warm up in Vegas shuffling index cards, or putting washers in slot machines. I need every second I spent in motion to count.

Pulled muscles and torn ligaments happen this way, but if you know you've only got so many minutes in you, you can't waste a one. We had ten dollars riding on this, and my diminishing pride.

"Let's go," I said.

He had never forgotten what I said about him not being tough, tough like me. The truth is I'm not that tough. I don't even know if I ever had anybody fooled. But it was too late. Some things lay like a splinter in a boy's head.

He went at me hard from the first drumbeat of that ball on the gleaming hardwood floor, raking my face, jumping into me, landing on my toes, on top of a foot. He tumbled to the floor twice, but bounced up immediately, as if he was made of hard rubber instead of flesh and bone. I drove on him but he stuck his body in front of me like a mail-

238

box post. I banged hard with my shoulder, lifting him off the ground, but in no time I was so tired I couldn't shoot, or find a rhythm, or even breathe.

He went for the ball—supposedly—as I tried a clumsy layup, and he dug a groove with his fingernails across my arm.

"If you do that again I'm gonna put you down hard," I told him, and as soon as he got the chance he did it again. I mustered the last energy I had and ran over him. It hurt me a lot more than it did him. I was done.

He was still just a thirteen-year-old growing into his big feet, and he missed seven-eighths of his shots. I could have beat him still, I swear I could, if I had not been in the kind of shape where even putting on my socks made me see stars. I missed a short jump shot and we both leapt up for the rebound, but I am not sure my feet actually cleared the floor.

He did not gloat or dance, at the end.

I always had.

He just held the ball and looked at me.

"Want to go again?" he asked.

"Sure," I said. "Gimme a minute."

I staggered to a bench to rest, and to wish I were dead. I have always loved the cliché, the one about being careful what you wish for. I staggered through another game. He drew blood again.

"You're not trying," he said.

He knew how to hurt an old man.

Then, white of face, I staggered to the parking lot.

I threw my arm around his shoulders, like I did when he was little.

He wrapped his arm around my waist.

Together, me leaning on him, we made it to the truck.

"Good boy," I said.

I patted him, like an old woman.

He patted me back.

"You okay?" he asked.

"You didn't hurt me too bad," I said.

He grinned. When he does, you see the little boy again.

He is not gone. He never will be. This boy's heart will always be young, soft, or at least I hope it is. The little boy just lives inside the armor of this big boy, this young man. There was never anything hiding, lurking. There was never anything out there, not for him.

One of the first trips we ever made home when he was still a little boy was in cool weather, early December. People told me not to even try to fish the pond, the fish would be so sluggish, but the boy wanted to fish. My first cast I snagged a five-pound bass—it was probably just four pounds, but it was a nice fish, even allowing for lies. The boy asked if he could touch it, and I told him sure, and he ran one finger down its lovely green scales. He is fascinated with fish. I tried to work the hook out but she had taken it deep, almost in her guts, and I have hated all my life to kill a fish that way. I could see a look on his face very much like panic, and I worked harder. If it had been a single hook and worm I would have bit the line in two and let it go, trusting the hook to rust out, but it was a plug, with eight barbs, and if she choked it down she would surely die.

"Run to the house and get my pliers," I told him, and he took off like it was his life in my inept hands, not the fish.

The woman had bought him some new jeans and they fell down twice as he ran, and it would have been funny any other time. It was all uphill, about three hundred yards, and that might not seem far to you, but you try it, holding to your pants.

He half killed himself getting up that hill, to save a fish. I knelt down in the mud and eased the fish, still hooked, into the water, and rocked it back and forth. I tried again and again to get the hook out, my fingers numb and slipping, and was just about to give up when the hook came free, and I eased the fish into the water, alive.

I wish he could have seen it, seen that whorl of mud, seen it streak away.

But instead, as he ran up, his lungs on fire, I was already casting for a new one.

"Never mind," I said.

His chest was heaving. Sweat ran down his face.

"Did it die?" he said.

"No," I said.

He might have cried if it had, or wanted to.

CHAPTER SEVENTEEN

The Circle

T HE TWO-DOLLAR PROPHECY came true. Sadie, the fortune-teller, said my mother's life would move in a circle, and I guess it did. As a young woman all her happiness depended on the mail. Now, in old age, she was still waiting, her life swinging on that mailbox lid. She walked to the box every day, a quarter mile and back along a driveway crisscrossed by redbirds, still with us after all this time. The mailman ran at one-thirty, so that was when she started her march, but being older now, she waited to read them when she could sit down. There was no surprise under the stamps now, just a postmark, a federal guarantee that her youngest son was alive for one more day. She prayed for the days to fly, wasteful, for a woman so old.

He had been doing time in the county lockup when he got out the last time, sick and thin. But she was at peace, and it seemed so was he. There was no catalyst we knew of, no evangelism. It was more like he just got tired, and decided he wanted to live quiet the rest of his days. She prayed he was truly over that life of self-destruction that took my father, but it didn't matter if it was permanent. Every day was a gift. Then an old charge, a dusty charge, resurfaced in the courts, and sent him off again. My mother was more stunned than brokenhearted, " 'cause he done so good," and it seemed like she just shrank in her clothes. He disappeared into the state system, to Atmore, and I thought it would kill her. Everyone says that about mothers and sons, but sons do kill their mothers that way.

I once believed I could make her happy with a house. I framed a book around that house, a symbol of some kind of victory over a life in borrowed houses. People traveled across the country to take pictures of it, because it meant something to them. But she would have been just as happy in a refrigerator box under the interstate, and just as sad.

I have never been all that sharp when it comes to learning from my mistakes. I caught her dreaming through a real estate magazine, and when she put it down I found a creased page. The picture showed a red cedar house and forty fine acres of wild, beautiful land. We got in the car and drove, just a few miles, then turned up a long driveway, lined with trees.

The other house was too close to the road, too big, and had too many lightbulbs to change. The house she dreamed about was really a cabin, made from squared-off logs, solid and faded to a bluish gray on the outside, still a rich, brownish red on the inside. But it was the land that mattered. The house perched on the side of a ridge, its yard sloping down to a fence and a pasture studded with water oaks, with a beautiful little stock pond just beyond. The pasture was still wild, filled with blackberry islands, and as we sat there a hickory nut fell from the branches overhead and rattled across the car hood. Sleek cattle grazed in the belly-high grass, and the ridge above the house was thick with hardwoods. I would learn that my grandfather made whiskey there when she was a girl.

We went a dozen times, to look. The pond was deep and clean and full of bream and big bass, and as I walked up to it the first time a snapping turtle the size of a hubcap crashed through the dead grass and weeds and into the water, roiling up the mud of the bottom. At dusk, a white egret waded at the shallow end, fishing. Egrets are rare here, up this high.

I handed my mother the deed.

Maybe it would help this time.

Maybe even she believed it would.

I bought it in fall, and in the changing season the frogs would sing so loud in the trees you had to shout to be heard. She would take walks at dusk, down the driveway, to listen to their music. Wild turkeys walked into her yard, and, afraid they might be hungry, she started putting out shelled corn. After a while, the turkeys stopped running when she came out the door, and she talked to them as they moved closer and closer. Deer tiptoed to the corn but crashed away when she swung open the door, and a giant rat snake she named Red Belly took up residence in the garage. We bought ducks and chickens, and I chunked rocks at the marauding possums, hawks and great owls.

It was good. The mornings sounded with bantam roosters, and at every dusk a parade of ducks, as regular as the ones in the Peabody Hotel, trekked up from the pond and squawked until my mother spread out a fresh sprinkle of corn. In spring she fished for bream with an honest-to-God cane pole and worms she dug herself, and caught fish the size of a salad plate. As her first summer neared she talked over and over about how she would have a real garden, a showplace garden, when her boy came home.

For her birthday I got two miniature donkeys, which are like any other donkeys except, well, smaller. My mother laughed out loud as they burst out of the trailer. The thing about miniature donkeys is they do not know they are. They think they are big, and bite, holler and demand attention. I watched her pet them, watched her spoil them with sweet feed till they almost foundered.

It is hard to find a perfect place, but this seemed like it. At sunset, I liked to sit on the steps and just look at it, at the wakes cut by the snapping turtles across the still pond. Some nights I take my spinning rod and try to catch a monster bass that my brother has already caught once. You have to run the donkeys off, or they will sneak up and bite you when your back is turned. So I fish with eyes in the back of my head, and cast until past dark. I am descended from great fishermen, in a culture where a man who cannot catch fish is more pathetic than a man who cannot change a tire.

"I think I've been happier here than I've ever been in my life," she told me, and it was as sweet a lie as I have heard.

They counted down the days, mother and son, as if they were scratching it on the walls: 200, 199, 198 . . . He called her from inside, but sometimes there were lockdowns and sometimes he just couldn't get to it, and sometimes when he did call she could hear the jailhouse sounds on the other line, screams, catcalls, crashing doors, and it scared her. But every day, there was a letter, to tell her that he was okay.

As the days crept by she began to talk about what they would do, him and her, on their farm.

She showed me the place, a place thick with weeds and impenetrable hedges and blackberry bushes, as if they wanted the hardest place in creation, to test them. It was the blackberry bushes that worried me. They were thicker than my thumb at the base, and tough as green hickory. "It looks a little wild," I told her, but she said she could clear it easy, her and Mark. This would be their garden.

Now, every day's letter was about soil and seeds and fertilizer. "He wrote the same thing over and over, like your daddy when he used to write to me," she said. They all began with: "When I get home . . ."

. . . the garden comes first. I want you to think about what you want us to plant when I come home. Me and you will try to plant something every day we can. I will be glad when I can see it growing. We're going to plant beans, cucumbers, and lots of tomatoes, potatoes and onions. I will plant you a pumpkin patch, because you said you wanted some pumpkins. Ma, I try only to think of good things. Sometimes that ain't easy. But that's okay and I'll be home soon. I want you to only think of good things and happy things. We will do a lot when I come home. I would like to put a gate at the top of that hill in the second pasture. We'll walk and look when I come, but our garden comes first. I can do all this other stuff when it rains . . .

I spent the first day of our honeymoon in Montgomery, begging for his early release in front of the Board of Pardons and Paroles. The board listened to my excellent lawyer, then they listened to me as I tried to tell them how every day hurt my mother a little more. The clerk warned me not to even bring up mommas, because everybody's momma hurts when their boy is in such a place. The board denied it, after deliberating about fifteen seconds. "This is the best place for him now," a board member said. I walked out and swung one stupid, pointless punch at the air. I am sick of this, I thought, sick of this cycle, sick of being at the mercy of something as insignificant as a drink of alcohol.

HE WAS RELEASED IN WINTER. The woman and I drove southwest on Interstate 65, deep into the pine barrens and flatland along the Florida line. Early the next morning we waited outside a chain-link fence on a flat, dull landscape, in what has to be one of the most desolate-feeling places on this earth. When he walked out I noticed he had aged years in that year and change. I shook his hand, like he had sold me some life insurance, and we went home. My mother rushed out the front door when the car pulled into the drive but just stopped when she saw him, and they stood for a minute there, awkward, till she reached her arm around his neck and patted him once, twice. "Your hair's gone gray," was all she said.

THE MODERN WORLD, e-mail, cell phones, all that clutter, stopped at the garden gate. The ghost of Bob must have slept in this ground. My brother worked pale and coughing, his insides giving up the food he ate more often than he kept it down, because a lifetime of drinking leaves you that way. But he hacked and cut at the underbrush and burned it clean, her beside him, until they both just gave out. He killed snakes with his hoe as he tore at the brush and plowed up their dens, and strung barbed wire around the plot, to keep the damn donkeys out of the corn. After about two months they had a space about thirty yards wide and forty yards long, not red clay but rocky mountain soil, a yellow-gray. They combed the rocks out together, pulled the roots up and cut them in two, and fertilized the soil. In May they planted what they had written each other about, planted white corn, hot pepper, red and white potatoes, turnips, Kentucky Wonder pole beans, yellow squash, okra, Vidalias, Texas Sweet and purple onions and two kinds of tomatoes, Better Boys and Rutlers Old Timey, and cleared more ground for a pumpkin patch and peas. They didn't have a good rain for two months so they toted water to irrigate the plants, and when I asked them why they didn't just get a long hose and run it down from the house, they both looked at me funny, like I had asked them to cheat.

I was gone almost a month, working, and when I came home I rolled past the garden and stopped my truck. Everything there—everything—was not just growing but thriving. They had already picked and canned forty-nine pints of turnip greens, and the onions were already beginning to make. Everything was either in bloom or further along, and as I walked beside my little brother through the rows I realized I was a poser, a fake country boy, and that driving a truck and shooting a gun is a lame statement next to what he knew about the ground. Unlike me, he had paid attention walking beside the old people in our family, and when I asked how he knew what to do, he just looked at me funny, again. "I've always knowed," he said.

In the squash, he reached down and pinched off a bloom, and I wondered why he would do that—you needed a bloom to grow a squash. "It's a false bloom, on the end of a little-bitty squash. If you leave the false blooms on there, it won't make a squash. You pinch it off, and it lets the new squash grow."

He lectured row by row. You pinch off the first little pepper pods that show. That makes the whole plant react by producing more pods, instead of a single pod or two on a plant that never fully develops. With okra, you cut off the first pod and leaf. You keep the dirt pulled back from the onions once they begin to grow, because the packed dirt will slow or stop them from developing. I told him it was amazing what they had done, and I meant it.

"I had my doubts," he said, smiling, "when I saw them black-berries."

I asked him why he would work so hard on something like that, but he never answered.

"Everybody that sees it says it's the prettiest garden they ever seen," my mother said.

They live together, the two of them. I have a room there and my name is on the cable bill, but I always feel like a tourist when I come, with the woman and boy. Sam and his wife Teresa and their daughter Meredith, with her family, visit a lot, and we eat that food—fried squash, boiled okra, new potatoes, stewed sweet corn—all seasoned with Velma's magic, and at dusk we fish the pond and fend off the jackasses. My aunts and uncles and cousins come when they can, but time is catching up with us, and we are fewer now.

I think a lot about my daddy's people now. The last time I saw Bob, he was Christmas drunk in '65 and sitting next to me in the backseat of my father's car. He and Velma had words, and he threatened to cut her with his new pocketknife. "I told your daddy not to give Bobby a knife for Christmas," my mother said. But he snapped it closed, grinned at me, pinched my arm blue, and we rode, a family. Velma, I saw for the last time in the funeral home in Jacksonville. The young preacher told us Velma had come to him near the end of her life, and told him she was never saved. He said he prayed with her, and he was with her when she was. But I think the young minister had it wrong. I think she was saved all along.

Their youngest son lies near them, in a grave we rarely visit. One day Sam came by, covered in sweat, and told me he had gone to the cemetery to cut the weeds off the family plots on my mother's side—our grandfather, grandmother, others—the people he considers real family. "I walked over and I cut Daddy's," he said. "I mean, I was already there."

The garden at my mother's house thrived all summer and into the fall, bore its fruit, and died, but as it withered my baby brother was still fine, still gaunt and old before his time, but living inside that peace he had found, and allowing her to live inside it, too.

They broke that circle, together. "Everything we wrote about in them letters has come true. Everything we dreamed about has come true, this time," my mother said. "How often does something like that happen in this world?"

———·—·———

THE NEXT SPRING they started over. Fearful of snakes in the tall grass of the pasture, my brothers used mowers to cut a clean path for her from the yard to her pond, and from the yard to her garden. In one week the path was covered in wildflowers. "Everywhere Momma walks is flowers," Sam said, and he didn't mean it to sound pretty but it was. It has acres of flowers, her new Eden, and not one rose.

She prayed it would last forever, but even for an old woman, forever can take too long. My little brother stumbled and fell. But what fine minute she lived in, before he did. Some days, she did not check the mail at all.

The Boy

———·———

FUNNY THING, about that silver sports car.
No one ever bought it.

It may be because, when people called to ask about it, I would sometimes neglect to call them back.

I guess I never called anybody back.

The boy says that's all right.

He plans to drive it to prom.

"You don't even know how to shift gears," I said.

"Teach me," he said.

He is three years away from a driver's license, but there is no harm in knowing early.

We crawled in, and I turned the key.

The sound of it, Lord, it just hums in your blood.

The wind blows the rust off a man.

I worked the clutch but I let the boy shift through the gears from the passenger seat, telling him to listen for a change in that growl, that roar, and he figured it out quick, like he was born to do it.

We were in Fairhope, in a dwindling summer. We idled along Mobile Bay, then went due east on those needle-straight country roads, a respectable fifteen miles over the speed limit.

"You know," I said, "if you ever drive reckless, I'll whip you like you were mine."

He just laughed.

"I mean it," I said. "You can't."

"Okay," he said.

"You don't understand consequences," I said. "Your life's been too safe, too easy . . ." and before I knew it I was deep into my rant, again. I think I will always do that, because someone has to be afraid for this boy.

I geared down and nudged the accelerator a little more. The timbre of the engine changed, sweetened, and the telephone poles went by like fence posts.

The boy raised his hands into the wind, like a little kid.

For a second, just a brave second, the car split the air under its own volition, and I raised mine, too.

ACKNOWLEDGMENTS

Before I can begin to thank the people who made this book possible, I must first offer apologies to my mother and brothers for having to endure my questions about a past that was hard to relive. I can let things lie now.

And, though it is far too late, I must say how sorry I am for letting my feelings for my father keep me for so long from his people, from my grandmother, especially. I am told she loved without condition, loved my mother, and loved us boys. I never gave her reason. It was just the kind of person she was.

———·+·———

It is a cliché, to say it will be impossible to thank all the people who made this endeavor possible, but it is nonetheless true.

First, I must thank the storytellers who were generous enough to put a more human, complicated face on my father. Jack, Carlos, Shirley, Billy, Bill Joe, so many others . . . I would never have known him, if not for you.

Others built the stage that my family's story is played on. Jimmy Hamilton told me the best story I ever heard of my grandfather. Homer Barnwell made the Jacksonville of his boyhood come alive. Ruby England, my father's sister, told me how pretty my mother looked on her wedding day. Wayne Glass told me one of the finest whiskey-running tales I ever heard.

And as with every book I write about home, I must thank my aunts Juanita, Jo, and Edna, and my uncles Ed and John, for once again lending color, drama, and substance to the past. Your stories have filled the very air around me with pictures, all my life.

Before I could begin piecing together their remembrances, I needed more distant history. This book, like so much of what I have tried to write in my lifetime, attempts to peer into the pasts of blue-collar Americans, specifically the mill and mountain people of the foothills of the Appalachians. Chapter two, the story of where we come from, would not have been possible without the genuine historians who have already chronicled that history.

I must begin with Wayne Flynt. In *Poor but Proud* and other works on the poor, rural people of my state, he educated me on my own soil, and revealed the sweat and blood spilled into it by generations. By reading his works, I began to better understand the gut-tearing contradictions in my people in the years before, during and after the Civil War. His exhaustive research into the deprivations of the postwar period—from dejection-filled letters to damning statistics—put flesh and blood on dim history. I had heard that Alabama soldiers marched into battle without shoes, had known that women back home cried for bread, but never really saw it, in my mind's eye, until I read it in his books.

I found more historical gems in the most unusual places. A history of Jacksonville compiled in my youth by the First National Bank provided a glimpse into what was done and said as young men of the town marched off to war.

Hardy Jackson's works took me even deeper into my state's history, back to the time of the Creeks. I know more than ever about my people thanks to him and to so many other historians whose works gave voice to the men and women who were here before.

This history of the Jacksonville cotton mill alone is upheld by more sources than I can count. The memoirs of Knox Ide gave me entrée to the people who shaped the future here. Peter Howell, who tried to save the mill from the wrecking ball, provided, literally, a trunkful of information. The most official history of the mill and its founders, written in an application for historic status by David B. Schneider (compiling information from local historians such as Jack Boozer and others), showed me its origins, its founders, more. Dozens of first-person accounts of life in the village, from Donald

Garmon, Odell Knight and others, provided beautiful insights into life there in the first half of the twentieth century.

I also have to thank the reporters, most of them long gone, of the *Anniston Star* and the *Jacksonville News,* who chronicled our history one faded page at a time, and took me—with the help of flesh-and-blood sources—inside the tragic killing of Chief Whiteside.

And I have to thank the people who loaned me their legs, and minds, in gathering first-person remembrances and press and historical accounts of the cotton mill village and the surrounding town—most of which will find a home in a book yet to come, but a small part of which helped me in these pages: Jerry "Boo" Mitchell, Greg Garrison, Lori Solomon, Megan Nichols, Jen Allen, James King, Taylor Hill, Ryan Clark, Beth Linder and Cori Bolger.

As with every book I write, I must thank my editor, Jordan Pavlin, for taking this imperfect work and turning it into something I am proud of. I have never minded a good editor. In this book, I would have drowned without one. And again, I want to thank my agent, Amanda Urban, for giving me a book life to begin with, at a level I never even dreamed.

I have never been the kind of writer who needed a perfect place to write, a willow tree, a seaside cottage. I could write just as well—or just as poorly— on an upside-down oil drum. But the University of Alabama gave me a place to write that looks out over massive oaks and green lawns, within earshot of the chimes. I am now spoiled.

Perhaps most of all I thank the readers who have found value in the stories of my people, and—more important—found value in their time on this earth.

Finally, I must thank the boy, for forgiving me for all that I have fumbled, broken and lost, and the simple fact that, sometimes, I just don't have good sense.

A NOTE ABOUT THE AUTHOR

Rick Bragg is the author of two best-selling books,
Ava's Man and *All Over but the Shoutin'*.
He lives in Alabama with his wife,
Dianne, and stepson Jake.

A NOTE ON THE TYPE

This book was set in a typeface called Bulmer. This
distinguished letter is a replica of a type long famous in the
history of English printing which was designed and cut by
William Martin about 1790 for William Bulmer of the Shake-
speare Press. In design, it is all but a modern face, with vertical
stress, sharp differentiation between the thick and thin strokes,
and nearly flat serifs. The decorative italic shows the influence of
Baskerville, as Martin was a pupil of John Baskerville's.

COMPOSED BY *Creative Graphics,*
Allentown, Pennsylvania

PRINTED AND BOUND BY *Berryville Graphics,*
Berryville, Virginia

DESIGNED BY *Iris Weinstein*